Front & back cover illustrations : Daniel C.K. Lau, *Harmony* (details), 2010 (cat. no. 1)
封面及封底作品：劉澤光《和》（局部），2010（展品1）

HARMONY

Synergy between Tradition & the Contemporary

Chinese Calligraphy and Seal Engraving

by Daniel C.K. Lau

和：劉澤光古今相生書法篆刻

Daniel Chak-kwong Lau

劉澤光

With contributions by Wan Qingli, Peter Y. K. Lam, Vincent K. T. Tong, Vivan Wing-yan Ting, Chris Rothermel, Emma Watts, Lolita Cheung and Jack Luo

特邀論文作者：萬青屴、林業強、唐錦騰、丁穎茵、羅斯麥　、屈艾瑪、張楚筠及羅屹昀

Harmony : Synergy between Tradition and the Contemporary
和 ： 古今相生

In the long history of Chinese culture, the concept and philosophy of harmony has always been dominating the leading values of society through time and space. Dr. Daniel C.K. Lau re-interprets the concept of "equilibrium and harmony" in an innovative and contemporary way.

The large-scale calligraphic installation "Harmony" (cat. no. 1) accentuates the framework of this book. Through a collection of various script styles and other styles from ancient and modern times, this work exemplifies the purport of harmony, the lifeworks of our ancestral scholars, and the synergy between tradition and the contemporary in a modern look.

Dr. Daniel Lau's unique artistic approach integrates the past and the present; with strong and solid skills in brush and ink, he creates works that are contemporary and refreshing by utilizing visual elements of multiple media in visual arts, and incorporates contemporary thoughts and content into his work. This book presents quintessential works from Dr. Lau's past decade of oeuvre. Works are grouped into four categories to investigate four kinds of relationship: "Heaven and Man", "Give and Receive", "Black and White" and "Elegance and Vulgarity"

Heaven and Man

There is love between heaven and earth. The resources and blessings from mother nature are no doubt free gifts, yet the response from human varies: sometimes awestruck by the wonders of nature, sometimes enlightened, yet sometimes damaging. For instance, revealing the artist's incisive admiration of the natural object, the jerky brushstrokes on *Awestruck* (cat. no. 2) reinforce the coarse texture of a piece of weathered teak wood and the momentum generated from its twisting form. By contrast, *Walking in the Mystifying Haze* (cat. no. 22), *Louis Vuitton & Porsche* (cat. no. 23), and *Service for Renminbi* (cat. no. 24) present the lamentation on the distorted relationship between man and nature such as environmental pollution and man's endless desires for materialism, fame and profit.

Give and Receive

This part focuses on how like-minded people maintain friendship by giving and receiving seals. At the same time, by embracing reciprocal cognizance on the thoughts expressed by the seal and shared values, these people established an in-group identity quite unknowlingly.

Black and White

This part explores the concept of "void-solid reciprocity" in Chinese art. Experimental calligraphy *Emptiness* (cat. no. 128) is the best example to demonstrate this concept. The Chinese character *"kong"* (空emptiness) is written in seal script in a hollow-out way with flowing and dripping ink on a piece of thin and transparent chiffon. What's more, the brushstrokes and the consciousness of space also extend out of the work in a manner of subverting the tradition; "*Emptiness*" integrates with the view outside the glass wall of the gallery, generating a compellingly synergistic effect.

Elegance and Vulgarity

Lau illustrates that this pair of concepts could be highly integrated with each other in calligraphy in a forward-looking way of thinking and creative practice. For example, *What?* (cat. no. 140) is a three-dimensional work inspired from the Cantonese dialect. Lau transforms the two Chinese characters "咩話" into a visual effect resembling a stone monument rubbing, and evokes an additional sense of historic association through a forcefully archaic and austere calligraphic style, thus taking the age-old and richly vernacular Cantonese dialect through the caverns of time into the dramatic present. In this way, Lau encourages us to think about the local identity constructed by Cantonese dialect and culture in the modern society.

在源遠流長的中國文化中，和諧的觀念和哲學一直支配着社會的主導價值觀，並貫穿着不同時空。本書以「和」為核心，劉澤光博士以創新、現代的手法對此中國文化極為重視的觀念，作出嶄新的演繹。

巨幅書法裝置展品《和》（展品1），點出了全書綱領。作品集結古今不同書體及風格，以現代的面貌，體現全書「和諧」、「集大成」及「古今相生」的旨趣。

劉博士獨特的藝術途徑融和古今，在其深厚的筆墨功力上注入跨藝術媒介的視覺元素及當代的思想和內容，作品充滿時代感，令人耳目一新。本書精選了劉博士近十年的傑構，共分四部份，探討以下四種關係："天與人"、"施與受"、"黑與白"及"雅與俗"。

天與人

天地有情，大自然給予人的資源及祝福，無疑是一份白白得來的禮物，人對大自然的回應，時驚嘆，時感悟，但有時卻是傷害。例如，作品《驚嘆》（展品2）以生澀的筆觸增強了風化柚木紋理的粗燥感，「勢」從木材扭曲的形體奔湧而出，展現了劉澤光對自然的深深禮贊。然而，《走進撲朔迷離的「煙霞」》（展品22）、《LV與波子》（展品23）和《為人民幣服務》（展品24），則透露了作者對人與自然關係被扭曲了的回應，如環境污染、對無止境的物欲及名利的追求等等，而發出的悲嘆。

施與受

此部份集中思考一種特別的人際關係維繫模式，探討志同道合者如何透過印章的惠贈及接受，以維繫彼此間的情誼，並藉彼此認同印章內容所表達出的思想，以擁抱共同價值觀，並在不知不覺間建構內群體身份認同。

黑與白

此部份探討中國藝術虛實相生的精神和概念。實驗性書法《空》（展品128）是一佳例，流暢淋漓的筆觸和墨韻，在輕透的雪紡上意外地以縷空的方式書寫出篆書「空」字。觀者需以虛實倒置的概念方可解讀出以留白方式出現的「空」字筆劃。更有趣的是，作品中的筆墨痕跡與空間概念，以巔覆書法傳統的姿態，伸延至畫面之外 —《空》與玻璃牆外的景物彷彿融為一體，產生富震撼力的協同效應。

雅與俗

劉澤光以嶄新並富有前瞻性的思維方式及創作實踐，打破「雅」與「俗」的疆界，探索雅俗協同而有別傳統的另類關係。《 咩話？》（展品140）是一件參用港式粵語而創作的立體書法作品。劉澤光將「咩話」二字轉化為石碑拓本的視覺效果，並藉沉雄古樸的書法風格拱托出一種格外的歷史聯想，將歷史猶久而富濃厚地方色彩的粵方言，帶到戲劇化的現在。本來難登大雅之堂的港式粵語，如今結合新式的書法表現形式，搖身一變，成為一種另類的學術工具，探究有深厚歷史文化底蘊的粵方言，以及本土文化在當代社會建構出的本土身份認同。

Harmony | 和

Synergy between Tradition and the Contemporary
Chinese Calligraphy and Seal Engraving
by Daniel Chak-kwong Lau
劉澤光古今相生書法篆刻

Daniel Chak-kwong Lau
劉澤光

AVA Refereed Publication
This publication has been assessed by
international academics
本出版之內容經國際專家學者評核並推薦

Assistant Editors: Lolita Cheung,
Chen Ying, Roger Kho
助理編輯：張楚筠, 陳鶯, 許天星

Design: Roger Ng
設計：伍啟豪

Photography: TY Yeung,
Tsui Chung Wei Ray, Brian Chong
攝影：楊沛鏗 徐重偉 莊恩羣

Co-published by Academy of Visual Arts,
Hong Kong Baptist University and Asia One Books
香港浸會大學視覺藝術院及宏亞出版聯合出版

香港浸會大學
HONG KONG BAPTIST UNIVERSITY

視覺藝術院
Academy of Visual Arts

asiaone

Asia One Books 宏亞出版

ISBN 978-988-19716-4-7

資助
Supported by
香港藝術發展局
Hong Kong Arts Development Council

This book is dedicated to my Heavenly Father
謹以此書獻給我的天父

The Poems Glorifying the Lamb (cat. no. 8)
《詩贊羔羊》（展品8）

Acknowledgements

I would like to express my deepest gratitude to Professor Wan Qingli, Professor Vincent K. T. Tong, Professor Peter Y. K. Lam, Dr. Vivian Ting, Mr. Chris Rothermel and Ms. Emma Watts for reviewing this book and contributing their essays. I am especially grateful to Dr. Vaughan Mak and Mr. Roger Kho for reading the draft of this book and offering insightful comments for the completion of the manuscript. Sincere thanks go to Professor Peter Sturman and Professor Wan Qingli for their enlightening mentorship throughout my academic career, and to the late Mr. Han Yunshan who took me as his calligraphy student at a time when my enthusiasm for calligraphy was matched only by my superficial knowledge and skills.

I would like to thank Members of Publication Committee of Academy of Visual Arts, HKBU for their review and approval of this publication, and their eventual recommendation of this book to be published as a refereed publication after a double-blind international peer review.

Acknowledgement should also be made to Ms Lolita Cheung, Mr. Roger Ng, Mr. Roger Kho and Miss Chen Ying for their editorial assistance. Special thanks go to Mr. Peter Lau, Mr. Ramon Leung, Ms. Sue So and other professionals of Asia One Books for their great effort in making the publication possible.

Great encouragements have also come from Mr. Andy Lee (Vice-President (Administration) and Secretary, HKBU), Professor Harold Mok, Professor Lee Yun Woon, Professor Helen Shen, Mr. Koon Wai Bong, Mr. Hui Lai Ping, my family and my wife.

There are also a number of offices and organizations that I wish to recognize for their generous support: Academy of Visual Arts of Hong Kong Baptist University, Office of the Vice-President (Administration) and Secretary (HKBU), Estate Office (HKBU), and Communication and Public Relations Office (HKBU) and the Hong Kong Arts Development Council.

CONTENTS/ 目錄

A Glimpse of *Harmony*: The Evolution of Chinese Script Types

Harmony (cat. no. 1) presents itself as a perfect example to illustrate the various characteristics of the major Chinese script types. Based on previous research on the history of calligraphy and archaeological findings, the following descriptions of the wide spectrum of script types applied in this series of the same Chinese character *he* ("harmony") endeavor to trace the evolution of Chinese calligraphy through the ages.[1]

01 Oracle-Bone Script (*Jiaguwen* 甲骨文)

Literally "shell-and-bone writing," refers to ancient Chinese writing engraved on animal bones or turtle shells by sharp knives. Dating from the fourteenth to the eleventh centuries B.C., oracle-bone writing were largely records of divination of the royal house. Characterized by the ubiquitous pictorial elements, the primitive appearance of the writing reminds the modern audience of the early effort to record through carving abstract lines in imitation of natural objects, lives and phenomena, and even much more abstract concepts like "harmony." Executed in ink on paper, the modern interpretation of oracle-bone writing seeks to relive the spontaneity in wielding the knife and create thin lines with rough aura that stems from speedy and uneven brush movement.

02 Great-Seal Script (*dazhuan* 大篆)

Also known as bronze script (*jinwen* 金文) or *zhouwen* 籀文, the great-seal script largely appeared as the inscriptions of the bronze ritual vessels of the Shang and Zhou dynasties (ca. 1600-256 B.C.) The size of the characters can vary drastically and dramatically within the whole work or even on the same line. Retaining a lot of pictorial elements, the character structure is complex, constructed on the basis of more curvilinear lines, hence embodying a feeling of classical elegance.

03 Small-Seal Script (*xiaozhuan* 小篆)

Being a product of the unification of China under the Qin dynasty (221-206 B.C.) established by the first emperor Shi huangdi 秦始皇帝, the small-seal script represents a conscious effort of unifying the writing system. Characterized by the thin and curvilinear lines and symmetrical and relatively less complex character composition, the emergence of the small-seal script as the later form of the archaic script witnessed an early decision to simplify writing. Expressed with brush-and-ink that is clean and neat, the modern interpretation is handsome and airy as a result of rendering slight brush modulation within the prevailing centered-tip brush method.

04 Clerical Script (*lishu* 隸書)

Popularly used in the Qin and Han dynasties (221 B.C.- A.D. 220), the clerical script is a bridge between the archaic scripts and the modern scripts. The clerical script is marked by the outwardly flaring shape of the horizontal strokes, and the right and left downward slanting strokes. The further simplification of character structure and reduction of the number of strokes in characters successfully catered to the ever-increasing need of clerical efficiency in the Han dynasty. Aesthetically, the emphasis on the rhythm of the conscious brush movement reflects a growing interest in the expressive potential of the brush. This subtle dynamics within the brushstrokes of the clerical script, in a sense, facilitated the subsequent evolvement of the more modern scripts.

05 Draft-Cursive Script (*zhangcao* 章草)

An abbreviated form of the clerical script, the draft-cursive script originated around the second century B.C. It was developed by writing the clerical script in a speedy manner, hence it is also known as cursive-clerical script.

06 Cursive Script (*caoshu* 草書)

Cursive script matured in the third and fourth centuries. Fluidity and speed are emphasized in cursive writing. Relatively more abbreviations and linkages are used within and between characters. Though cursive calligraphy is the least constrained of all the scripts, the order of the strokes, the manner in which abbreviations of characters are created and the movement of the brush remain largely governed by rules and conventions.

07 Standard Script (*kaishu* 楷書)

The standard script matured between the second and fourth centuries. With a conscious effort to regulate spacing, the characters of the standard-script writing become more uniform in size and orderly in appearance. On the other hand, the characters are square structured. Individual strokes are clearly and subtly executed. The high degree of legibility makes it best used in printing, and the script is commonly employed for official or public functions nowadays.

08 Semi-Cursive Script (*xingshu* 行書)

A simplification of the standard script, semi-cursive script developed as a form of casual writing. The semi-cursive writing is written in a rather speedy manner, usually showing the links between the strokes within a character. Executed in a noticeably spontaneous way, personal touches are created with relatively more freedom of the brush.

1 The following discussions on various Chinese script types are adapted from Lau Chak-kwong, "The Calligraphy Couplet as the Embodied Image of Literary Game," in *The Auspicious Image*, edited by Lau Chak-kwong (Hong Kong: Academy of Visual Arts, Hong Kong Baptist University, 2007), *vi-ix*.

01

02

03

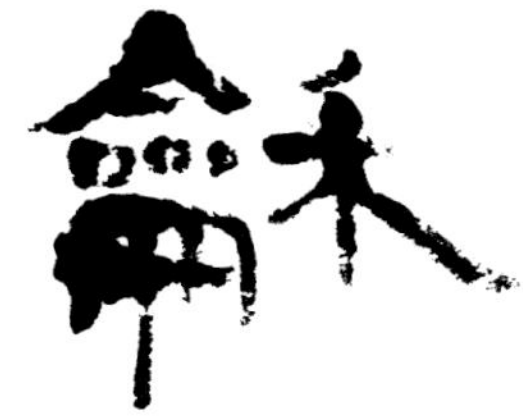
04

05

06

07

08

《和》之一瞥：中國書體之演變

《和》（展品1）是一件最能説明中國書體於不同年代演變的佳例。[1]

01 甲骨文

以利器刻在動物之骨甲上的甲骨文，是大約公元前14至11世紀時商代王室用於占卜記事的文字。字中經常出現的象形元素以及其原始之貌，在在使現代觀者想起先民用鐫刻的抽象線條，以模擬自然現象及生命，甚至如 “和諧” 等抽象概念。甲骨文之現代演繹是以墨書於紙上，出鋒尖削，以迅捷及略帶生澀的用筆，追求古人鐫刻細劃時急就之刀意。

02 大篆

殷商、周時期（約公元前1600-256年） 出現於青銅禮器上的文字通稱金文，又作“鐘鼎文”或“彝器款識”，書體則稱為大篆，有時又稱籀文。通篇書法，甚至出現於同一行中的文字，大小不一，而且富自然美。書法保留了較多象形元素，結體頗繁複，用筆凝重，其變化較多之曲線蘊含古典優雅之感。

03 小篆

秦朝（公元前221-206年）國定的標準書體，今稱小篆，它是秦始皇帝統一度量衡和文字等國策的時代產物。小篆用筆細長而多有弧線，簡化大篆較繁複的字形、結構，結體勻圓整齊而左右對稱。小篆之現代演繹，以中鋒用筆為主，輔以間中側鋒用筆，使字體在秀美中更顯靈活之感。

04 隸書

盛行於秦漢時期（公元前221年-公元220年），隸書是古體和今體的一道橋樑。從篆書簡化演變而形成的隸書，筆法逆入平出，呈“蠶頭雁尾”之筆勢 — 長劃起筆時，回鋒之筆法，使筆鋒藏於筆劃裡而不外露，形如蠶頭；波磔收筆時，已向下按的頓筆斜起，形如雁尾，體勢開張。這種強調“提”、“按”互補的筆法，刻意強化了運筆時的韻律感，其中所體現到毛筆的寫意抒懷的潛力，有助演變出後來較現代之書體。

05 章草

漸形成於公元前2世紀的章草，是一種簡化隸書。以較迅捷或潦草的行筆書寫隸書，寫成的“章草”書法，筆劃中蘊含隸書波磔，故又稱草隸。

06 草書

草書於公元3至4世紀發展得至為成熟。講求流暢性及速度的草書，筆劃及偏旁極為簡化，同行中，上一字的收筆與下一字的起筆，上下呼應，甚至以連筆或牽絲牽連在一起。

07 楷書

於公元2至4世紀發展得至為成熟的楷書，結構勻稱，字形方整。形態平穩、端正。因其撇撩分明，筆劃清楚，易於辨字，故今通用於印刷及一般公文。

08 行書

簡化了楷書的規矩，行書予人簡便、隨意之感。行筆迅捷，直抒胸臆，盡顯書者之個性。

1 以下有關中國書體演變的討論是根據 Lau Chak-kwong, "The Calligraphy Couplet as the Embodied Image of Literary Game," in *The Auspicious Image*, edited by Lau Chak-kwong (Hong Kong: Academy of Visual Arts, Hong Kong Baptist University, 2007), *vi-ix*，並略作調節。

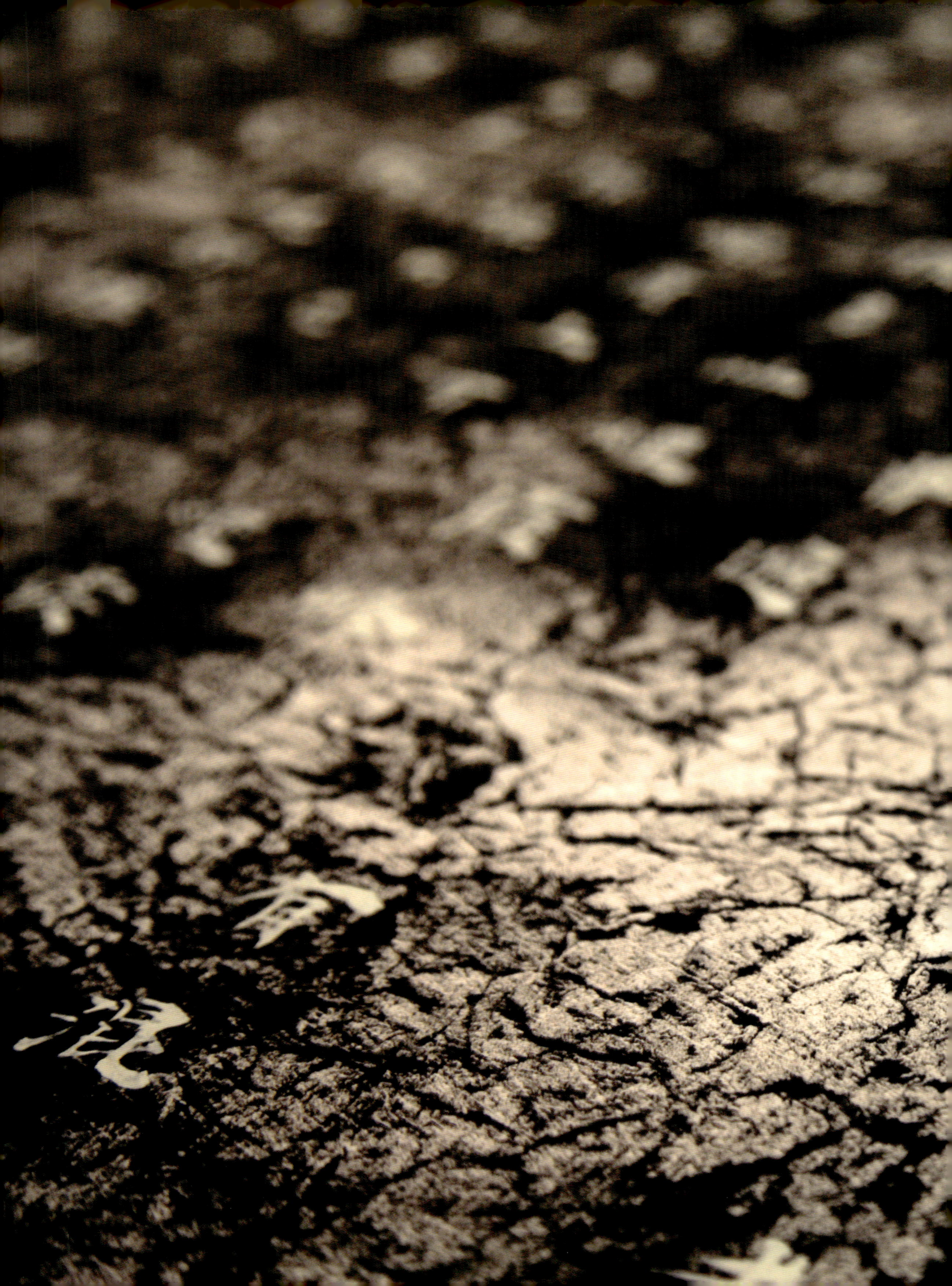

東藝西看

PROLOGUE/前言

Eastern Art through Western Eyes

The Pioneering Spirit of the Integration between Academic Theory and Creative Practice as Embodied in a Three-Dimensional Format: The Potency of Daniel Lau's Art

Chris Rothermel
Assistant Professor
Hong Kong Baptist University

When viewing Dr. Daniel Lau's work in his recent solo exhibition I am again taken back by the fluidity and potential risk that he expresses within and beyond his discipline. My impression as a layman is that in order to use these techniques in such a free and expressive manner one must spend much time technically learning and becoming fluent with the brush, the ink and the cutting of the seal. This is of course on top of a seemingly endless study of the thousands of different scripts and their expressive stylistic possibilities. Furthermore, the historical significance and, in Daniel's case, the contemporary relevance all contributes to his interest in giving us a glimpse of where theory meets practice and where the written word or character gathers new possibilities when presented in a three dimensional format.

It is at this point that I find Daniel's work so intriguing. Like myself, I believe in taking risks with my work and ideas. I believe that the answers to my interests do not only lie in the three-dimensional sphere but must coexist between the image and a space. It is here that Daniel's work seems to thrive and transform. Earlier I mentioned risk, what I mean is that Daniel's work, is in some cases, riding the line of the tradition and pushing forward into new areas of knowing within and beyond his discipline. In fact I don't think of him as merely a calligrapher, Chinese painter and seal-engraver. He is in fact a Visual Artist that embraces all of these areas and more to transform them into something completely new and unique.

Daniel's work has left the wall and has come into our space. His work has challenged our understanding of the written character and pushed it into real experience. He has taken naturally formed materials and given it back to the Creator with such humble yet eloquent writing. As a sculptor I find his work refreshing and accessible. His work breathes and moves in the space with honesty and strength.

體現於三維空間之學術理論結合藝術實踐的拓荒精神：劉澤光藝術之感染力 ◣

羅斯麥
香港浸會大學助理教授

觀賞劉澤光博士最近的個人展覽，令我再次驚訝到他所表現於其藝術領域，以致超越其範疇所顯現的流暢性與潛藏的勇於冒險精神。作為門外漢，我感受到的是，要做到如斯自由奔放而富於表現力，其於書畫篆刻的造詣必然下個不少苦工。加上他對古今書畫風格體變鍥而不捨的深入研究，在在顯出其在歷史意義上，以至於當代關聯中，都促使劉博士展現在我們眼前的，那種對理論結合實踐的探求，及於書寫字體於三維空間展示的新探索。

由於這特點，我發現劉博士的作品意趣盎然。就仿如在我自己的作品與理念裡，我相信於險中探索，不單在於三維空間，而是同時存藏於形象與空間之中，去找尋答案，正是於這裡，劉博士的作品繁衍蛻變。 剛才我提及的冒險精神，就是劉博士於其一些作品中表現出那種跨越傳統，推陳出新的精神，因此我不獨將他視為書法家，國畫大師以及篆刻家，而是抱持各家於一身，融和貫通，追求革新的一個視覺藝術家。

劉博士的作品跳出牆垣，走入空間，挑戰我們對文字的既定認知，推進嶄新的體驗。他將樸實而富表現力的書法書於渾然天成的自然物料中，以有説服力卻又謙遜的文字回饋造物主。作為雕塑家，我發現他的作品新穎脱俗，平易近人，淳樸而雄厚的氣息，縈繞於空間之中。

Harmony – Through the Journey of a Western Eye

Emma Watts
Lecturer
Hong Kong Baptist University

To the Western eye the calligraphy and the characters of the Chinese language are a mystery. We know we are looking at a visual language of words, with meaning and instruction, but what we see are abstract images that defy interpretation and yet hold the viewer in captive focus. The ink-formed characters provide the viewer with the association of the irresistible mystery, the ultimate puzzle of a visual language and the human pursuit for understanding.

The forms and structure of calligraphy, created with ink and brush, are sublime in their ability to create space and dynamic motion. The energy of each character presents a visual anticipation, which forces interpretation without knowledge of the language. The art challenges the western reading of the characters in both visual form and their literal meaning.

How we decipher and decode the characters of the calligraphy, without comprehension of individual meaning, embodies the synergy between the chapters of the Harmony body of work; Heaven and Man, Give and Receive, Black and White, Vulgarity and Elegance.

Throughout Harmony, Dr Daniel Lau combines the art of calligraphy in a compilation of mediums; paper, sculptural forms, maze installation and seal engraving. These four mediums present the navigation for a course of discovery in the journey for western interpretation.

The essence of calligraphy, and the articulation of the word, is the beginning of the Western journey. The use of ink on paper is not solely or exclusively a Chinese practice but its application, and intentions, transforms perception of the most basic function of writing and reading. Too often in Western culture we see ink as machine printed on paper, handwriting has become a rarity. As such the art of Chinese calligraphy carries a weight of inferred meaning, reinforcing a symbol of culture through the art of individual skill and tradition.

In Western culture the use of the 'word' is similarly loaded with expectation and cultural perceptions. Within the historiography of Western art, letters from the English alphabet have been frequently used, from Cubist newsprint collages to Fluxus and the visual manipulation of concrete poetry. However, letters often appear as sign posts, merely elements, presented in artistic format. By contrast the characters of calligraphy are the subjects of the art, transforming the ordinary into the extraordinary.

The differences in English and Chinese language add to the complexities of definition. The word letter is used to describe the symbols from the English language alphabet, the word suggesting a near clinical function, to provide a framework for the formation of words and written communication. By contrast the English definition of character presents a multifaceted meaning combining the nature of positive qualities and individuality of spirit, to aspire and inspire.

Tranquillity (cat no.144) possesses the qualities of the English definition of character. Moving beyond the instruction of the title, the image of the script takes the viewer through the physical formation of the character and leaves us with a vision of the journey the art has taken. The imagery explores the pathways and mysteries of the ink, creating a visual experience that demands contemplation and alludes to the sense of a spiritual core and a deeper dimension as our eye follows the ink as it trails away and off the paper.

Lau's Harmony pieces present calligraphy characters that go further than merely explaining, rather they extend the dimensions of visual language. Each work explores the significance of form to present the viewer with calligraphy central to an image of balance and meditative power. Lau's use of medium explores this relationship in a fundamental and elemental combination between character and material.

The glass piece, *A Deep and Tranquil Mountain* (cat no.5) explores this concept in delicate, yet dramatic, organic form. Described by Lau as experimental calligraphy utilising the character shan or mountain, the piece provokes the essence of the mountain. The physicality suggested in the title echoes in the fluid solidity of the form, and is further loaded with a sensory experience that possesses an untouchable and ethereal quality. The piece contains meanings that are layered in a voyage of interpretation through the medium, the shape of the character shan and translation of the mountain evolve through these layers, exploring the multi faceted experience of personal interpretation, ideas, memory and physical recollection of the mountain.

Lau further explores his use of calligraphy as an elemental connection point, creating unusual unions between mediums. *Awestruck* (cat no.2) introduces seal script to a piece of raw teak wood, resulting in a piece that seems to grow as it is viewed. The elegance of the script, literally, is the character of the fronds and tendrils of nature and contrasts with the raw un-worked piece of teak. The union of the mediums echoes the fundamental relationship of life, the connection between man and nature. The objectivity of both the wood and the ink evolve into an elemental subjective synergy of a natural organic Harmony.

The installation piece of ink, water and paper on wooden boxes; *Walking in the Mystifying Haze* (cat no.22) is a physical maze, expanding the boundaries of calligraphy and introducing another dimension for interpretation. The intention is the deviation from the predetermined way of reading traditional calligraphy works. For the Western viewer the maze is akin to a learning structure and reinforces the mystery and depth in each character. The pictorial element of the characters are bound in an installation of scale and dimension which expands the voyage of discovery with a near musical interpretation of tones and notes that echo from the floor structure in an interactive experience which further pushes the boundaries of convention and understanding.

The seal engravings intensify the focus of the script and reveal an intimate invitation for enquiry. Small and beautifully formed, these pocketsize articulations contain story, personality and the specificity of the individual. They link to the works of calligraphy as the mark of authorship and provide the viewer with an association of personal connection with the art and creativity. The intimacy of the seals becomes slightly voyeuristic in nature, which initiates an intense personal connection. The visual, personal bond echoes across the walls and floor of each of the pieces, through the individual personality of each of the seal's characters, linking the viewer to the art. Meaning and definition, which define the Western eye, become insignificant in the face of the art.

The dichotomy for the Western eye is intertwined with breaking through the barriers of difference and, at points, the barriers of ignorance, to decode the art via the aesthetic of the image; tracing the shapes in the corners of the memory, to acknowledge the character of the script. The pathway for resolution is found in the articulation of the character, which loaded with the Western meaning of depth and positive qualities, becomes the focus and, moreover, the vessel of the visual journey as the art is visually broken down into its constitute parts. The application of the ink transforms into a character, the character evolves into script, and the subsequent interaction with each of the differing mediums completes the experience of discovery.

Lau's body of work presents calligraphy, script and seal as Harmony, which guides the un-educated through the puzzle of language. His intense and powerful expression of each character focuses the possibilities of interpretation and resonates through the depth and spirit of Western definition to inspire.

西方人觀和之旅

屈艾瑪
香港浸會大學講師

於西方人眼中，書法與中文字猶如一個謎團。我們知悉所看到的是一種滿有意義而有所指的視覺語言，但觀者雖難以解讀所見的抽象形像，卻令人全神貫注。由墨跡所描繪出的字形，令觀者聯想到一種不可抗的謎團，那種源於對視覺語言的迷亂與人類對認知的追求的聯繫。

以墨與毛筆，作為的形式與結構，書法可提昇成藝術正是其對空間的演化與躍動的能力。每個字體的神態形成了一種視覺期待，從而道出一種不求於語意層面的演繹，中國書法這種藝術，對西方以視覺形式與語意層面的去解讀字體，提出了質疑。

我們如何能在個別意義的不了解中，解讀書法中字體(個性)，具體表現在"和 -劉澤光 古今相生書法篆刻"的作品篇章中的：天與人，施與受，黑與白，雅與俗。

通過"和"，劉博士於書法藝術中結合了一系列的媒介包括：紙，雕塑，迷宮裝置，篆刻。透過這四種媒介，刻劃出西方演繹的發現之旅的一本指南。

西方對書法認知的起點，正在於書法的本質與字的清晰度。於紙上用墨並非中國獨有的習性，但中國書法於應用與意味方面，卻轉化了我們對讀寫的基本認知。 在西方文化中，墨往往被視為紙上的機械印刷，手寫本已見稀少，於此中國書法藝術卻通過個人技藝與承傳，成為了強化文化的符號。

在西方文化中，單字的運用同樣隱含著期許與文化覺差。在西方藝術史學中，從立體派的報刊拼貼到激浪派及詩文的視覺運用中，文字以至英文字母都經常被引用，但文字往往只以標示或純原素表現於藝術形式中。相對地，中文書法的字體本身，從平凡中蜕變出超凡，而成為藝術的主體。

英文與中文的差異，更令定義複雜化。英文字中 letter 是用於描述英文字母中的符號，表示其提供一個文字形成的框架及書寫傳意功能。相對地，於英文定義中的 character 卻呈現了多方面意義，結合了正面的素質，個性，渴望，觸發靈感等意義。

《寧》(展品144) 作品中，富有英文定義中的 character (個性)的質素。超越了主題標示，以字體的形象，觀者被牽引到字體的藝術創作的形成旅程，這意象探索了墨跡的奧妙，藉著我們的眼追隨著墨的游走至跳出紙張，營造出視覺經驗中對沉思的追求，以致暗喻其核心精神面貌與深度。

劉博士的作品中，書法字體的表現超越了純粹解説，擴張了視覺語言的深度，每件作品探索了造形的重要性，呈現給觀者一種以書法為主體的對稱與感染力，於媒介的運用中，探索了對字體(個性)與質料的基本關係。

《山深杳杳》(展品5)的玻璃作品以細緻，富戲劇性而有機地探索了這些概念。劉博士將此形容為實驗性書法，以山字於作品中，引發起對山的精髓，其質感顯出主題中固體形態的流動性，進而暗視了那種不可觸碰與輕盈的觸覺質素，作品承載著於媒介中層層疊疊的演繹，山字的字型與通過這些層次的演繹，探索了多方面對山的個人演繹，理念，記憶與親身經歷。

劉博士更以書法作為原點，創作出非一般的混合媒介作品。 《驚歎》(展品2)，將篆書引用到一柚木原材，使作品在觀賞中衍生，字體的優雅形象正如自然中的蕨類葉片與蔓藤，與原材無雕琢的柚木形成比對，不同媒介的融合，反映出生命的基本關係，人與天的結合，木材與墨的客體性，相生出原形主體，自然而有機的融和。

《裝置作品走進撲朔迷離的"煙霞"》(展品22) 以迷宮形式，用墨水描繪於木盒上的紙，擴展了書法的疆界，引入新演繹，並意圖使人脱離閱讀傳統書法作品的預定方法。對西方觀者，迷宮形同學習結構，而且強化了每個字謎的深度，象形文字被裝置的比例與規範束縛，卻擴展出一種近乎音樂演繹音色與音符的發現之旅，回盪於樓板的互動體驗，將習氣與認知推出疆界。

篆刻作品則強化了字型的焦點，揭開了知性的追求，小巧而優雅的設計卻載滿了故事，個性，個人的偏愛。印章以作者的記號的形式連繫到書法作品，使觀者能夠將個人聯繫到藝術創作上。印章的小巧親切，使人有窺探的感覺，觸發強烈的個人聯繫，視覺上與個人的結合縈繞在每件作品，每個印章字體的個性，都將觀者連繫到篆刻藝術。西方看重的意思與定義，於篆刻藝術變得無關宏旨。

西方人眼中的二分法， 糾纏於突破差異的障礙，或於某些方面，突破無知的障礙，所以試圖將這藝術，透過影像的美學，追逐於記憶中的形狀，甚或認知手稿中的字體去解讀，解決的途徑在於，專注於字體的節理，這隱含了西方所說的深度與正面素質，再加上以這視覺旅程的載體作為藝術，被分解為組成部份，將墨轉化為字體，由字體衍生出手稿，以至其後不同媒介的互動，就完滿了這經驗。

劉博士以“和”呈現其書法，手稿及印章作品，帶引未知者穿越語言字謎，其於每個字體強而有力的表現力，聚合了演繹的可能性，就如西方精神中所謂的觸發靈感。

天与人

CHAPTER 1/ 第一章

Heaven & Man

Harmony:
Meditations on Culture, Art and Life

Daniel C.K. Lau
Assistant Professor
Hong Kong Baptist University

Tracing the Origin of Harmony

In the long history of Chinese culture, the concept and philosophy of harmony has always been dominating the leading values of the society through time and space. Confucianism, as an important pillar of Chinese culture, considers "harmony" the universal philosophy of life, as well as the core of ideological system to build a harmonious society. Hence, Chinese people often say: "everything prospers in a harmonious family" (cat. no. 20).

There are two versions of the Chinese character "harmony" (*he*和) in modern Chinese language: a simple version *he* 和 and a complex version *he*龢. Their meanings are indistinguishable; however, they were two distinct words in ancient times. According to *Shuowen jiezi*說文解字 (A Lexicon of Chinese Characters, circa. 100A.D.), *he*龢 means "tune", denoting harmonious music; while 和means "echo". Today the two words are interchangeable, meaning harmony and mediation. Hence, the two variations of the Chinese character *he* ("和"and "龢"), as commonly used nowadays, are apparently related to harmonious music. To understand the latent meaning of the Chinese character *he*龢, one needs to examine how the ancients created the character *yue* "龠",which is the radical of *he*龢, and its relevant meanings. According to Guo Morou's (1892-1978) *A Research on Oracle Bone Script*, the character *yue* "龠"was first created as a pictograph — one of the six-principles theory of Chinese script (*liushu*六書); the pictographic character resembles the form of pipes arranged in order. The character *yue* "龠" in bronze script (great seal script) consists of pictographic symbols indicating the openings of the pipe ends.[1] Hence, in ancient time, the character *yue* "龠",which is the radical of *he*龢, was used to indicate a kind of musical instrument produced by arranging bamboo pipes in order. *Erya* (an ancient dictionary) even points out that the character *he* (和) was the name of a kind of ancient musical instrument called *sheng*.[2] *Sheng* is a wind instrument. Since the two Chinese characters *he* (和) and *he* (龢) were closely related to music in ancient time, they mutually convey the meaning of harmony in music in present time.

Entitled "Harmony", the first work in this catalogue (cat. no. 1) accentuates the framework of the whole publication. The work consists of 50 small pieces (30.5 x 30.5 cm each), 49 of which are calligraphy rendered in different types of script (oracle bone script, great and small seal scripts, clerical script, draft cursive and modern cursive scripts, semi-cursive script and standard script) and styles for the Chinese character harmony (*he* 和, and龢); and one for inscription from Matthew 5:9 "Blessed are the peacemakers, for they will be called children of God." The pieces, ink on paper, are mounted in transparent, crystal clear plexiglass, which are supported by cylindrical metal tubes of various lengths to produce a relief sculpture that stands out from the huge peach wood wall. A collection of various script styles and styles from ancient and modern times, this large scale calligraphic installation work exemplifies the purport of harmony, the lifeworks of our ancestral scholars, and synergy between tradition and the contemporary in a more modern look.

This work was created for the Chung Chi Christian Festival (2010) organized by Chung Chi College, The Chinese University of Hong Kong. The exhibit is a large scale work comprises of "seven" groups of "seven" single Chinese characters. As the number "seven" repeatedly symbolizes completeness or perfection in Scripture, this work's theme of harmony is sublimated with a biblical symbolism of completeness. Moreover, this work emphasizes the natural harmony of different colors and the interaction between brushstroke and space. The synergistic effect created by various visual elements further interprets the meaning/ idea of harmony.

1 See *Hanyu da zidian* (A Dictionary of Chinese Language) (Wuhan and Chengdu: Hubei cishu chubanshe and Sichuan cishu chubanshe, 2001), vol. 4, p. 4807.

2 Zheng Chao, *Erya zhu* (Annotation of Erya) (*Siku quanshu* version, hereafter SKQS), *juan zhong*, pp. 7b-8a.

This artwork was created as a response to a growing societal issue of family violence. The news may only be revealing a small fraction of cases, and I am afraid there are many more hidden in the society. In this city life which is full of tension, many people are filled with resentment, and the families have lost their harmony. The repeated character "Harmony" in this work and their interwoven relations remind the audience that one must treasure human relationship.

The Aesthetics of "Equilibrium and Harmony"

In the Yong Chapter of *The Analects of Confucius* by Kong Zi, "Perfect is the virtue which is according to the Constant Mean (Zhongyong)!"[3], so he sees "the constant mean" as the highest state of self-cultivation. "The Mean" is expanded to the ideology of "equilibrium and harmony" in *The Book of Rites*, "this equilibrium is the great root from which grow all the human actings in the world, and this harmony is the universal path which they all should pursue. Let the states of equilibrium and harmony exist in perfection, and a happy order will prevail throughout heaven and earth, and all things will be nourished and flourish."[4] "Harmony" implies the meaning of "order". Therefore, "harmony" means not only a state of unison and completion, but also the utopia where the overall conformity as well as order is emphasized. This Confucius ideology of "equilibrium and harmony" has a profound influence on the later aesthetics.[5]

"Equilibrium and Harmony" in Calligraphy

Calligraphy scholar, Xiang Mu, from the Ming Dynasty interprets the "beauty of equilibrium and harmony" in calligraphy by the interaction between "square" and "round", and using "odd/ deviant" to complement the "standard". "Roundedness in square, and square yet rounded/ curved; the standard can embrace the odd while the odd would not relinquish the standard. They all come together in equilibrium and harmony, and this is what beauty and goodness are[6]."

Kang Youwei (1858-1927) supplemented the above square-round concept in the art of calligraphy, and had concrete interpretation towards the aesthetics of this "equilibrium and harmony". He believes that the logic of square-round concept can be embodied in the "the used of brush," or brush method, and the visual effect by the consequent brushstrokes. "The wonders of calligraphy lie entirely in the use of brush. The essence is in the square-round interaction. Once the technique is mastered, it will be accomplished. Pressing to get square, lifting to get roundedness.[7] "Pressing" here refers to a downward motion of the tip of the brush, while "lifting" refers to a slight vertical upward movement of the brush with the brush tip still touching the paper throughout the writing. Kang further exemplifies the aesthetic sense resulting from these two ways of use of brush, "Lifting results in elegance and coherence, pressing results in preciseness. Rounded brushstroke is disperse and free; square brushstroke is congealed, orderly and calm." Kang also explains the femininity and masculinity connotations of "round brush" and "square brush" in a metaphorical way: "Lifting is like gossamer curling up in the air, while pressing is like a lion cub squatting on the ground." Kang emphasizes that both square and round are necessary, "the brilliance lies in the use of both square and round, they are neither square nor round, but at the same time they are both square and round." [8] The "lifting" and "pressing" of the brush reflect a rhythm upon which the calligrapher's thoughts and feelings flow naturally onto the paper in the form of complimentary ink shapes from the "lifting" and "pressing" motions.[9]

Entering the Past, Exiting the Present

On the basis of examining the brush methods and aesthetics of equilibrium and harmony in Chinese calligraphy, inheritance and innovation in calligraphy are undoubtedly two major aspects of the author's active exploration. "Entering the past, exiting the present" is the author's manifesto of his creative endeavor in Chinese calligraphy, which lucidly expresses the author's aspiration to earnestly study the spirit and skills of Chinese calligraphy, and at the same time, inject contemporary thoughts and content in his art. *Louis Vuitton & Porsche* (cat. no. 23) is an intriguing

3 *Lunyu zhushu* (Commentaries on the Analects, SKQS version), *juan* 6, 16. Translation of *The Doctrine of the Mean*, Zhong Yong, is by James Legge, in The Chinese Classics, vol. 1 (reprinted by Hong Kong University Press, 1960). http://www.international.ucla.edu/eas/documents/lunyuCh6.htm.
4 *Liji zhushu* (Commentaries on The Book of Rites) (SKQS version), *juan* 52, 2. Translation of equilibrium and harmony (*zhong he*), is by James Legge, in The Chinese Classics, vol. 1 (reprinted by Hong Kong University Press, 1960). http://www.chinaknowledge.de/Literature/Classics/zhongyong.html
5 The major arguments of this paragraph is adapted from Lau Chak-kwong, "The Embodiment of Confucian Aesthetics in Kang Youwei's (1858-1927) Theories and Practice of Calligraphy", in Conference Proceedings of "The Modern Interpretation of the Confucian Aesthetics: The First Mainland China, Taiwan, Hong Kong Chinese Aesthetics Academic Conference" p. 79.

6 Xiang Mu, *Shufa Yayan* ("SKQS version), p. 19.
7 Kang Youwei, *Guang yizhou shuangji* (shanghai: Shanghai guji chubanshe, 1996), p. 83
8 ibid.
9 The major arguments of this paragraph are adapted from Lau Chak-kwong, "The Embodiment of Confucian Aesthetics in Kang Youwei's (1858-1927) Theories and Practice of Calligraphy" p. 79-80.

work that witnesses the artist's practice of his manifesto. This work's inspiration comes from *Seven-character-line Couplet in Seal Script* by Zhang Huiyan (1761-1802):

> *Between heaven and earth, the Songs and Documents, are most precious.*
> *Within a family, filial piety and fraternal love take precedent.*[10]
> 天地間詩書最貴
> 家庭內孝弟為先

However, *Louis Vuitton & Porsche* presents a humorously twisted literary content of this couplet:

> *Between heaven and earth, LV is the most expensive.*
> *Amidst the busy city, Porsche is genuinely showy.*
> 天地間 L V 最貴
> 鬧市中波子真威

Hong Kong people like to refer to the famous French fashion brand Louis Vuitton as "LV". Meanwhile, the famous sports car brand Porsche is commonly pronounced by Hong Kong people as "*bozi*" "波子"— the Cantonese homophone that represents a similar speech sound as the English pronunciation of Porsche.

In traditional Chinese society, the cultural value of poetry writing and book learning and the virtues of filial piety and fraternal love highlighted in the five basic human relationships in Confucianism had been emphasized. However, these traditional values have been frequently ignored in contemporary metropolitan situations, as exemplified by the phenomena that consumerism and hedonism are all the rage in Hong Kong — while there are always long queues in front of the LV flagship shops without a moment's pause, the ubiquitous Porsche sports cars in eye-catching shimmering yellow speedily swagger around town.

Rendered in a bitterly satirical manner, *Louis Vuitton & Porsche* subverts the tradition of the practice of Chinese calligraphy. First, works of traditional Chinese calligraphy are usually executed in black ink against white paper which accentuates the honest and unadorned aesthetics and the modest and self-effacing spirit treasured by the Chinese. By contrast, *Louis Vuitton & Porsche* utilizes the colors that allude to the typical colors of the products of Louis Vuitton and Porsche — mud yellow monogram against brown color for classic Louis Vuitton products and the bright yellow commonly painted on showy sports cars.

Second, traditional calligraphic couplets are mounted as hanging scrolls to be symmetrically hung on the left and right of the wall. In contrast, *Louis Vuitton & Porsche* deviates from the tradition of reading the couplet vertically from top to bottom and from right to left in that each character from the original couplet was brushed on individual canvas frame and eventually hung on a huge wall (approximately 6m (height) x 9m (width)) to form a random pattern in an overwhelming configuration (see photo showing this work at 1/F, Koo Ming Kown Exhibition Gallery, Communication and Visual Arts Building, Hong Kong Baptist University) (cat. no. 23). It is intriguing to note that the strict parallelism governing the traditional couplet is obviously noticeable in *Louis Vuitton & Porsche* in that the mirroring effect between the irregular shapes of arrangement of the frames on the upper wall and the lower wall tellingly suggests that the pairing of different constituents from the upper line (*shang lian* 上聯: Between heaven and earth, LV is the most expensive) and the lower line (*xia lian* 下聯: Amidst the busy city, Porsche is genuinely showy) achieves a strict parallelism: while "heaven and earth" and "the busy city" are matched nouns indicating the spaces or places where the strange phenomena take place, "between" and "amidst" are matched prepositions, "LV" and "Porsche" are matched nouns (brand names), and "expensive" and "showy" are matched adjectives.

A Celebration of Life (cat. no. 15) and *Walking in the Mystifying Haze* (cat. no. 22) are two other examples of calligraphic works that transform the traditional mounting method and mode of display into a contemporary approach of installation that can effectively accentuates the concepts, ideas and content of calligraphic works. For *A Celebration of Life— A Diary Witnessing the Loving-one-another Spirit Amidst the Great Sichuan Earthquake*, the original album of 24 leaves of handwriting in small-character stand script was transformed into an aerial and mobile installation. The reflection of light on the plexiglass complements the naturally air/ wind-driven mobile installation to efficaciously intensify the latent rhythm embodied in the ode-like diary — *A Celebration of Life*.

10 This couplet is featured in Jason C. Kuo & Peter C. Sturman (ed.), *Double Beauty: Qing Dynasty Couplets from the Lechangzai Xuan Collection* (Hong Kong: Art Museum, The Chinese University of Hong Kong, 2003), cat. 82. Please note that the expression of "*Songs and Documents*" in the couplet is a translation denoting the meaning of The Book of Songs(詩經) and The Book of Documents (書經). This translation of *shi* 詩and *shu* 書 ("*Songs and Documents*") can alternatively be replaced by the literal meanings of the two words *shi* 詩and *shu* 書 — "poetry" and "book".

Walking in the Mystifying Haze (cat. no. 22) is intended to break away from ideas, conventions and the method of display for traditional calligraphic practice. Created in the style in "imitation of rubbing from stone carving in clerical-standard script," the paper-based artwork is mounted on 16 square prisms of varied heights. The prisms are spread out on the gallery wall and floor, specially arranged into a maze-like installation space. The artwork, consisted of 14 Chinese characters and a long inscription, will need to be viewed by walking along a specially designed meandering path of the "maze". The physical "maze" alludes to the evasive deviation from the predetermined way of reading traditional calligraphic works.

The literary content of the artwork is a modern poem composed by the artist:

Haze has shrouded the city.
In the romantic veil,
health is
fading…
away!

The poem satirizes the Chinese term "*yanxia*", or haze (literally smoke and colorful glow), used in Hong Kong Observatory's weather reports to refer to "polluted air". Such a description has romanticized the urban air pollution problem, since the term "*yanxia*" embodies a poetic sentiment and inspires picturesque imagination. Being continually immersed in such romanticization, people's vigilance of the problem is numbed, and their health consciousness keeps being undermined. In the artwork, the massive maze-like installation space mocks the widespread obfuscation of the public message. The artwork provides a unique interactive experience as the audience physically and literarily strolls through the poem

Harmony: Four Types of Relationship

There are four chapters in this book; each chapter comprises works of calligraphy and seal engraving and academic essays to investigate the following four types of relationships:

Chapter 1 – Heaven and Man

This chapter, on the one hand describes the relationship between man and nature or the environment, on the other hand expresses the valuable relationship between men. There is love between heaven and earth. The resources and blessings from mother nature are no doubt a free gifts, yet the response from human varies: sometimes awestruck by the wonders of nature, sometimes enlightened, yet sometimes damaging. For instance, revealing the artist's incisive admiration of the natural object, the jerky brushstrokes appeared on *Awestruck* (cat. no. 2) reinforce the coarse texture of a piece of weathered teak wood, and the "momentum" (*shi* 勢) generated from its twisting form. Every single element in nature is the subject of human appreciation as this is tellingly exemplified by the picturesque imagery portrayed in *Eight-character-line Couplet in Oracle-bone Script* (cat. no. 7):

The morning sun rises up above the woods,
shining on the playful mountain finches.
The setting sun goes down beyond the trees,
casting light upon the homeward ox herds.
初日出林燕雀追逐
斜陽在樹牛羊下來

As the Daoist philosophy emphasizes very much on the harmonious relationship between humanity and the cosmos, *Meditating on the Wisdom of Laozi* (cat. no. 13) compellingly reflects that both the artist's act of transcribing the whole text of *Laozi* (the Daoist philosophy) and the viewer's act of reading the text are processes of meditation on this harmonious union between nature and man. In fact, natural phenomena always embody an intense sense of wisdom that can enlighten the human mind as this is revealed in *Seven-character-line Couplet in Clerical Script* (cat. no. 12):

Scenery stays still no matter how rapidly the water flows.
A quiet mind is always kept no matter how frequently the flowers wither and fall.
水流任急景常靜
花落雖頻意自閒

Moreover, works presented in this chapter profoundly reflect that human relationship needs to be supported by love and care. *Everlasting Love* (cat. no. 18) commemorates not only the love mutually experienced by the artist and his wife but also a sense of togetherness when sojourning in Southern California in 2004. Indeed, "love" is the most exalted reflection among human relations. The quest for reunion with love ones is subtly expressed in *Seven-character-line Couplet in Seal Script* (cat. no. 19):

Man becomes an experienced traveler for there have been thousands of miles that he goes;

Mid-Autumn Festival comes again easily as one year has passed very quickly.
萬里因循成久客
一年容易又中秋

The inscription of this couplet further delineates how the artists treasured every moment with his students and family:

> I wrote this pair of couplets occasionally when talking with my students on the Mid-Autumn Day in the year of *gengyin* (2010). I don't know in what kind of manner the couplets were executed, for they were neither in seal script nor in clerical script. I intended to finish this work as a demonstration for my calligraphy class, but after I finished writing, I started to think that it was not suitable for the students to follow, because the untrammeled brush and ink were too hard for the beginners to perceive, hence can merely for my own amusement. I have sojourned in the United States for six years. This year when I came back, I suddenly realized that how good it is to be at home. Nothing else can give me more love and joy than spending the Mid-Autumn Day with my beloved familiy.

The love between individuals becomes more intense in the face of natural disaster. This is especially evident in the Sichuan earthquake in 2008 as altruistic sentiments and behavior were touchingly documented in the form of a diary written by a life-rescuer first and later transcribed by the calligrapher who was deeply moved by all the heroic and selfless spirit of the rescuers (cat. no. 13).

Alas! Man's lofty aspirations and the pure heart sometimes get lost in the face of the materialistic city. The rest of artworks featured in Chapter one present a lamentation on the distorted relationship between man and nature as a result of both man's lack of awareness of environmental pollution (*Walking in the Mystifying Haze* (cat. no. 22)) and man's endless desires and the lost in vanity in contemporary Hong Kong as exemplified by *Louis Vuitton & Porsche* (cat. no. 23) and *Service for Renminbi* (*People's Currency*) (cat. no. 24)

Chapter 2 – Give and Receive

This chapter focuses on how like-minded people, especially those who are passionate and study traditional Chinese painting and calligraphy, maintain friendship by giving and receiving seals. Seals are mainly used to symbolize the seal owner. Whether for commercial contracts or for paintings and calligraphy, the seal impression serves as the evidence of commitment and promise, since the seal impression reminds the viewer of the seal owner as a person. Both Chinese words and pictorial images can be used to express the content of the seal. Apart from showing the names of individuals and organizations, seals can also be symbolic images and text to convey self-referential ideas, which not only reveal the seal owner's personalities, aspirations, hobbies, special life experience, personal values and religious beliefs and commitments, but also serve as a symbolic token of like-mindedness between the giver and the recipient of the seal.

For example, *Little Friend of the Ox-Shed* (cat. no. 111) is a set of two seals engraved with words and pictorial image respectively. The sobriquet seal reading "Little Friend of the Ox-Shed" 小棚友was engraved by Dr. Daniel C.K. Lau (author of this catalogue), while the portrait seal of Professor Wan Qingli was engraved by Miss. Mancy Li. These two seal impressions are shown together as a collaborative work: The red legend image seal, which looks lighter, is put above, while the white legend sobriquet seal, which looks heavier, is put below. Prof. Wan, a well-known art historian and artists, is now Chair Professor of Visual Arts, and Founding Director of Academy of Visual Arts, Hong Kong Baptist University. During the Cultural Revolution, Prof. Wan met with Li Keran (1907-1989) and other artists in ox-shed unexpectedly, and his sobriquet seal is meant to commemorate this marvelous life experience.[11] Furthermore, the relationship between the recipient and the givers of the "Little Friend of the Ox-Shed" seal also deserve to be mentioned. Prof. Wan (the recipient) was the supervisor of Dr. C.K. Lau (giver 1) when he studied for his master's degree at the University of Hong Kong, while Mancy Li (giver 2) was a student of Lau. Therefore, both the sobriquet seal by Lau and the portrait seal by Mancy are brimmed with their respect for their teachers and grand teacher. Genuine feelings stream down into the point of carving knives — In Mancy's eyes, Prof. Wan, her grand teacher, is both a respectable scholar, and an innocent and lively artist. She vividly captures the naughty facial expression of Prof. Wan, expressing his dual identity of both scholar and artist, and conveying his philosophy of life. Meanwhile, for Dr. C.K. Lau, his sobriquet seal is with double meaning too. "Little Friend of the Ox-Shed" not only represents Prof. Wan's extraordinary meeting with masters in the ox-shed, but also reminds Lau of his unfadable

11 Daniel C.K.Lau, *Impression: Seals Engraved by Daniel C.K. Lau* (Hong Kong: Academy of Visual Arts, Hong Kong Baptist University, 2009), p.17.

memory of meeting Prof. Wan, his abecedarian of the history of Chinese art at the University of Hong Kong. In sum, from the givers' perspective, seals can be used to commit their emotions for the receiver; and from the receiver's perspective, impressing the seal received on his own art work, also suggests a certain kind of in-group identification. Especially in the case mentioned above, as an outstanding artist and an art historian who enjoys distinguished reputation in the academic world, Prof. Wan is very strict with the seals imprinted on his paintings, because only selected seals can reach harmony with the content of the painting. Therefore, undoubtedly, impressing the image and sobriquet seals on his art works indicates his approval of the givers' artistic achievement. Hence, the giving and receiving of seals can illustrate the subtle interactions inside the art circle, as well as the latent cultural phenomenon.

Chapter 3 – Black and White

This chapter moves its focus from social network to a pair of abstract artistic concept: the relationship between "void"虛 and "solid"實, to discuss the concepts of "void" and "solid", "*yin*"陰 and "*yang*"陽, "black" and "white" as visual elements in Chinese art. The elements in each pair of concepts are of mutual attraction and opposition, and they are subtly applied in all the artworks shown in this chapter.

Emptiness (ca t. no. 128-1) is the best example to demonstrate the concept of "void-solid reciprocity" used in this chapter. In this experimental calligraphy, the Chinese character "*kong*" 空 (emptiness) is written in seal script in a hollow-out way with flowing and dripping ink on a piece of thin and transparent chiffon. Thus, when facing this work, audience have to read the abstract character with the help of their own imagination: They can no longer read as they are used to read black brushstrokes in the past, instead, they need to draw support from the concept of "void and solid reciprocity", and read the white and blank part so as to see the strokes. What's more, besides the interaction of "void" and "solid" used within the work, the brushstrokes and the consciousness of space also extend out of the work. This piece of calligraphy, exhibited in the Koo Ming Kown Exhibition Gallery in the Academy of Visual Arts, Hong Kong Baptist University, communes with the view outside the glass wall of the gallery. Its rhythmic ink and brushes interact with the outdoor environment under different angles of sunshine, and echoes to the ripples in the pond and trees in the distance (cat. no. 128-2,3) . The frame of the work is like a window, leading the audience's sight into a mysterious world: Are the ink, the brushes, the view, the time, and the existence of the audience themselves eternal or momentary? Are they real or just illusion? The work "Emptiness" invites its audience to think about such philosophical questions.

The relationship between "emptiness" and "fullness" then comes into the audience's mind. Perhaps it is just like what Laozi shares with us in Chapter 21 of *Dao De Jing*: "The Dao in its acting is something, highly inconceivable, highly incomprehensible. Incomprehensible, alas, inconceivable, alas: in its inside, there are images; inconceivable, alas, incomprehensible, alas: in its inside, there are beings."[12] Alas! How hard it is to define "void" and "solid"!

Chapter 4 – Elegance and Vulgarity

This series of artworks aim to go beyond the boundary of "elegance" and "vulgarity" and to explore a new relationship for them with experimental artistic approaches. Calligraphy was naturally related to "elegance", and totally unconnected with "vulgarity". The works in this chapter, however, illustrate that this pair of concept could be highly integrated with each other in calligraphy. For instance, *What?* (cat. no. 140) is a three-dimensional work inspired from the Cantonese dialect. The Cantonese expression " 咩話" has a twofold meaning: an exclamation of surprise or a question asking literally "what dialect?" Cantonese is a dialect that has "surprisingly" defied the fate of extinction of most minority languages and continues to remain in dominant use in Hong Kong even after the 1997 handover; it helps foster a strong sense of local identity and pride.

To celebrate Cantonese as a distinctive social and cultural phenomenon, the artist transforms the two Chinese characters "咩話" into a visual effect resembling a stone monument rubbing, and evoke an additional sense of historic association through a forcefully archaic and austere calligraphic style, thus taking the age-old and richly vernacular Cantonese dialect through the caverns of time into the dramatic present. In this way, Cantonese, which was unqualified to take its place in the higher circles, has integrated with calligraphy and transformed into an offbeat tool of academic inquiry, encouraging us to think about the local identity constructed by Cantonese dialect and culture in the modern society.

12 Laozi,*Dao De Jing*. Translation from: http://www.tao-te-king.org/.

和：文化、藝術與生活的沉思 ◣

劉澤光博士
香港浸會大學助理教授及視覺藝術碩士(藝術行政管理）課程總監

和諧朔源

在源遠流長的中國文化中，和諧的觀念和哲學一直支配着社會的主導價值觀，並貫穿着不同時空。作為中華文化重要支柱的儒家學説，以“和”為其宇宙人生觀及思想系統的核心，致力建構和諧社會。是故，中國人愛説：“萬事以和為貴”及“家和萬事興”(展品20)。

現代漢語中的“和”字，有簡單的“和”及繁複的“龢”兩種寫法，意思相通，但在古時卻本來是兩個不同的字。根據東漢許慎《説文解字》，“龢”解作“調”，意指協調、和諧；“和”字則解作“相應”，今二字相通，有“和諧、調和”之意。故今日通用“和”、“龢”二字，明顯的與和諧悦耳之音樂有關。要了解“龢” 字的最早含義，就得先研究古人創造 “龠” 字（即“龢” 的部首）時的造字法與相關的字義。據郭沫若（1892-1978）《甲骨文字研究》的考證，“龠” 是“象形”字，形似編管，金文(大篆)“龠”字中有表示“管頭之空”的形符。[1] 所以，“龠” (即龢字部首) 古時常用以表示一種用竹管編成的樂器。《爾雅》(一部古代詞典)更指出“和”是一種古代樂器名稱：“大笙謂之巢，小者謂之和”。[2] 笙是吹管樂器。正因“和”、“龢”二字在古時皆與音樂有關，所以它們今天都有音樂和諧的含義。

本書第一件作品（展品1）以“和”為題，點出了全書綱領。作品由50個小幅（30.5x30.5厘米）組成，分別為49幅以甲骨文、大篆、小篆、隸書、章草、今草、行書和楷書等不同書體、不同風格書成的“和”或“龢”字，以及1幅寫有《馬太福音》第五章第九節：“使人和睦的人有福了，因為他們必稱為神的兒子”的作品題識。水墨紙本的書法裝裱在晶瑩通透的有機玻璃中，長短不一的圓形金屬支柱使整套作品以浮雕形式突出桃木巨牆。集結古今不同書體及風格，此巨幅書法裝置，以較現代的面貌，在在體現全書“和諧”、“集大成”及“古今相生”的旨趣。

1 參見《漢語大字典》(武漢、成都：湖北辭書出版社、四川辭書出版社，2001)，卷4，頁4807。
2 鄭樵《爾雅註》（《四庫全書》本），卷中，頁7b-8a。

本作是應香港中文大學崇基學院邀請，為其基督教文化節（2010）而創作的參展作品，以“7”組、每組“7”個單字建構成一整體的巨幅作品。“7”是聖經中常用以象徵完全的數字，借用於此作時，能將“和諧”的主題昇華至“完全”之境。再者，此作強調不同顏色的自然調和並筆觸與空間的互動。各種視覺元素產生的協同效應，進一步詮釋了和諧之意。

這件作品的創作動機，是對社會上愈見頻繁的家庭暴力事件作出回應。從新聞裏看到的個案都是被報導的少數，隱藏在社區裏的恐怕更多。在緊張的都市生活中，許多人充滿怨氣，家庭也失去和睦。此作以不斷重複的“和”字，以及它們交織出的關係，提醒觀眾必須珍視人與人之間的關係。

“中和”美學思想

孔子《論語 · 雍也》説：“中庸之為德也，其至矣乎。”[3] 可見他視“中庸”為一種修養的最高境界。《禮記· 中庸》將“中庸”擴展至“中和”的思想：“中也者，天下之大本也；和也者，天下之達道也。致中和，天地位焉，萬物育焉。”[4] “和”蘊含“秩序”的含義。因此，“和”不單是和諧、圓滿的狀態，更是一種著重整體協調而有秩序的理想境界。儒家的“中和”思想對後世審美觀影響頗深。[5]

中和書法

明代書論家項穆以“方”、“圓”互動和“正”、“奇”互補的概念闡釋書法需具備的“中和之美”：“圓而且方，方而復圓，正能含奇，奇不失正，會於中和，斯為美善。”[6] 康有為對以上有關書法藝術的方圓概念作了一些補充，並對“中和”審美觀作出具體的演譯。他認為方圓之理可體現於“運筆”方法

3 《論語注疏》（《四庫全書》本），卷6，頁16。
4 《禮記註疏》（《四庫全書》本），卷52，頁2。
5 此段大部份論點曾載於劉澤光《論康有為(1858-1927)書法理論及實踐中蘊含的儒家美學思想》，載《儒家美學思想的現代闡釋— 岸三地首屆中國美學學術研討會論文集》，頁79。
6 項穆《書法雅言》（《四庫全書》本），頁19。

及其產生筆觸的視覺效果："書法之妙，全在運筆，該舉其要，盡於方圓，操縱極熟，自有巧妙。方用頓筆，圓用提筆，提筆中含，頓筆外拓，中含者渾勁，外拓者雄強。"[7] "頓筆"指以毛筆書寫時，將筆鋒用力向下按，"提筆"則指行筆時，將已按下的筆鋒垂直向上提起，但筆尖不離紙面。康有為更進一步説明這兩種運筆方法分別產生出相應的美感："提筆婉而通，頓筆精而密。圓筆者蕭散、超逸，方筆者凝、整、沉著。"康氏又以比喻説明"圓筆"和"方筆"流露出陰柔和陽剛的意蘊："提筆如遊絲裊空，頓筆如獅狻蹲地。"康氏更 調方圓兼備，缺一不可："妙處在方圓並用，不方不圓，亦方亦圓"。[8] 運筆時的"提"、"頓"其實反映一種節奏感，在"提"、"頓"互補的筆墨中，書者在創作時的思緒和感情自然地傾流於紙上。[9]

入古出今

在探究書法的用筆及中和美學的基礎上，書法的承傳與創新，無疑是本書作者努力探索的兩大課題。《入古出今》（展品123）是作者書法創作的宣言，明確表達作者既有潛心鑽研傳統書法精神和技法的志向，亦同時在作品的內容和形式注入當代的思想內容和面貌。《LV與波子》(展品23) 是一有趣的"入古出今" 實踐。創作靈感源於張惠言 （1761-1802） 的《篆書七言聯》:

天地間詩書最貴
家庭內孝弟為先[10]

然而，《LV與波子》幽默的將聯文改為:

天地間 LV最貴
鬧市中波子真威

香港人常以LV簡稱法國名牌時裝Louis Vuitton；波子則是港人以粵語諧音稱名牌跑車Porsche。中國傳統社會重視的詩書、學問、修養等文化價值以及強調孝弟的儒家人倫觀，在當代都市的處境中經常被人忽視。相反，消費及享樂主義在香港大行其道，LV旗艦店外無時無刻不大排長龍；顏色鮮艷奪目的 "波子" 跑車 ，在大街小巷裡風馳電掣的招搖過市。

7 康有為《廣藝舟雙楫》(上海 ： 上海古籍出版社， 1995)，頁83。
8 同上。
9 此段大部份論點曾載於劉澤光《論康有為(1858-1927)書法理論及實踐中蘊含的儒家美學思想》，頁79-80，茲略有修訂。
10 參看郭繼生，石慢合編《合璧聯珠：樂常在軒藏清代楹聯》(香港: 香港中文大學文物館，2003)，展品82。

《LV與波子》以戲謔的手法強烈顛覆了書法傳統。首先，傳統書法大多以黑白色為主，強調樸實無華的美學與中國人崇尚的內斂精神；此作則大膽地加入了暗示LV產品上經典的顏色 — 深褐色及泥黃色，以及跑車常用的奪目鮮黃色。第二，傳統書法對聯一般裝裱為兩幅掛軸，對稱地懸掛在牆上的左右方；此作則打破了傳統書法對聯直線的由上而下的閱讀習慣，把聯語中每一個單字分開書寫在獨立的布本畫框上， 然後由左至由在巨牆 (高約6米闊約9米)上，以排山倒海之勢，震撼地排出高低起伏的圖案(見拍攝於香港浸會大學傳裡視藝大樓顧明均展覽廳一樓之照片(展品23))。有趣的是，傳統對聯講求上下聯中的字詞對仗，在《LV與波子》，竟能看出排列形狀的對稱與詞性、字義上對仗的關係 — "天地" 對 "鬧市"、"中"對 "間"、"LV"對"波子" 、 "最貴"對 "真威" 。

《生命禮贊》（展品15）和《走進撲朔迷離的「煙霞」》(展品22）是另外兩件改變傳統書法裝裱及展示模式的例子；它們以較富時代感的裝置手法去強化作品思想內容 — 前者將原來二十四幅記錄了2008年四川地震的小楷日記冊頁，改裝成吊掛式自然流動裝置。隨空氣流動的裝置，結合了燈光在膠片上的反射，大大加強了日記內容如頌歌般的《生命禮贊》的韻律感。

《裝置作品走進撲朔迷離的"煙霞"》(展品22) 擬突破傳統書法創作理念及展示方式—— 雖以仿石刻隸楷拓本(黑老虎)為基礎風格,但紙本作品裝裱於16個高度不一的方形柱體。柱體以特定的排列方法裝置於展館牆上和散佈在地上，並建構出狀似"迷宮"的裝置空間（"迷宮"亦暗示因違反傳統書法中預設的閱讀方式而產生的 "模糊性"）。觀者需以一特定的迂迴路線走完"迷宮" ，方可讀完以十四個大字寫出作者自撰的新詩:

"煙霞"瀰漫此地。
在"浪漫"中，
淡…
忘…
健康！

內容嘲諷香港天文台竟以"煙霞" 一辭表述"污濁空氣",把城市空氣污染問題 "浪漫化" ，因為"煙霞"一般予人詩情畫意之聯想。長久以來，市民在 "浪漫化"的敘述中不知不覺地淡化了問題，健康意識也變得模糊。作品以"迷宮"空間暗喻模糊化的公眾信息，其覆蓋面積之大暗喻信息蔓延之廣。觀者在緩慢的步伐中閱讀作品，與作品產生互動的關係。

和：四種關係

本書共分四章，各章中涵蓋的書法篆刻作品及論文分別探討了以下四種關係：

第一章：天與人

此章一方面描述人與大自然或其身處環境的關係；另一方面表達人與人之間關係的可貴。

天地有情 — 大自然給予人的資源及祝福，無疑是一份白白得來的禮物，人對大自然的回應，時驚嘆，時感悟，但有時卻是傷害。

例如，作品《驚嘆》（展品2）以生澀的筆觸增強了柚木紋理的粗燥感，"勢"便從木材扭曲的形體奔湧而出，展現了藝術家對自然的深深禮贊。自然界中的每一個存在，都應是人類欣賞的對象。《甲骨文八言聯》（展品7）中以詩畫般的語言繪出的一幅美景，便集中地體現了這種思想：

初日出林燕雀追逐
斜陽在樹牛羊下來

道家哲學非常強調人與宇宙世界的和諧關係。《老子的沉思》（展品13）表達了藝術家謄錄老子的道家學説文本，及觀者仔細閱讀，這兩種行為都是對人與自然和諧共處這一命題的思考過程。自然界中的各種現象，其實都蘊含了深刻的哲理，並照亮人心，一如《隸書七言聯》（展品12）所昭示：

水流任急景常靜
花落雖頻意自閒

此外，這一章中展示的作品，也深入反映了人與人之間的關係需要以關愛去維繫。《恩愛偕老》（展品18）不僅是藝術家與妻子間愛的見證，更包含了對2004年兩人旅居南加州歲月的回憶。事實上，"愛"是人倫中最崇高的體現。《篆書七言聯》（展品19）也巧妙地表達了藝術家對與所愛之人團聚的熱切希望：

萬里因循成久客
一年容易又中秋

同時，對聯側的題字更進一步説明了藝術家何等珍視與學生及家人共處的每個瞬間：

庚寅中秋，與諸生談笑間偶書此聯，非篆非草，不知何所似也。此雖欲為範作，然書後自覺逸筆草草，諸生切不可學。余曾客居美國六年，今夕驟覺回家真好。能與家人在中秋節共聚天倫，不亦樂乎。

人與人之間的愛常因面臨天災而增強。2008年的四川地震便是一個突出的例子。一位救援人員以日記的形式，動情地記錄了他所經歷的各種捨己為人的情感和行動。藝術家被其中的英雄氣概和無私大愛感動，遂以書法形式抄寫該日記，並以裝置手法展現此《生命禮贊》（展品15）。

唉！人高尚的志向、情操和純潔心靈，時常會迷失於物欲横流的都市表象中。《走進撲朔迷離的「煙霞」》（展品22）、《LV與波子》（展品23）和《為人民幣服務》（展品24），則透露了作者對人與自然關係被扭曲了的回應，如環境污染、對無止境的物欲及名利的追求等等，而發出的悲嘆。

第二章：施與受

此章集中思考另一種人際關係的維繫模式：即以專題形式探討志同道合的人，尤其是熱愛及研究傳統中國書畫者，如何透過印章的惠贈及接受，維繫彼此間的情誼，並藉彼此認同印章內容所表達出的思想，以擁抱共同價值觀，並在不知不覺間建構內群體身份認同。

印章基本上用以象徵用印者（即印章主人），無論用於商業契約或書畫創作，印章是誠信的憑記，因為"見印如見人"。印章的內容可以文字或圖像表達。除了刻上個人姓名或機構名稱之外，有直接表意作用或象徵意義的圖像及自我指涉的文字，既可以道出印章主人的個性、抱負、嗜好、特殊人生閱歷、個人價值觀和宗教信仰等，亦可以作為贈印者和受印者之間志同道合的象徵信物。

試舉一例：《小棚友肖像印》（展品111）是一組包括文字及圖像兩件石章的篆刻系列，刻有"小棚友"三字的印章是劉澤光（即本作品集的作者）所刻的萬青屴教授之別號印；另一方刻有萬青屴教授肖像的印章是利雪玲的創作。聯合起來的兩個印拓，以合作形式展示 —上面是感覺較輕的陽刻肖像印；下面則是較重的陰刻白文印。萬教授為著名藝術史學家及畫家，現為香港浸會大學視覺藝術院講座教授及建院總監。文革期間，萬教授竟然得以與老師李可染（1907-1989）和其他藝術家在牛棚相遇。而他的別號印用以紀念其牛棚生涯這一段難得的遇合。[11]值得特別注

11 劉澤光《印象：劉澤光篆刻》（香港：香港浸會大學視覺藝術院，2009），頁17。

意的是《小棚友肖像印》的兩位贈印者和受印者的關係：萬教授（受印者）是劉澤光（贈印者1）昔日在香港大學攻讀碩士學位時的指導教授；而利雪玲（贈印者2）卻是劉澤光的學生。故此，劉澤光為萬老師刻的別號印及利雪玲為她太老師刻的肖像印都標誌着濃厚的師生情誼。刀下留情 —— 在雪玲的眼中，太老師既是可敬的謙謙學者，亦是充滿童真、調皮又“爛玩”的畫家。雪玲的刀鋒刻出逼真傳神的萬老師容貌，不但敏銳地演繹出他兼有學者和畫家雙重的身份，而且深刻地捕捉了他既嚴謹亦淘氣的雙重處世態度；—— 對劉澤光而言，為萬老師刻“小棚友”別號印有雙重意義：此印不但暗指昔日萬老師於牛棚巧遇大師之經歷，而且還深刻地調起刻印者曾在香港大學初遇萬老師這位中國藝術史學大師這段難忘的回憶。總之，從印章內容及刻印者的角度看來，印章尤能寄託贈印者和受印者之間的情誼。再者，從印章之使用一特殊視角查察，蓋於用印者的書畫作品上的印拓，微妙地象徵著一種格外的內群體認同 —— 萬青屴教授是一位國際權威的藝術史學家兼資深畫家，他對所選用印章的藝術水平有頗高的要求，因為這樣方可達致印拓和他書畫作品內容的協同作用。是故，蓋於其作品上之別號印和肖像印，無疑意味着一種他對刻印者藝術水平的強烈肯定。由此看來，印章的送贈及接受能引申出以禮物“寄情”之外的微妙的藝術交流網絡及鮮為人察覺的文化現象。

第三章：黑與白

此章將焦點從社交網絡或人與人之間的關係轉移至較抽象的藝術概念和理論中“虛”與“實”之間的關係，深入探討中國藝術中虛實、陰陽、黑白等互相對立又相生相息的視覺元素和概念。

這些奇特的概念在在體現於本章所有作品中。《空》（展品128）是一佳例，最能揭示出本章中作品有意識的 調虛實相生的精神。實驗性的書法中，流暢淋漓的筆觸和墨韻，在輕透的雪紡上意外地以縷空的方式書寫出篆書“空”字。是故，觀者需以個人的幻想力去重建抽象化的“空”字 —— 改變以往欣賞書法黑色筆劃的習慣，並以虛實倒置的概念方可解讀出以留白方式出現的“空”字筆劃。有趣的是除了作品內部虛實空間的互動之外，作品中的筆墨痕跡與空間概念，以巔覆書法傳統的姿態，伸延至畫面之外，並與環境及觀者產生互動的關係 —— 置於香港浸會大學傳理視藝大樓顧明均展覽廳的《空》與玻璃牆外的景物彷彿融為一體；富韻律和節奏感的筆墨在不同日照角度下的環境中，與遠景搖曳的樹影及近景微蕩著的漣漪和水中景物的倒影，產生富震撼力的協同效應。作品的框架彷彿一扇窗子，引導觀者細看幻變的世界：筆墨、景物、時間及觀者自身的存在，常耶？變耶？真耶？幻耶？《空》向觀眾提出較隱諱而含意較深的發問。“空”與“盈” —— 直指觀者本心。也許老子《道德 》第二十一章可提供智慧的啟示：“道之為物，惟恍惟惚。惚兮恍兮，其中有象；恍兮惚兮，其中有物“。唉！難為“空”、“盈”、“虛”、“實”定分界!

第四章：雅與俗

此章以嶄新並富有前瞻性的思維方式及創作實踐，打破“雅”與“俗”的疆界，探索雅俗協同而有別傳統的另類關係。

本來書法予人幽雅和富學養的聯想，和“俗”的概念風馬牛不相及。本章中的作品體現出雅俗互參的高度包容性。雅俗共融的精神，一方面表現於書法風格及淵源，另一方面表現於作品的語言和內容。試舉一例：《咩話？》（What?）（展品140）是一件參用港式粵語而創作的立體書法作品。作品上有創作者的題識：“香港粵語中「咩話」一辭，既表達「驚訝」，亦可指「甚麼方言？」令人驚訝的是：粵方言破解了少數民族語言漸被淘汰的宿命，甚至97回歸後，仍在香港流通使用。這體現出 烈的本土認同和自豪感。為歌頌香港粵語作為獨特的社會和文化現象，我將「咩話」二字轉化為石碑拓本的視覺效果，並藉沉雄古樸的書法風格拱托出一種格外的歷史聯想，將歷史悠久而富濃厚地方色彩的粵方言，帶到戲劇化的現在。”本來難登大雅之堂的港式粵語，如今結合新式的書法表現形式，搖身一變，成為一種另類的學術工具，探究了有深厚歷史文化底蘊的粵方言及本土文化在當代社會建構出的本土身份認同。

01 *Harmony* | 和

Ink on paper, mounted on 50 plexiglasses (30.5 x 30.5 cm each) with metal tubes of different lengths, installed as a relief sculpture on the gallery wall.

紙本墨書，分別裝裱於50塊塑膠玻璃（30.5 x 30.5 厘米）中，再以長短不一的金屬管以浮雕形式設置於展廳牆上。

Artist's note:
In the long history of Chinese culture, the concept and philosophy of harmony has always been dominating the leading values of the society, and through different time and space. There are two versions of harmony(he和) in modern Chinese: a simple version和and a complex version 龢. The meanings are indistinguishable; however, they were two distinct words in ancient times. According to Shuowenjiezi 説文解字 (A Lexicon of Chinese Characters, circa. 100A.D.), 龢 means "tune", denoting harmonious music; while和 means "echo". Today the two words are interchangeable, meaning harmony and mediation.

This artwork was created as a response to a growing societal issue of family violence. The news may only be revealing a small fraction of cases, and I am afraid there are many more hidden in the society. In this city life which is full of tension, many people are filled with resentment, and the families have lost their harmony. The repeated character "Harmony" in this work and their interwoven relations remind the audience that one must treasure human relationship.

作者按：
在源遠流長的中國文化中，和諧的觀念和哲學一直支配着社會的主導價值觀，並貫穿着不同時空。現代漢語中的「和」字，有簡單的「和」及繁複的「龢」兩種寫法，意思相通，但在古時卻本來是兩個不同的字。根據《說文解字》，「龢」解作「調」，意指協調、和諧之音樂；「和」字則解作「相應」，今二字相通，有「和諧、調和」之意。

這件作品的創作動機，是對社會上愈見頻繁的家庭暴力事件作出回應。從新聞裏看到的個案都是被報導的少數，隱藏在社區裏的恐怕更多。在緊張的都市生活中，許多人充滿怨氣，家庭也失去和睦。此作以不斷重複的"和"字，以及它們交織出的關係，提醒觀眾必須珍視人與人之間的關係。

Harmony (Detail)
和（局部）

02 ***Awestruck*** | 驚歎

Seal script
Ink on teak, with metal stand
Height 78 cm
2009

篆書
柚木墨書，金屬架支撐
高78厘米
2009年

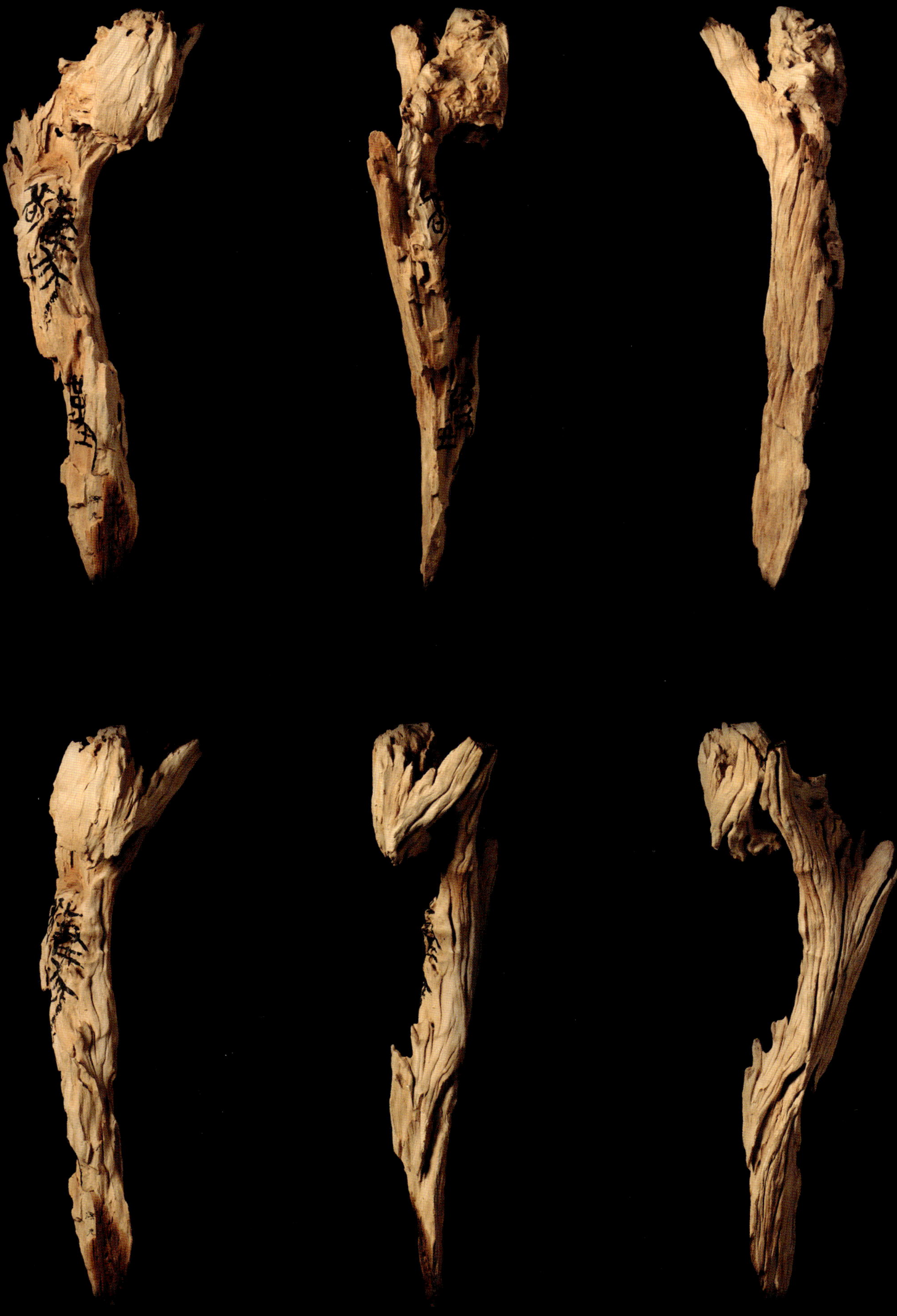

Awestruck (Detail)
驚歎(局部)

澤兇

03 *Natural Flavor* | 天趣

Cursive script
Ink on teak, with metal stand
Height 80 cm
2009

草書
柚木墨書，金屬架支撐
高80厘米
2009年

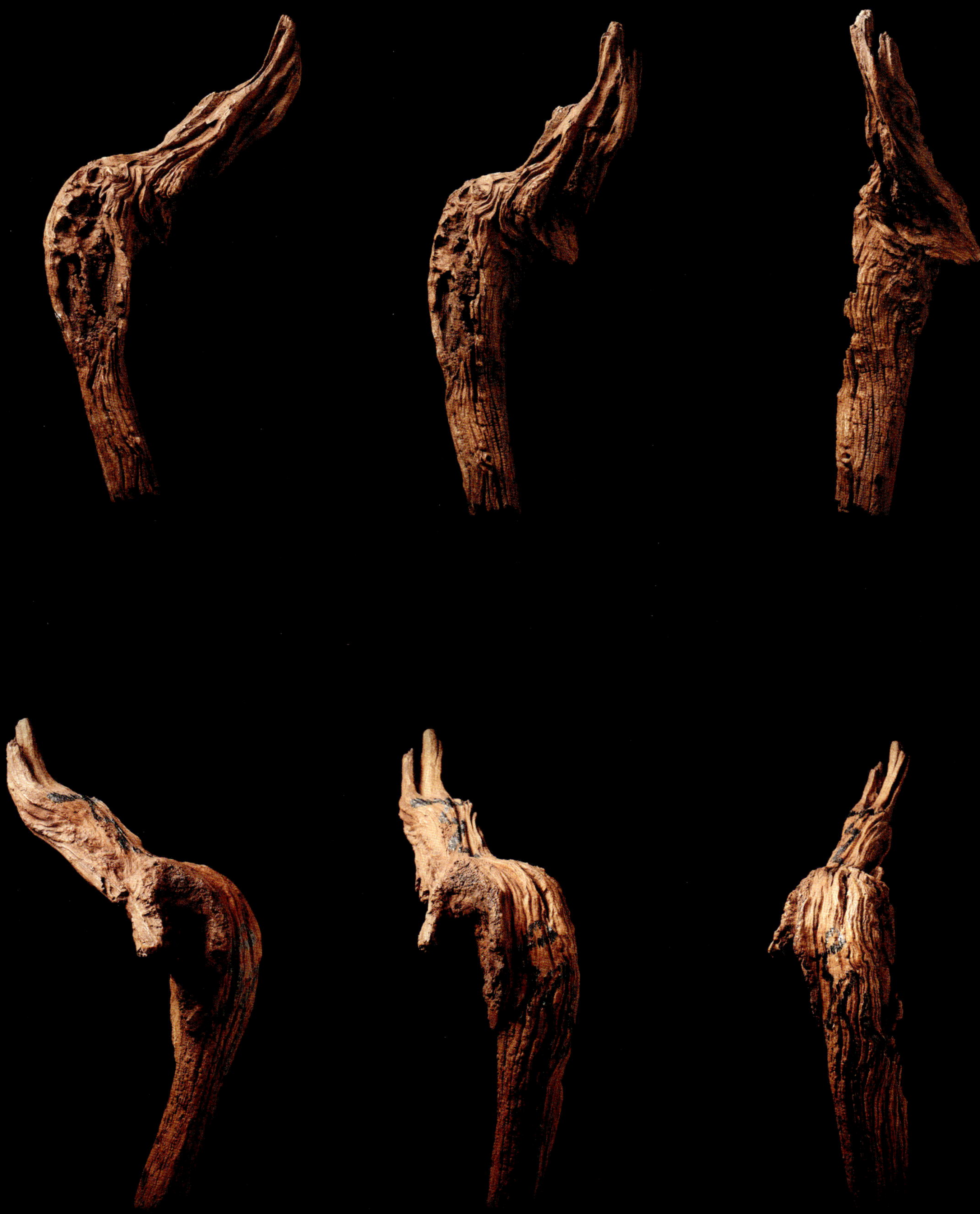

Natural Flavor (Detail)
天趣(局部)

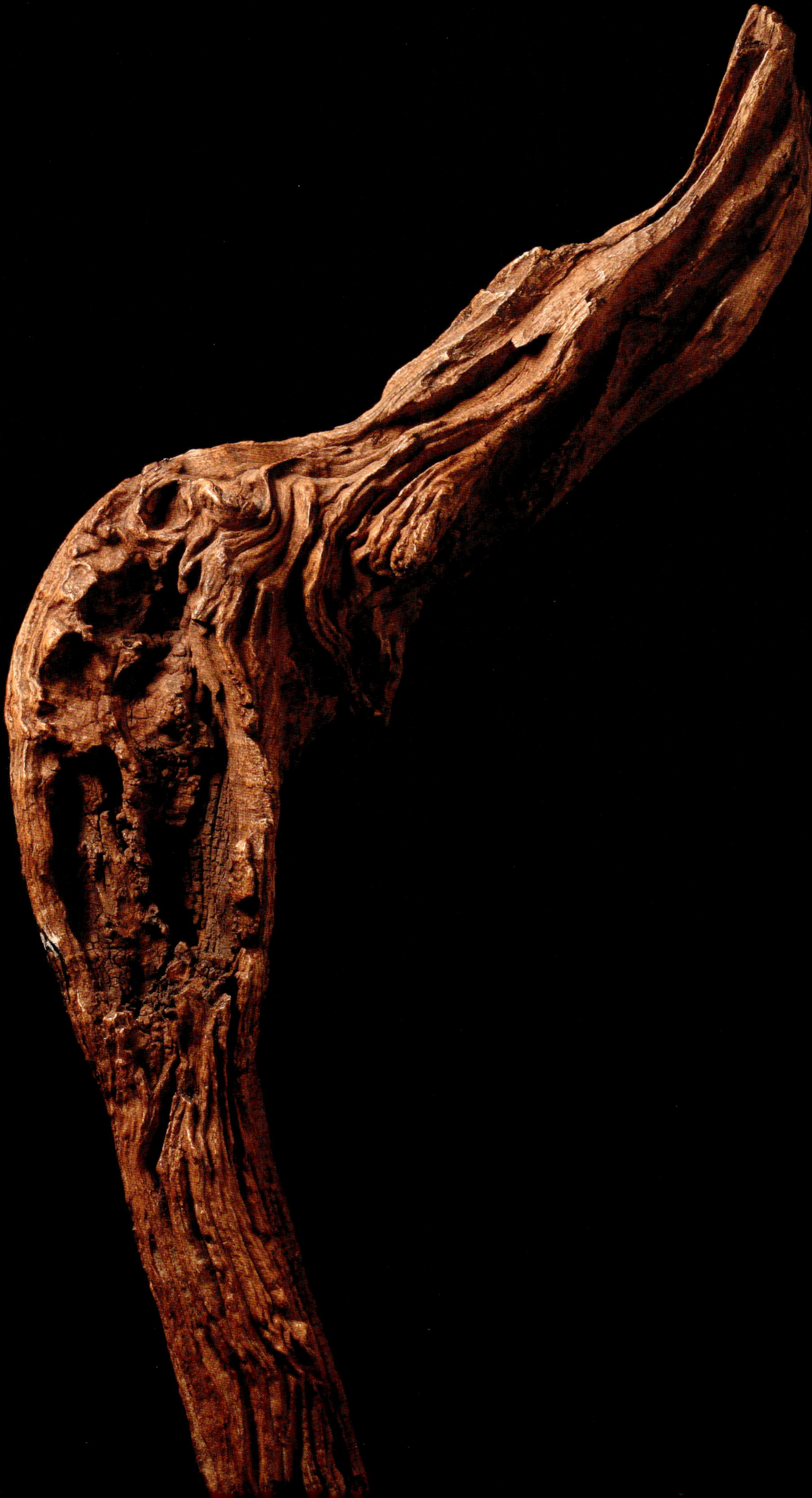

04 *An Endless Stream* |
川流不息

Experimental calligraphy
with the character *chuan* (川), or stream
Yellow rose wood (*Huanghuali* 黃花梨)
Height 16.5 cm
2009

實驗書法
“川”，墨書於黃花梨木
高16.5厘米
2009年

05 *A Deep and Tranquil Mountain* | 山深杳杳

Experimental calligraphy
with the character shan (山),
or "mountain", Glass
Height 9.5 cm, width 17 cm
2009

實驗書法
"山"，玻璃
高9.5厘米，寬17厘米
2009年

A Deep and Tranquil Mountain (Detail)
山深杳杳(局部)

06 ***Fledgling*** | 雛

Clerical script
Ink on paper, mounted and framed
95 x 70 cm
2009

隸書
紙本墨書，裱框
95x 70厘米
2009年

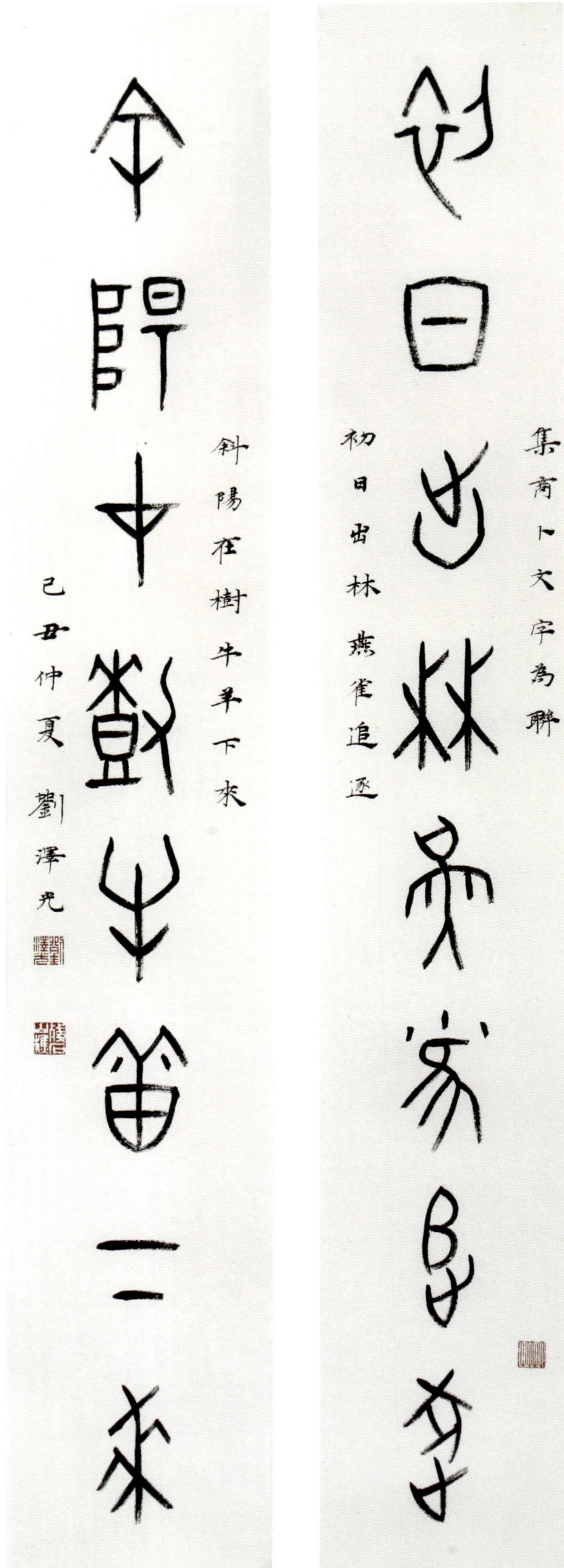

07 *Eight-character-line Couplet in Oracle-bone Script* I

甲骨文八言聯

Oracle-bone script
Ink on paper, hanging scrolls
137 x 34 cm (each)
2009

甲骨文
紙本墨書，立軸
各137 x 34厘米
2009年

Transliteration:
The morning sun rises up above the woods,
shining on the playful mountain finches.
The setting sun goes down beyond the trees,
casting light upon the homeward ox herds.

釋文：
初日出林燕雀追逐
斜陽在樹牛羊下來

牛羊下來
丑仲夏
劉澤光

08 *The Poems Glorifying the Lamb* |
詩贊羔羊

Oracle-bone script
Hand-carved characters (intaglio) on ox bone
33 x 2 cm
2010

甲骨文
牛骨陰刻
33 x 2厘米
2010年

Artist's note:

Also referred to as prophetic words from the ancient ruins of the capital of the late Shang Dynasty (14th-11th centuries B.C.), the oracle-bone script was the medium employed by the ancients to communicate with heaven. For such questions of the future as farming, fishing, warfare and climate, the royal family and rulers used oracle bones for the purpose of prognostication.

As a modern Christian, I transformed the ancients' prophetic words into voices of praise, and engraved the four Chinese characters *shi zan gao yang* ("The Poems Glorifying the Lamb") in oracle-bone script on a piece of ox bone. I sing hymns of thanksgiving to glorify Jesus Christ — the Lamb who was slain and sacrificed His life to save the world.

The line "the Poems glorifying the lamb" was originated from *Thousand Character Classic* (a Chinese poem used as a primer for teaching Chinese characters to children) by Zhou Xingsi (470-521). "The Poems" refers to *Shi Jing* (Book of Songs) in which the poem entitled "The Lamb" draws an analogy between the lamb and the lofty and virtuous gentleman. Although the expression "the Poems glorifying the lamb" was originally unrelated to the Christian faith, it literally connotes another type of significance for the calligrapher who is a Christian.

作者按：

商代甲骨文又稱殷墟卜辭 （約於公元前14至11世紀出現），是古人與上天溝通的媒介。對於未來之問題，包括農牧、漁獵、戰爭、氣候等，王室及統治者都以甲骨進行占卜。

作為現代基督徒，我將古人的卜辭化為讚頌之聲，在牛骨上以甲骨文書體刻 “詩贊羔羊”四字，並以感恩的詩歌，讚美那為世人犧牲性命而被殺的羔羊 — 主耶穌基督。

“詩贊羔羊”一語原出於周興嗣（470-521年）《千字文》。“詩” 是指《詩經》 。《詩經》中的“羔羊”篇以羔羊比喻品德高潔的君子。雖然“詩贊羔羊” 一語本來與基督教信仰無關，但對身為基督徒的書者卻有另一重意義。

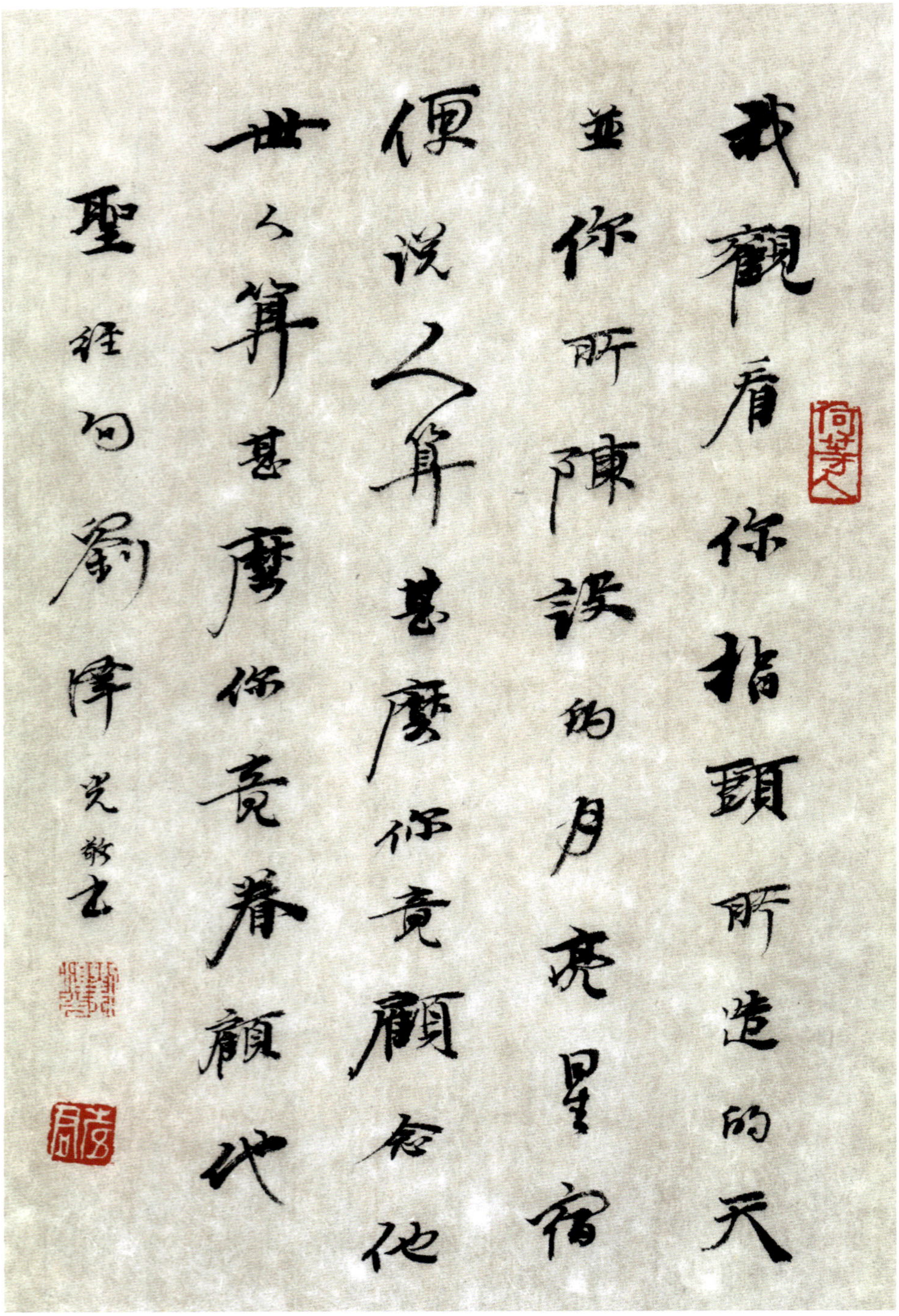

09 *What is Mankind* |
人算什麼

Semi-Cursive script
Ink on paper, mounted and framed
32 x 23 cm
2010

行書
紙本墨書，裱框
32 x 23厘米
2010年

Transliteration:
When I consider your heavens, the work of your fingers, the moon and the stars, which you have set in place, what is mankind that you are mindful of them, human beings that you care for them?
(Psalm 8: 3-4. New International Version, ©2010)

釋文:
我觀看你指頭所造的天，並你所陳設的月亮星宿，便說：人算什麼，你竟顧念他?世人算什麼，你竟眷顧他?
（《聖經》·詩篇 8: 3-4 ）

10 *Love Here (Love this Globe)* | 愛斯

Clerical script
Ink on paper, mounted and framed
32 x 23 cm
2010

隸書
紙本墨書，裱框
32 x 23厘米
2010年

Transliteration:
Artist's inscription: At the behest of my good friend Wang Nan. IPC dedicates its research on energy saving and emission reduction products. Aisi (愛斯), the Chinese name of IPC, means love this globe. Hence, IPC's name states its vision on environmental protection. I playfully transformed the English alphabets IPC as a rim to encircle the Chinese characters ai and si (愛斯) in an attempt to suggest the shape of the globe.

釋文：
題識：王南好友雅屬(囑)。愛斯工業科技公司(IPC)致力研發節能減排產品。"愛斯"即愛這地球。故愛斯之名闡明環保願景。余戲以英文字母為"愛斯" 二字加上圓框，以圓形喻地球之狀也。

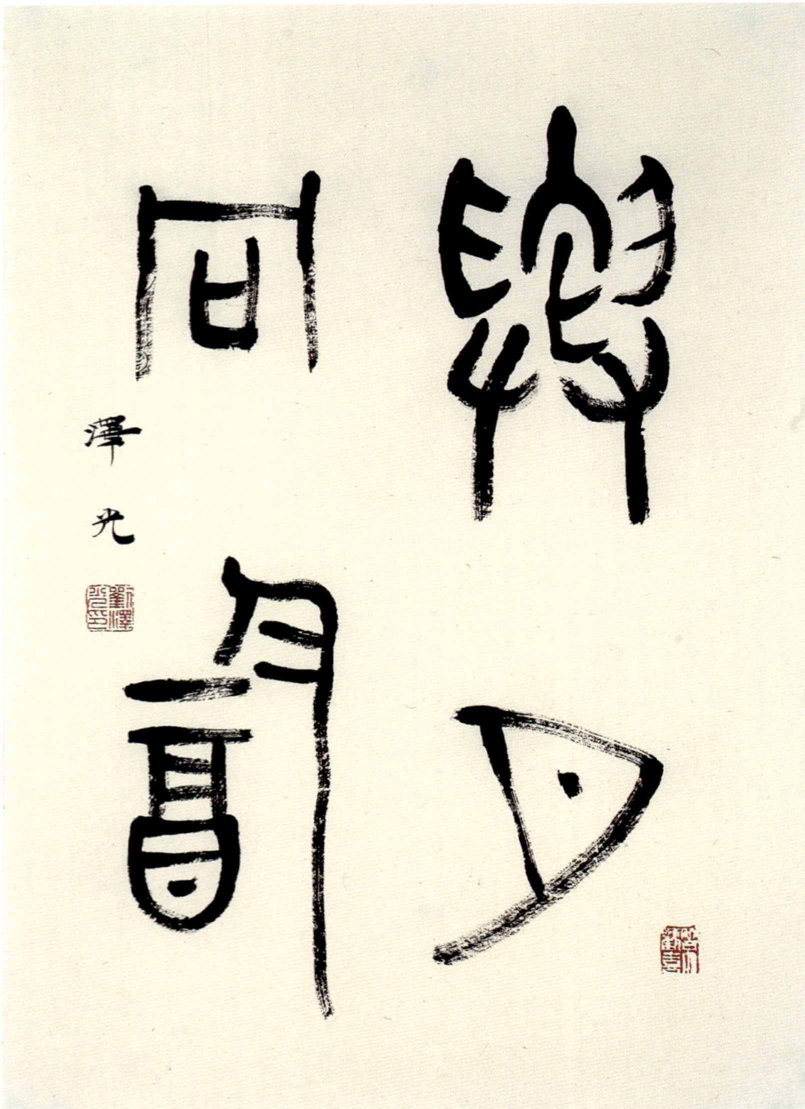

11 *Drink with the Moon* | 與月同飲

Great-seal script
Ink on paper, mounted and framed
42.7 x 29.7 cm
2009

大篆
紙本墨書，裱框
42.7 x 29.7厘米
2009年

澤

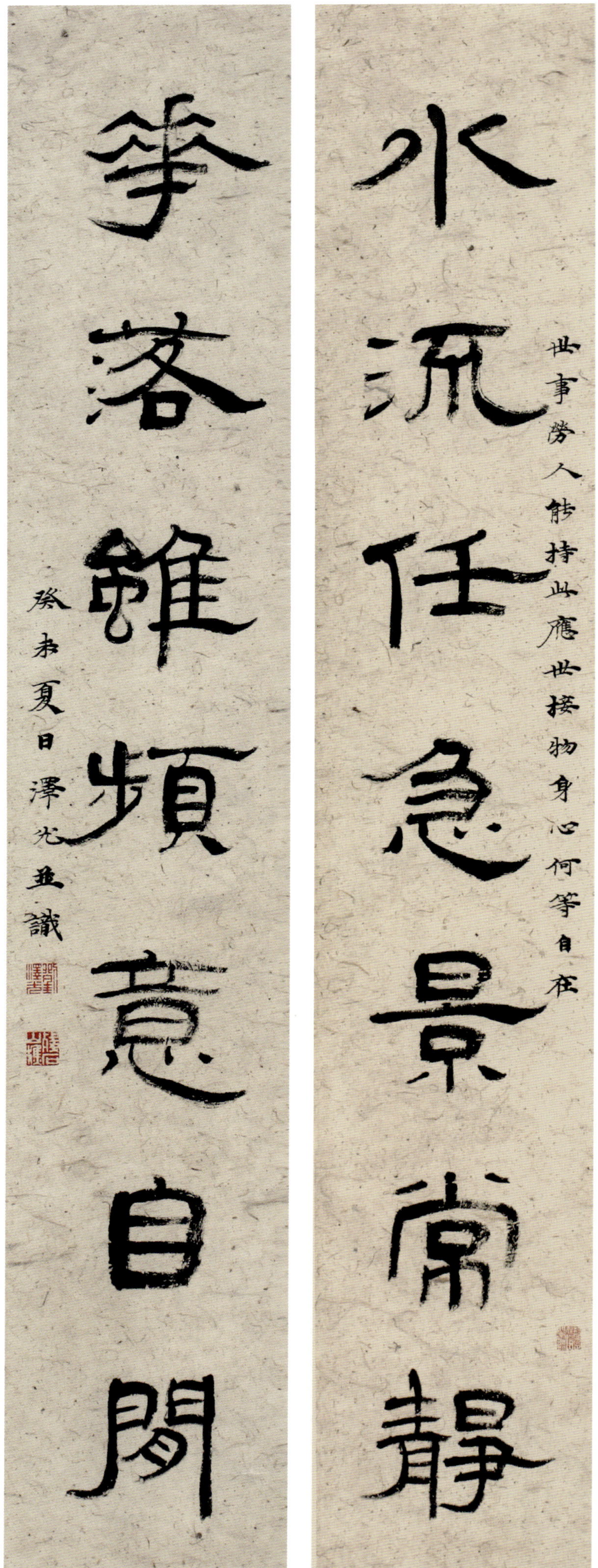

12 *Seven-character-line Couplet in Clerical Script* | 隸書七言聯

Clerical script
Ink on paper, hanging scrolls
135 x 33 cm (each)
2003

隸書
紙本墨書，立軸
各135 x 33厘米
2003年

Transliteration:
Scenery stays still no matter how rapidly the water flows.
A quiet mind is always kept no matter how frequently the flowers wither and fall.

釋文:
水流任急景常靜
花落雖頻意自閒

意

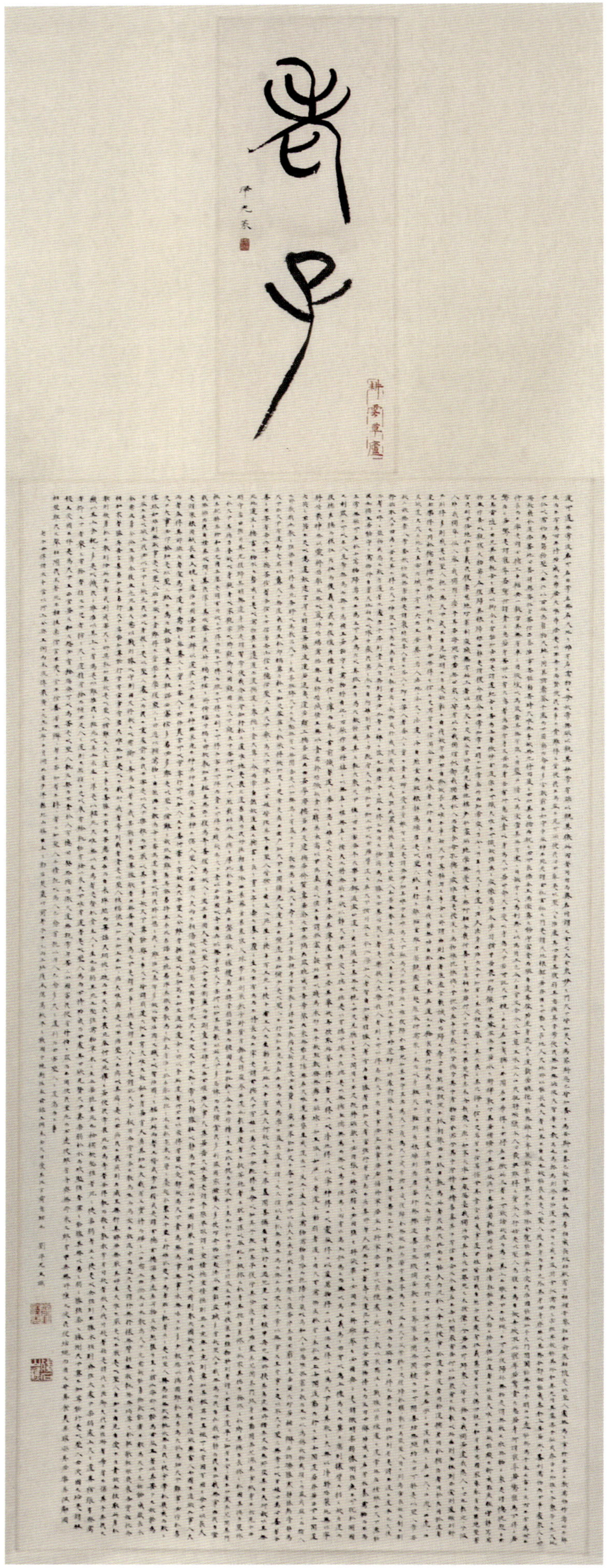

13 ***Meditating on the Wisdom of Laozi*** |
《老子》的沉思

Small-character standard script
Ink on paper, hanging scroll
210 X 70 cm
2009

蠅頭小楷
紙本墨書，立軸
210 x 70厘米
2009年

道名可名非常名無名天地之始有名萬物之母故常無欲以觀其妙常有欲以觀其徼
恃功成而弗居夫唯弗居是以不去不尚賢使民不爭不貴難得之貨使民不為盜不見可欲
芻狗聖人不仁以百姓為芻狗天地之間其猶橐籥乎虛而不屈動而愈出多言數窮不如守中
善地心善淵與善仁言善信正善治事善能動善時夫唯無爭故無尤持而盈之不如其已揣而
謂玄德三十輻共一轂當其無有車之用埏埴以為器當其無有器之用鑿戶牖以為室當其
謂寵辱若驚何謂貴大患若身吾所以有大患者為吾有身及吾無身吾有何患故貴以
其後執古之道以御今之有能知古始是謂道紀古之善為士者微妙玄通深不可識夫唯不可
復夫物芸芸各復歸其根歸根曰靜是謂復命復命曰常知常曰明不知常妄作凶知常容容乃
棄義民復孝慈絕巧棄利盜賊無有此三者以為文不足故令有所屬見素抱樸少私寡
人察察我獨悶悶澹兮其若海飂兮若無止眾人皆有以而我獨頑似鄙我獨異於人而貴
是以聖人抱一為天下式不自見故明不自是故彰不自伐故有功不自矜故長夫唯不爭
德者德亦樂得之同於失者失亦樂得之信不足焉有不信焉企者不立跨者不行自見
天王亦大域中有四大而王居其一焉人法地地法天天法道道法自然重為輕根靜為躁君
善救物故無棄物是謂襲明故善人者不善人之師不善人者善人之資不貴其師不愛其資雖智
吾見其不得已天下神器不可為也為者敗之執者失之故物或行或隨或歔或吹或強或羸或
或惡之故有道者不處君子居則貴左用兵則貴右兵者不祥之器非君子之器不得已而
之萬物將自賓天地相合以降甘露民莫之令而自均始制有名名亦既有夫亦將知止知止可

故大國以下小國則取小國小國以下大國則取大國故或下以取或下而取大
免邪故為天下貴為無為事無事味無味大小多少報怨以德圖難於
層之臺起於累土千里之行始於足下為者敗之執者失之是以聖人無為故無
式常知稽式是謂玄德玄德深矣遠矣與物反矣然後乃至大順江海所以
夫我有三寶持而保之一曰慈二曰儉三曰不敢為天下先慈故能勇儉故
不敢為主而為客不敢進寸而退尺是謂行無行攘無臂扔無敵執無兵
威則大威至無狎其所居無厭其所生夫唯不厭是以不厭是以聖人自知
者吾得執而殺之孰敢常有司殺者殺夫代司殺者殺是謂代大匠斲
強者死之徒柔弱者生之徒是以兵強則不勝木強則兵強大處下
攻堅強者莫之能勝其無以易之弱之勝強柔之勝剛天下莫不知莫
有舟輿無所乘之雖有甲兵無所陳之使民復結繩而用之甘其食
以其注言簡意賅也

劉澤光並識

澤光篆

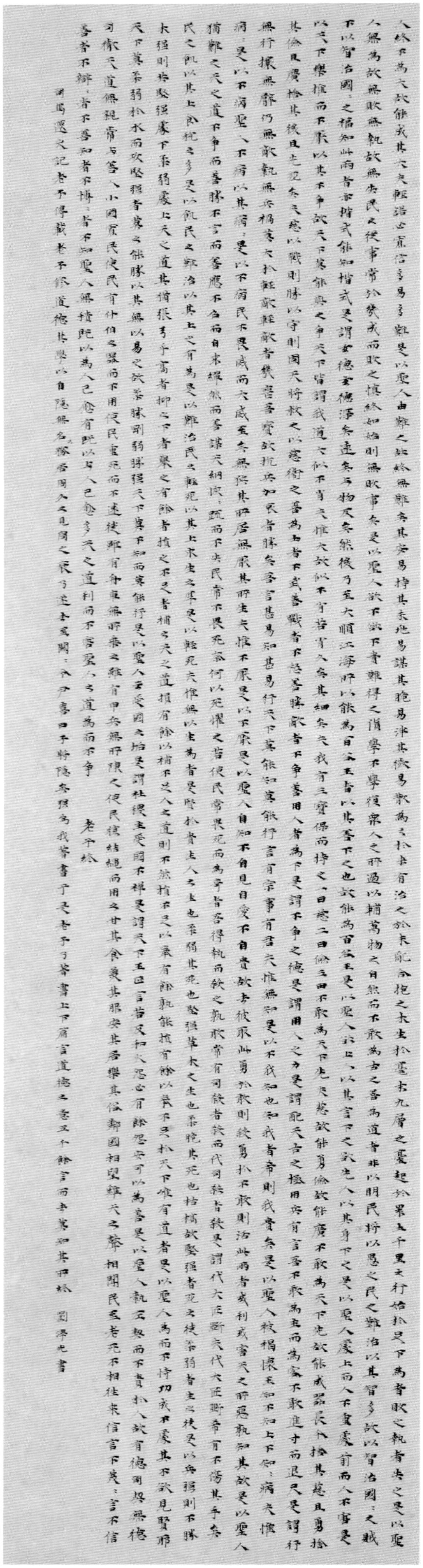

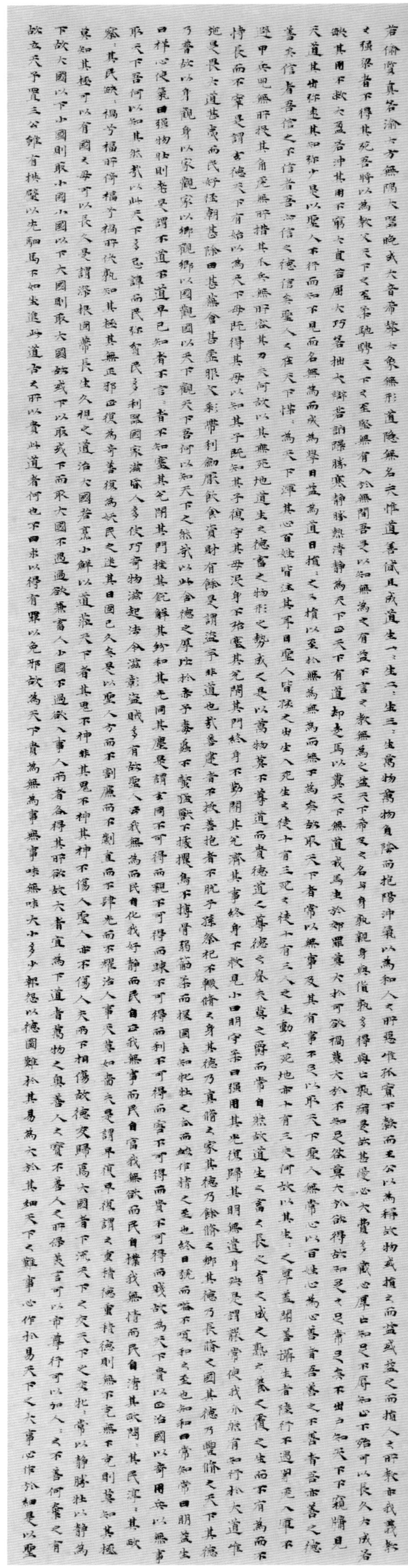

14 ***Laozi*** | 《老子》

Small-character standard script
Set of four hanging scrolls, Ink on paper
274 x 65 cm (each)
1999

蠅頭小楷
紙本墨書，四屏立軸
各274 x 65厘米
1999年

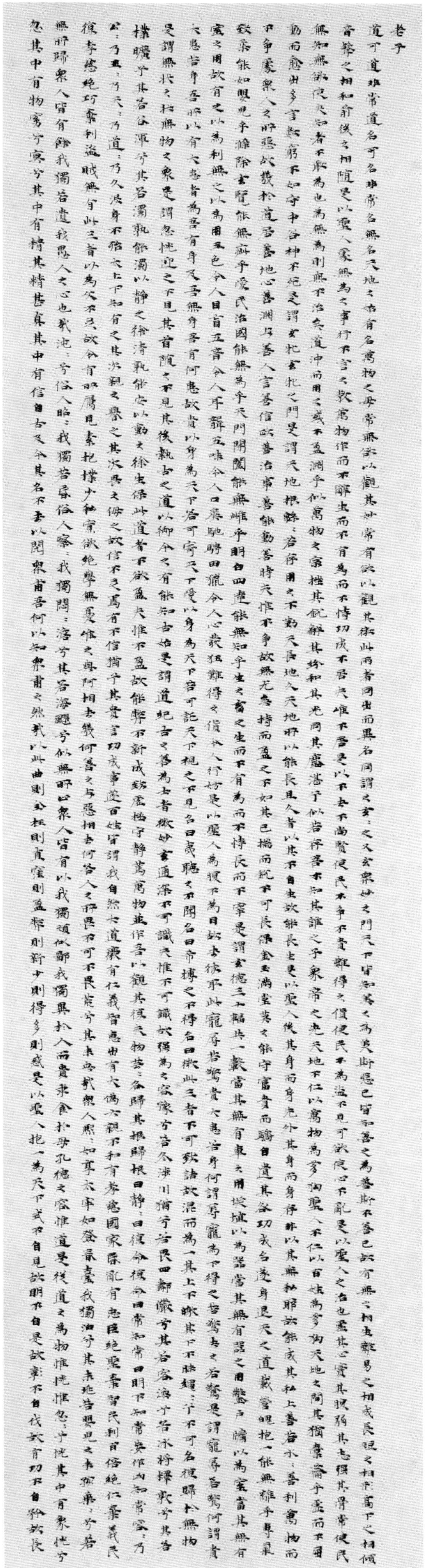
老子
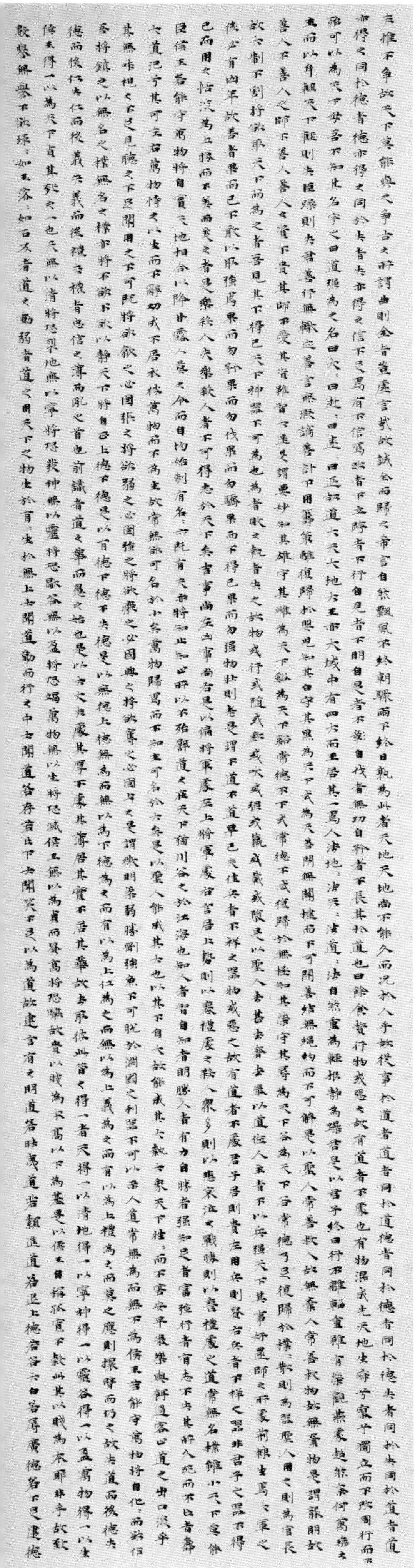

老子

道可道非常道名

音聲之相和前後

無知無欲使夫知者

誠全而歸之希言自然飄風不終朝驟雨不終日孰為此者天地天地尚不能久
跂者不立跨者不行自見者不明自是者不彰自伐者無功自矜者不長其於道
曰返故道大天大地大王亦大域中有四大而王居其一焉人法地地法天天法道
善計不用籌策離復歸於嬰兒知其白守其黑為天下式為天善閉無關楗而不
是謂要妙知其雄守其雌為天下谿為天下谿常德不下式常德不忒復歸於無
為也為者敗之執者失之故物或行或隨或歔或吹或強或羸或載或隳是以
而勿驕果而不得已果而勿強物壯則老是謂不道不道早已夫佳兵者不祥
得志於天下矣吉事尚左凶事尚右是以偏將軍處左上將軍處右言居上
始制有名名亦既有夫亦將知止知止所以不殆譬道之在天下猶川谷之於江海也
為主故常無欲可名於小矣萬物歸焉而不知主可名於大矣是以聖人能成其
欲弱之必固強之將欲廢之必固興之將欲奪之必固與之是謂微明柔弱勝剛
德不德是以有德下德不失德是以無德上德無為而無以為下德為之而有以為
前識者道之華而愚之始也是以大丈夫處其厚不處其薄居其實不居其
穀神無以靈將恐歇谷無以盈將恐竭萬物無以生將恐滅侯王無以為貞而貴
物生於有有生於無上士聞道勤而行之中士聞道若存若亡

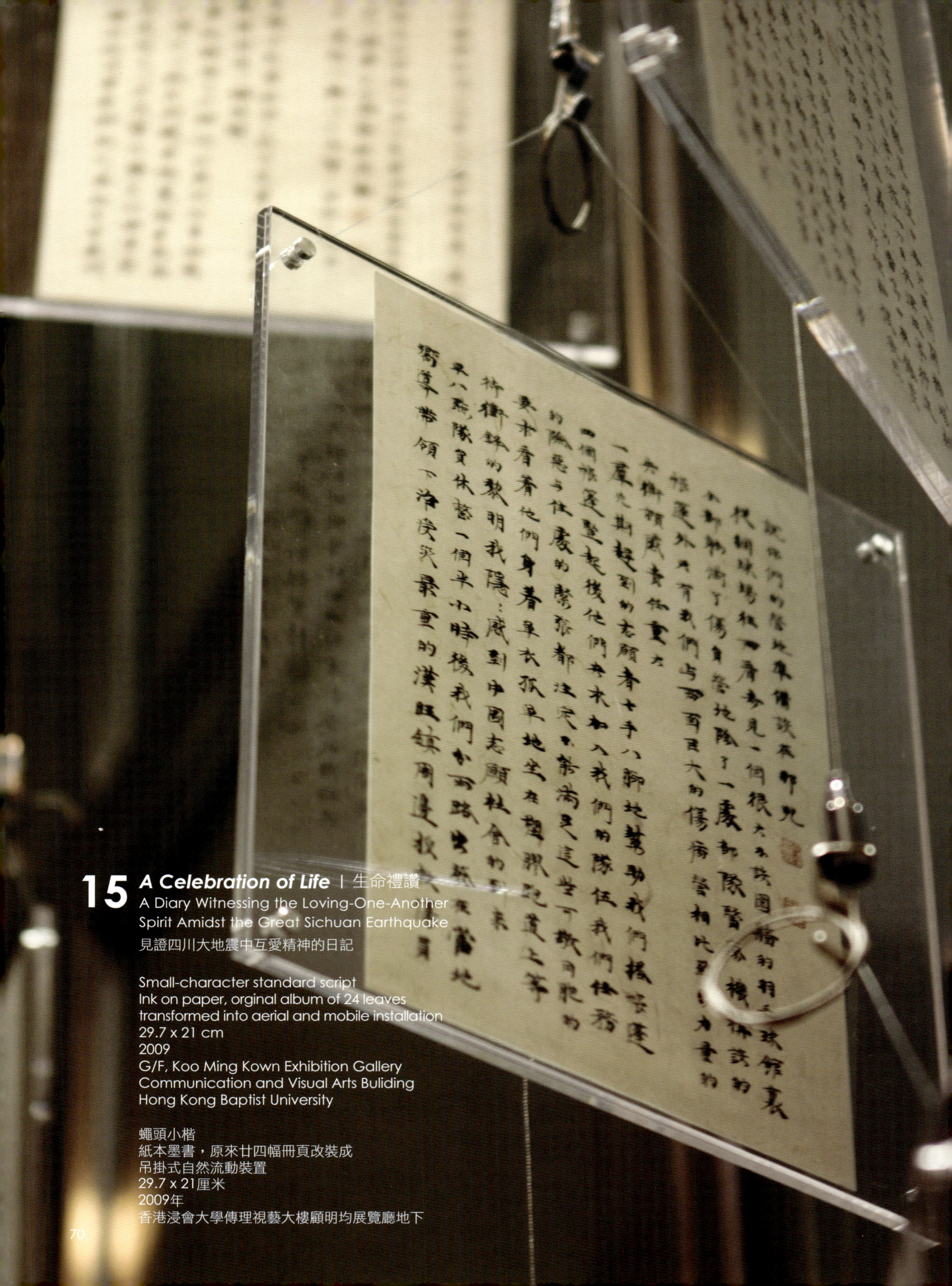

15 ***A Celebration of Life*** | 生命禮讚

A Diary Witnessing the Loving-One-Another Spirit Amidst the Great Sichuan Earthquake

見證四川大地震中互愛精神的日記

Small-character standard script
Ink on paper, orginal album of 24 leaves transformed into aerial and mobile installation
29.7 x 21 cm
2009
G/F, Koo Ming Kown Exhibition Gallery
Communication and Visual Arts Buliding
Hong Kong Baptist University

蠅頭小楷
紙本墨書，原來廿四幅冊頁改裝成
吊掛式自然流動裝置
29.7 x 21厘米
2009年
香港浸會大學傳理視藝大樓顧明均展覽廳地下

生命禮讚

999應急救援隊總指揮救災日記
作者為中國紅十字會999應急救援隊
領隊兼總指揮北京市紅十字會副會長
日記真實見證了國民永不言棄的精神
原文約一萬字略作刪節後刊於東方仁四川大地震一書
二〇〇九年五月十五日讀後有感遂書一過 劉澤光

5 of 24

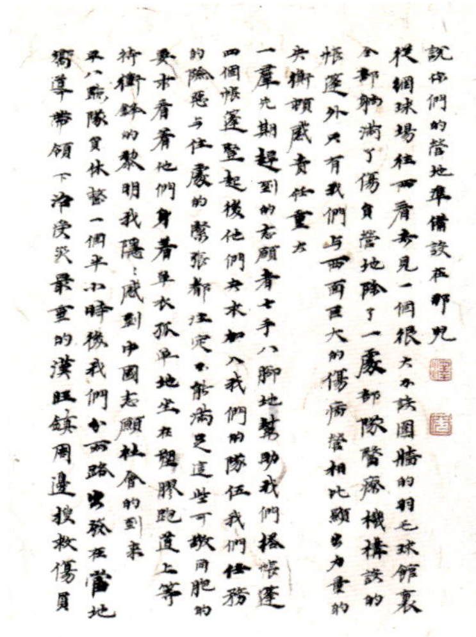
6 of 24

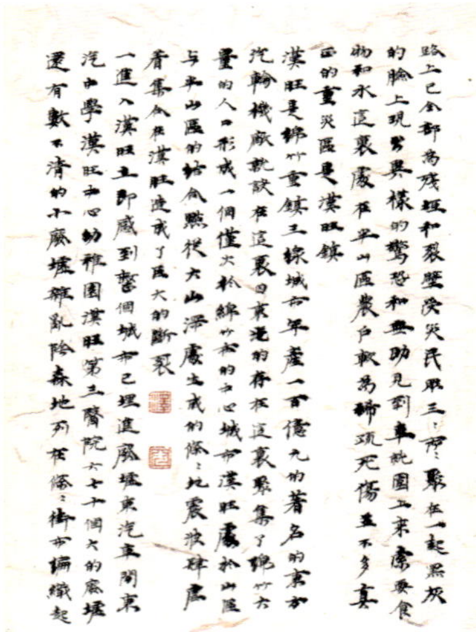
7 of 24

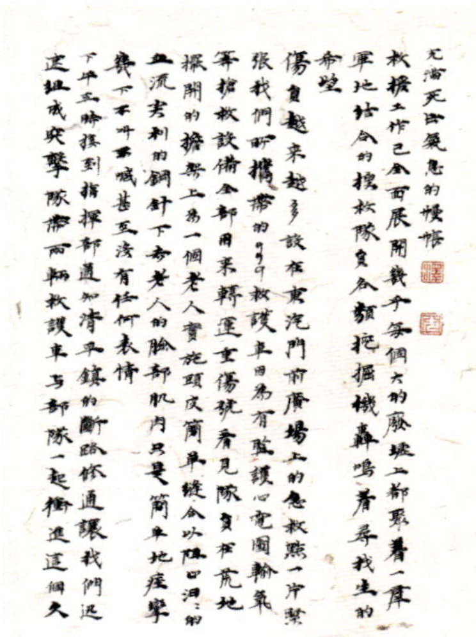
8 of 24

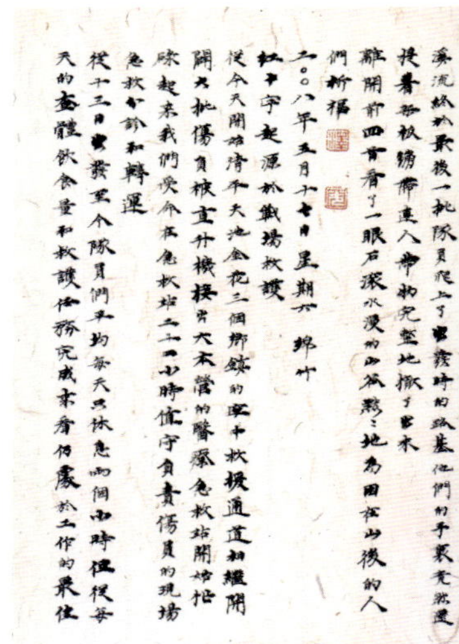
13 of 24

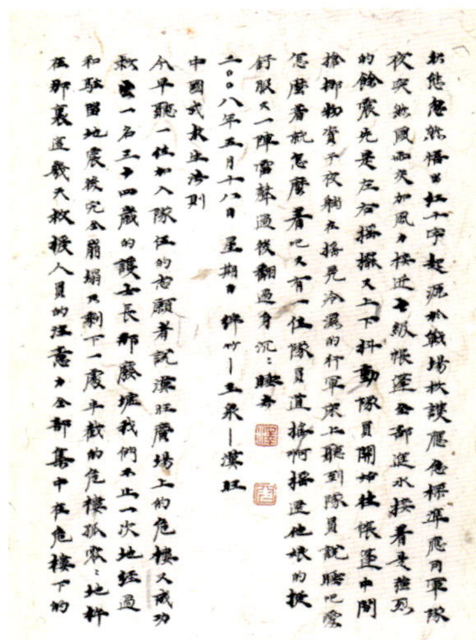
14 of 24

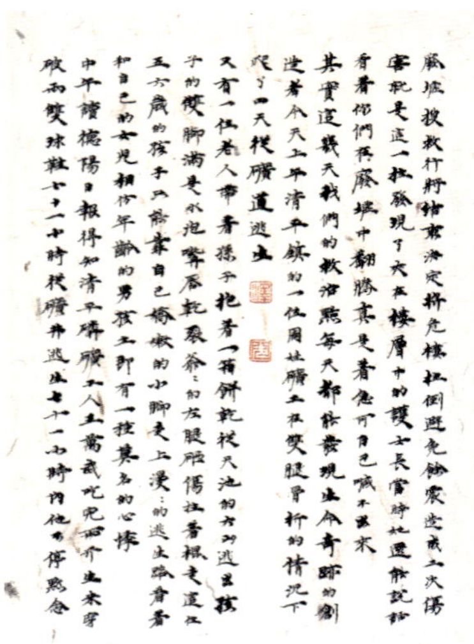
15 of 24

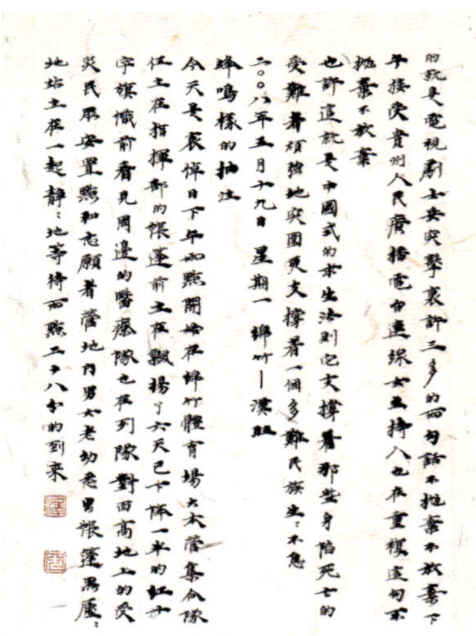
16 of 24

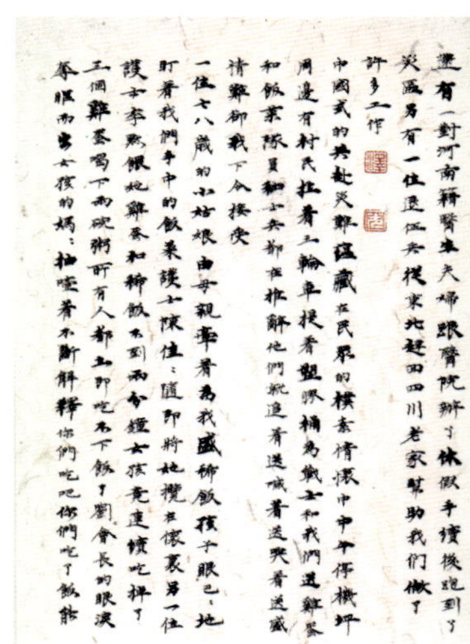
21 of 24

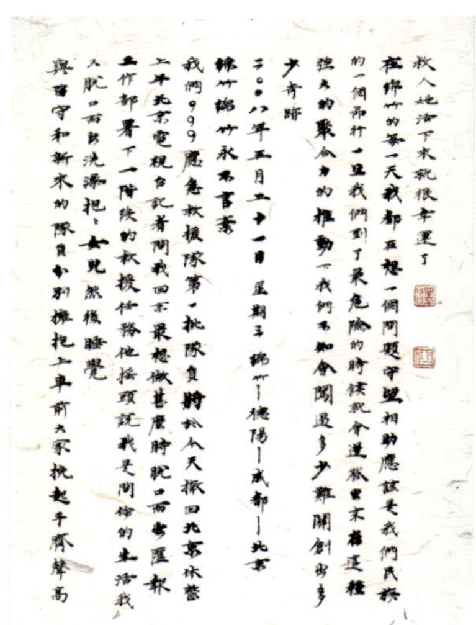
22 of 24

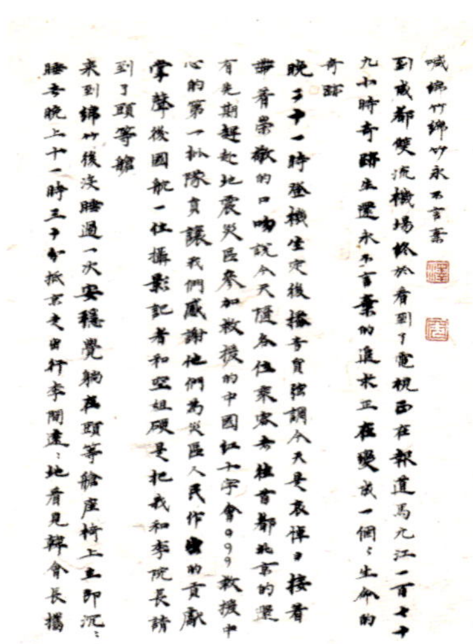
23 of 24

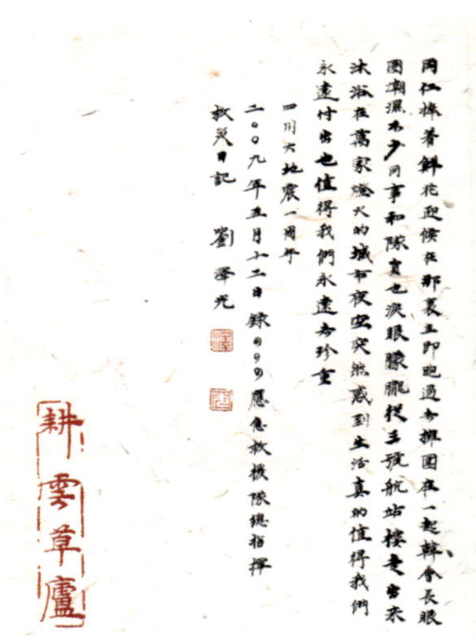
24 of 24

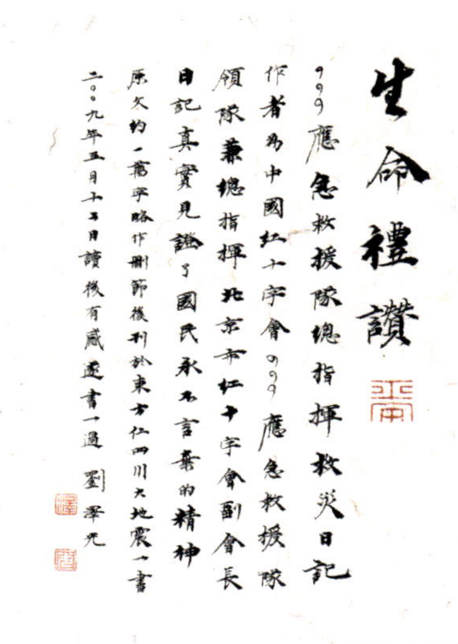

1 of 24

2 of 24

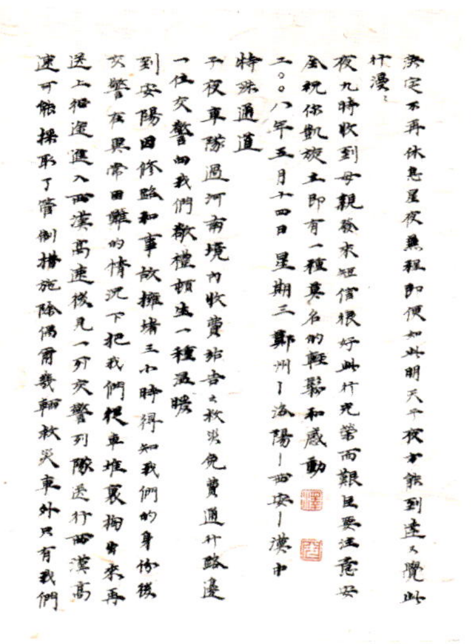

3 of 24

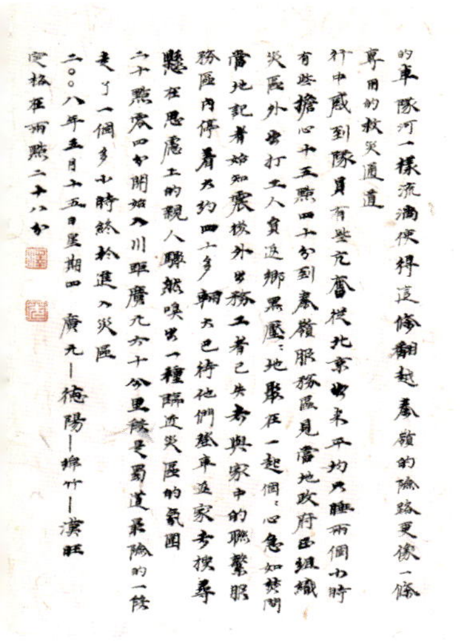

of 24

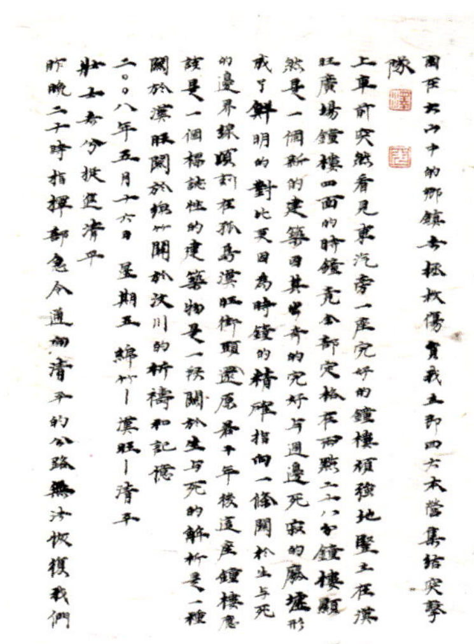

9 of 24

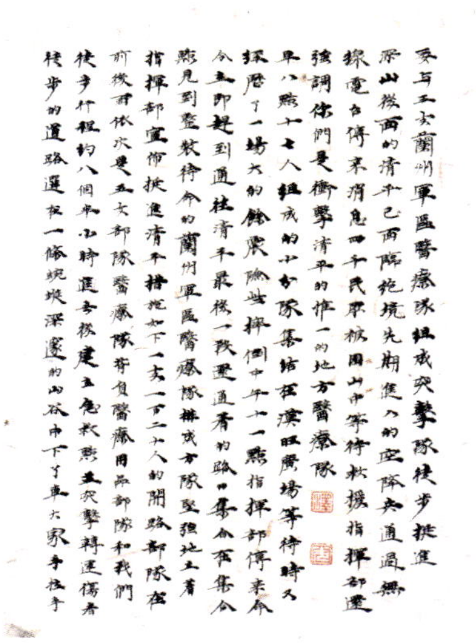

10 of 24

11 of 24

of 24

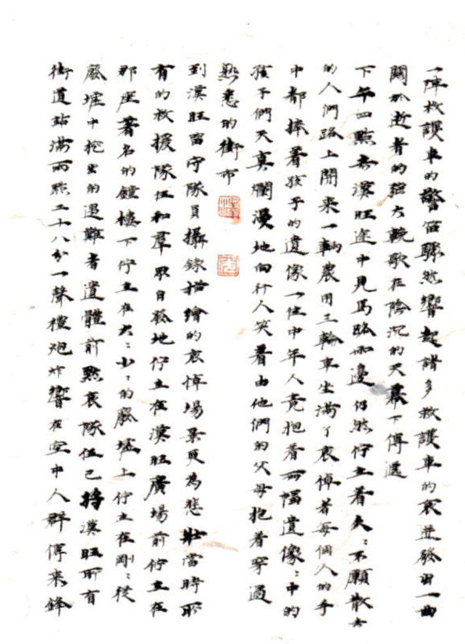

17 of 24

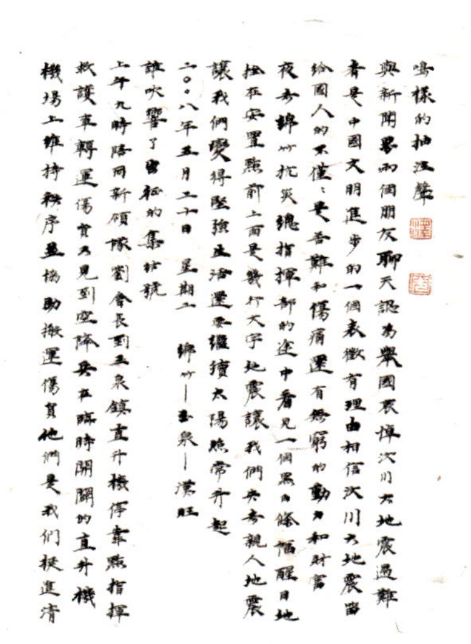

18 of 24

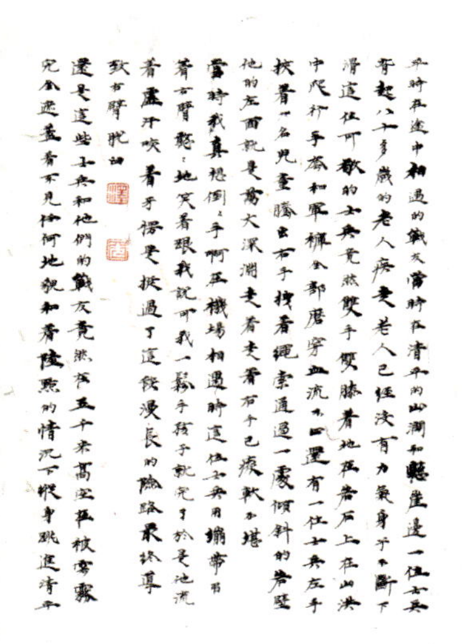

19 of 24

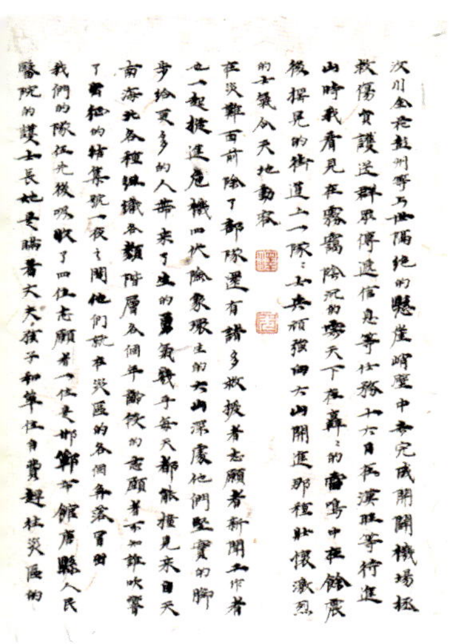

of 24

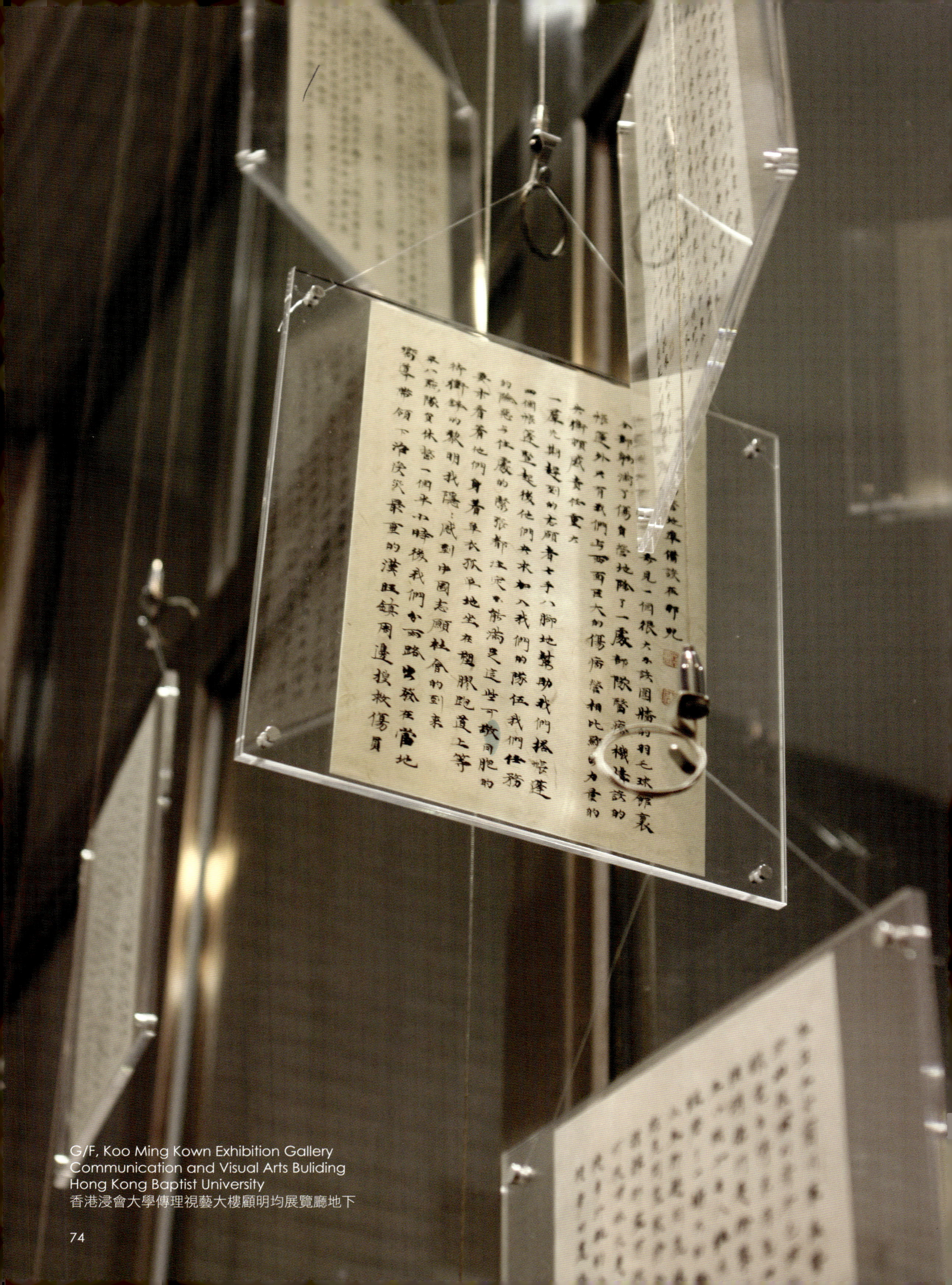

G/F, Koo Ming Kown Exhibition Gallery
Communication and Visual Arts Buliding
Hong Kong Baptist University
香港浸會大學傳理視藝大樓顧明均展覽廳地下

要求工兵蘭州軍區醫療隊組成突擊隊徒步挺進
廖山後面的清平已面臨絕境先期進入的空降兵直昇點
探電台傳來消息四千民眾被困山中等待救援指揮部更
強調你們是衝擊清平的唯一的地方醫療隊
早八點十七人組成的小分隊集結在漢旺廣場等待時人
經歷了一場大的餘震險些摔倒中午十一點指揮部傳來
命令即趕到通往清平最後一段[illegible]的路口集合[illegible]
官兵到達整裝待命的蘭州軍區醫療隊排成長隊[illegible]
指揮部即宣佈挺進清平措施如下一支一百二十八人的開路部隊
依次是五支部隊醫療隊背負醫療用品部隊和我們
徒步行程約八個半小時匯合後建立急救點並突擊轉運傷者
徒步的道路選在一條蜿蜒深邃的山谷中下了車大家手拉手

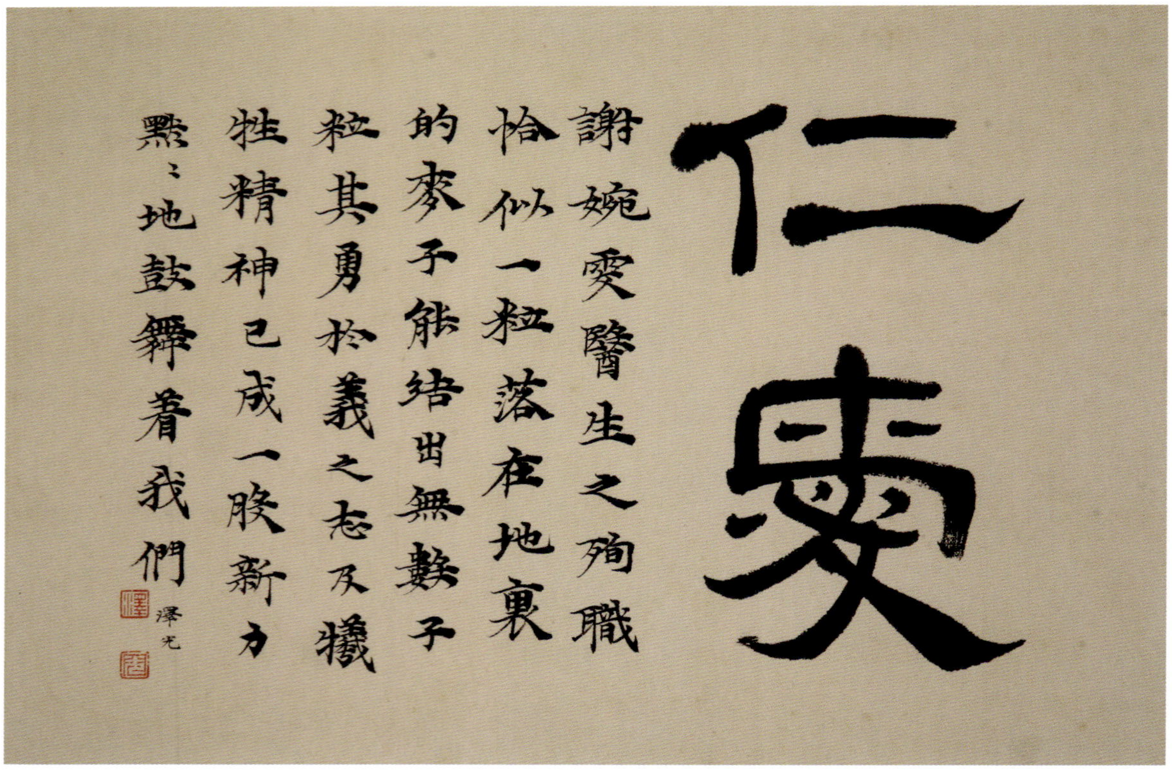

16 *Benevolent Love* | 仁愛

Clerical script
Ink on paper, mounted and framed
28 x 42 cm
2003

隸書
紙本墨書，裱框
28 x 42厘米
2003年

仁愛

謝婉雯醫生之殉職

17 *All of a sudden I turned about* I
驀然迴首

Ink on raw silk
Dimension varies
2010

生絲地墨書
尺寸不一
2010年

Transliteration:
Up and down the main streets, I must have run—
A thousand times or more in quest of one,
Who I have concluded, cannot be found;
For, everywhere, no trace of her can be seen,
When, all of a sudden, I turned about, That's her,
where lanterns are few and far between.

Translation from
http://www.shigeku.com/shiku/ws/sy/xinqiji.htm

釋文：
眾裡尋他千百度；
驀然迴首，那人卻在，燈火闌珊處。

養生

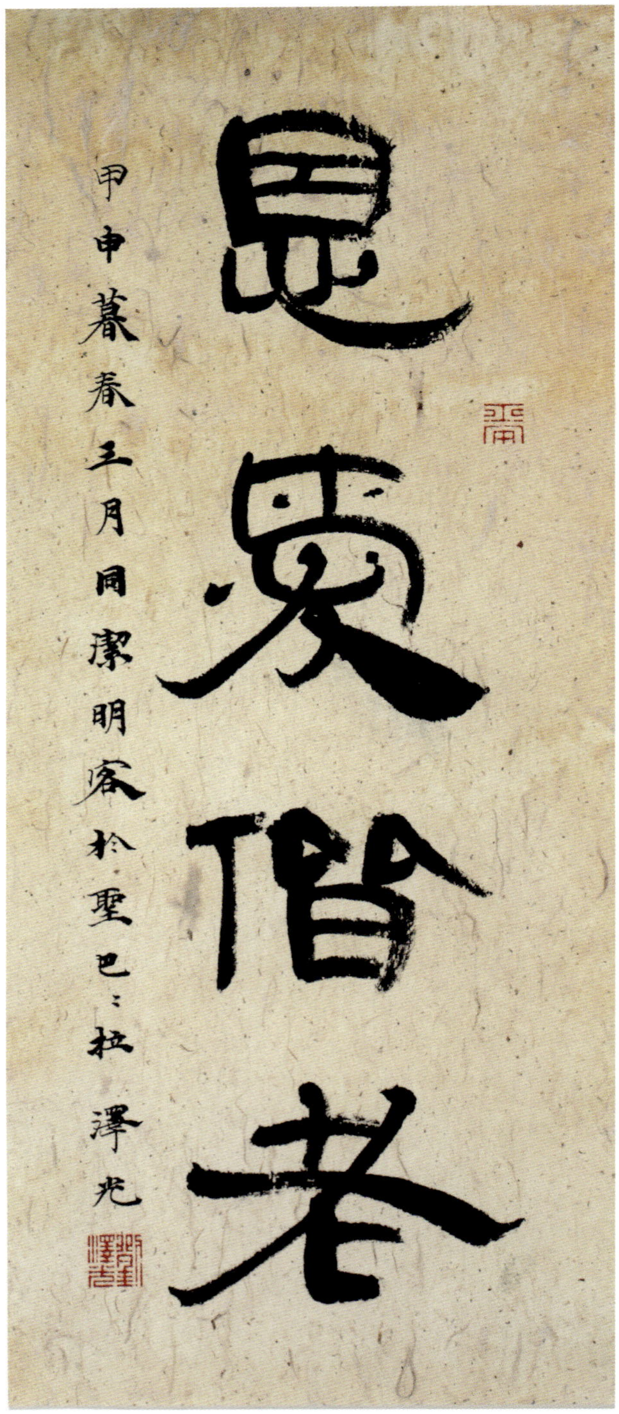

18 ***Everlasting Love*** | 恩愛偕老

Clerical script
Ink on paper, mounted and framed
30 x 85 cm
2004

隸書
紙本墨書，裱框
30x 85厘米
2004年

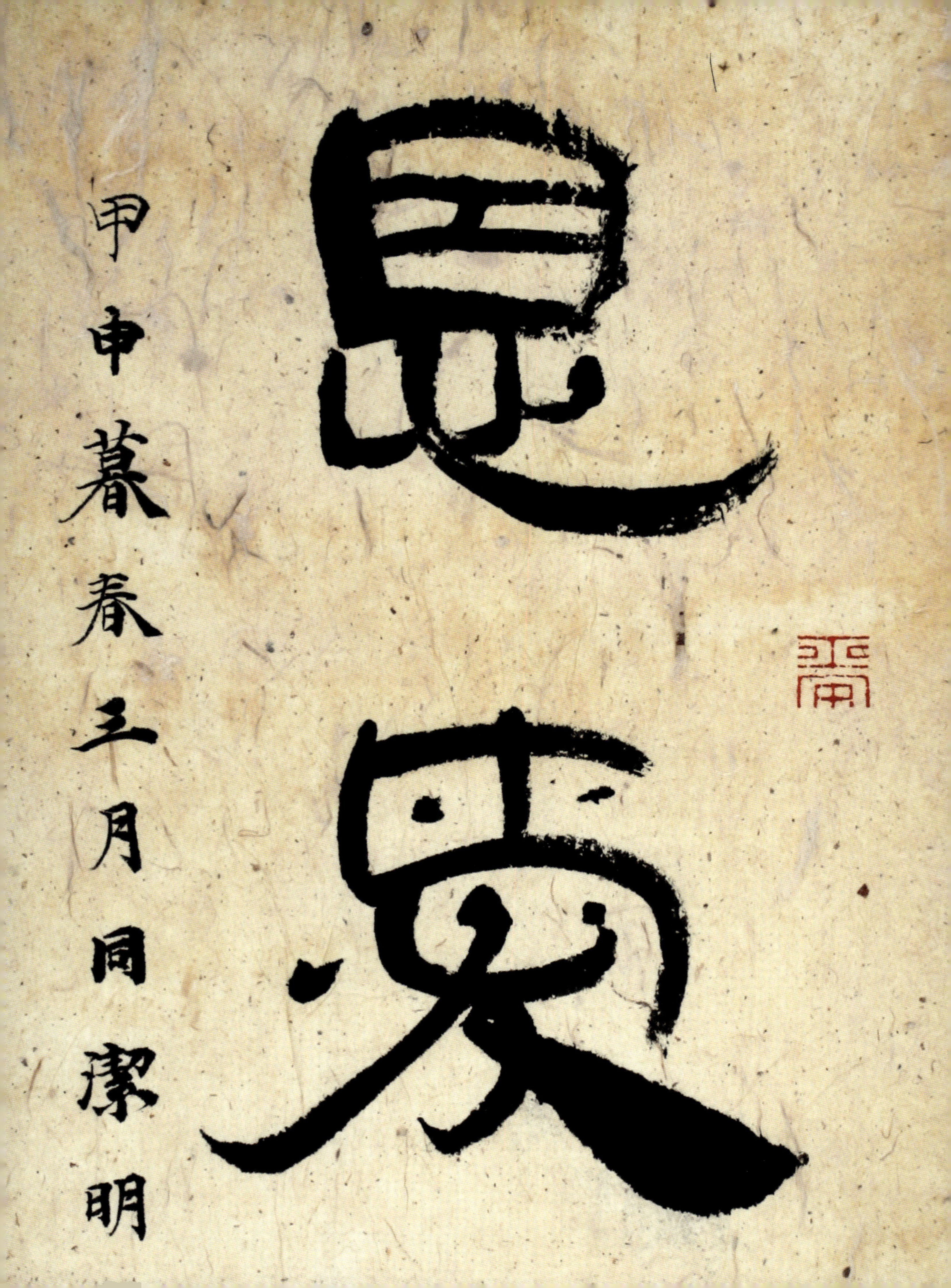
甲申暮春三月同潔明

19 *Seven-Character-Line Couplet in Seal Script* | 篆書七言聯

Clerical script
Ink on paper, hanging scrolls
138 x 35 cm (each)
2010

隸書
紙本墨書，立軸
各138x 35厘米
2010年

Transliteration:
Man becomes an experienced traveler for there have been thousands of miles that he goes.
Mid-Autumn Festival comes again as one year has passed very quickly.

釋文：
萬里因循成久客
一年容易又中秋

Artist's inscription:
I wrote this pair of couplets occasionally when talking with my students on the Mid-Autumn Day in the year of gengyin (2010). I don't know in what kind of manner the couplets were, for they were neither in Seal script nor in clerical script. I intended to finish this work as a demonstration for my calligraphy class, but after I finished writing, I started to think that it was not suitable for the students to follow, because the untrammeled brush and ink were too hard for the beginners to perceive, hence can merely for my own amusement.
I have sojourned in the United States for six years. This year when I came back, I suddenly realized that how good it is to be at home. Nothing else can give me more love and joy than spending the Mid-Autumn Day with my beloved family.

題識：庚寅中秋，與諸生談笑間偶書此聯，非篆非草，不知何所似也。此雖欲為範作，然書後自覺逸筆草草，諸生切不可學。余曾客居美國六年，今夕驟覺回家真好。能與家人在中秋節共聚天倫，不亦樂乎。

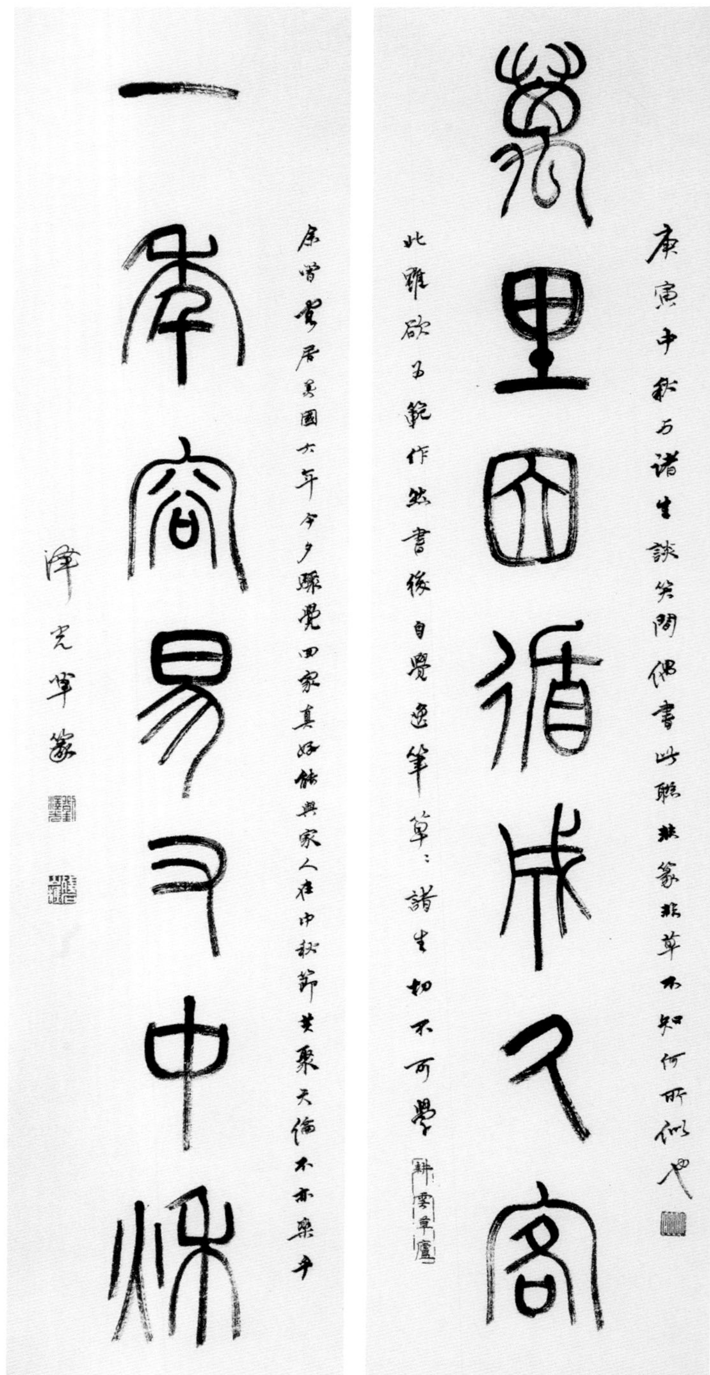

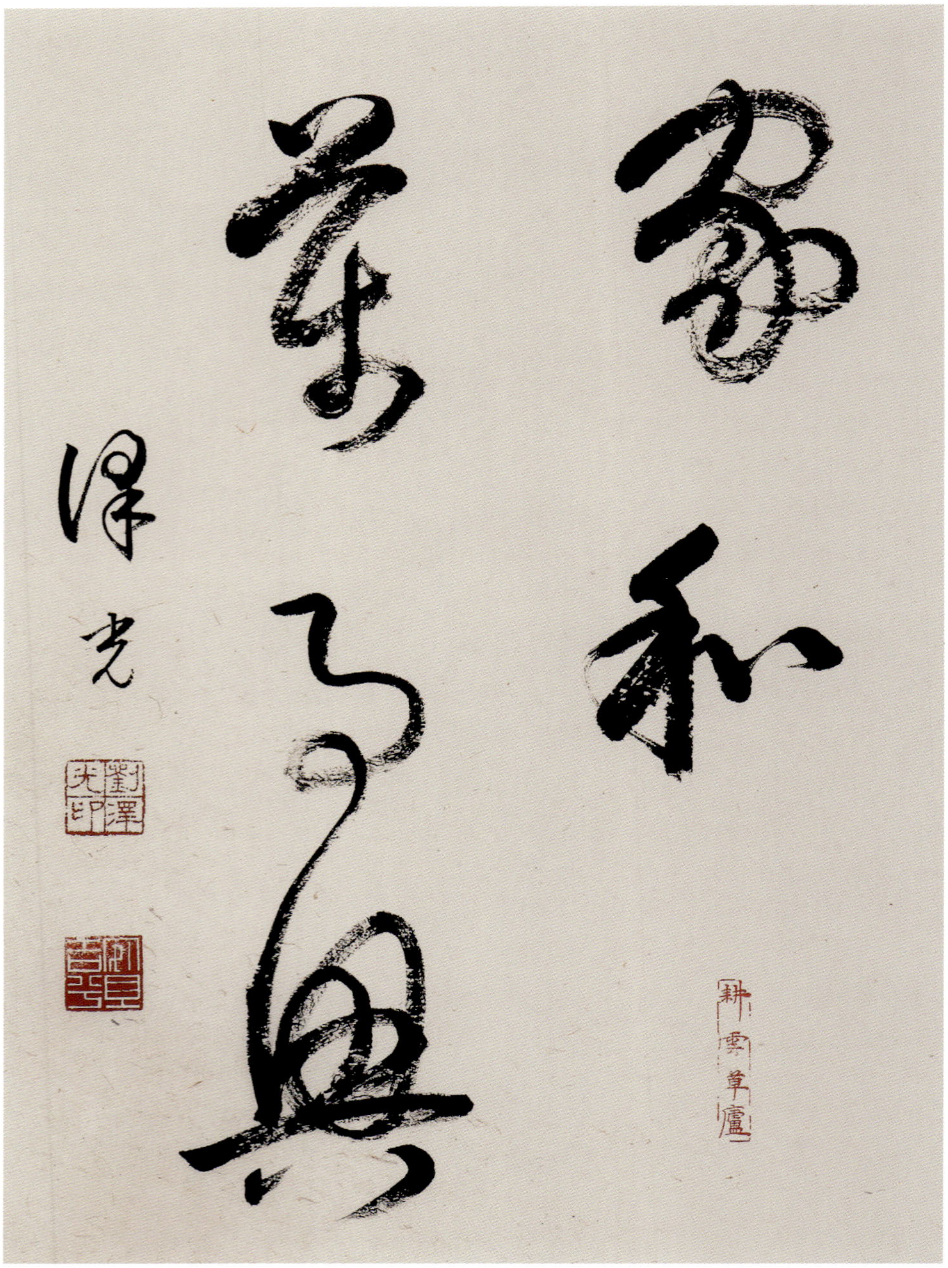

20 *Everything Prospers in a Harmonious Family* | 家和萬事興

Cursive script
Ink on paper, mounted and framed
95 x 70 cm
2009

草書
紙本墨書，裱框
95 x 70厘米
2009年

劉澤光印

21 *Give Thanks · Let's Have Tea* I
感恩吃茶去

A seven-year series comprising:
a hanging scroll (ink on paper, 94 x 20 cm, 2003) &
2 hand-engraved Chinese characters *gan en* 感恩 ("give thanks") in seal script on a *zhisha* (紫砂) teapot (height:9.5 cm, 2010)

七年系列：立軸（紙本墨書，94 x 20 厘米，2003年）及紫砂茶壺上之手刻隸書"感恩"二字（高9.5厘米，2010 年）

感恩

22 *Walking in the Mystifying Haze* | 走進撲朔迷離的“煙霞”

Installation: Ink and water on paper, mounted on 16 wooden boxes with variable size
A set of 16 wooden boxes with the same surface area of 145cm x 145cm but with different heights
2009

書法裝置 (仿石刻體)
裝置: 水墨紙本原作裝裱於
16個規格尺寸不一之木柱體之表面
1組16件木柱體，面積為145cm x 145cm，高度不一
2009

Artist's note:
This artwork is intended to break away from ideas, conventions and the method of display for traditional calligraphic practice. Created in the style in "imitation of rubbing from stone carving in clerical-standard script," the paper-based artwork is mounted on 16 square prisms of varied heights. The prisms are spread out on the gallery floor of about 27m x 9m, specially arranged into a maze-like installation space. The artwork, consisted of 14 Chinese characters and a long inscription, will need to be viewed by walking along a specially designed meandering path of the "maze". The physical "maze" alludes to the evasive deviation from the predetermined way of reading traditional calligraphic works.

The literary content of the artwork is a modern poem composed by the artist:

Haze has shrouded the city.
In the romantic veil,
health is
fading
away...

The poem satirizes the Chinese term "yanxia", or haze (literally smoke and colorful glow), used in Hong Kong Observatory's weather reports to refer to "polluted air". Such a description has romanticized the urban air pollution problem, since the term "yanxia" embodies a poetic sentiment and inspires picturesque imagination. Being continually immersed in such romanticization, people's vigilance of the problem is numbed, and their health consciousness keeps being undermined. In the artwork, the massive maze-like installation space mocks the widespread obfuscation of the public message. The artwork provides a unique interactive experience as the audience physically and literarily strolls through the poem.

作者按：
本作品擬突破傳統書法創作理念及展示方式──雖以仿石刻隸楷拓本(黑老虎)為基礎風格，但紙本作品裝裱於16個高度不一的方形柱體。柱體以特定的排列方法裝置於面積約 27米 x 9米的展館地上，並建構出狀似 “迷宮”的裝置空間（“迷宮”亦暗示因違反傳統書法中預設的閱讀方式而產生的 “模糊性”）。觀者需以一特定的迂迴路線走完“迷宮”，方可讀完以14個大字寫出作者自撰的新詩:

“煙霞”瀰漫此地。
在“浪漫”中，
淡…
忘…
健康！

內容嘲諷香港天文台竟以“煙霞” 一辭表述“污濁空氣”，把城市空氣污染問題 “浪漫化”， 因為“煙霞” 一般予人詩情畫意之聯想。長久以來，市民在“浪漫化”的敘述中不知不覺地淡化了問題，健康意識也變得模糊。作品以“迷宮”空間暗喻模糊化的公眾信息，其覆蓋面積之大暗喻信息蔓延之廣。觀者在緩慢的步伐中閱讀作品，與作品產生互動的關係。

Walking in the Mystifying Haze (Detail)
走進撲朔迷離的“煙霞”（局部）

1/F, Koo Ming Kown Exhibition Gallery
Communication and Visual Arts Buliding
Hong Kong Baptist University
香港浸會大學傳理視藝大樓顧明均展覽廳一樓

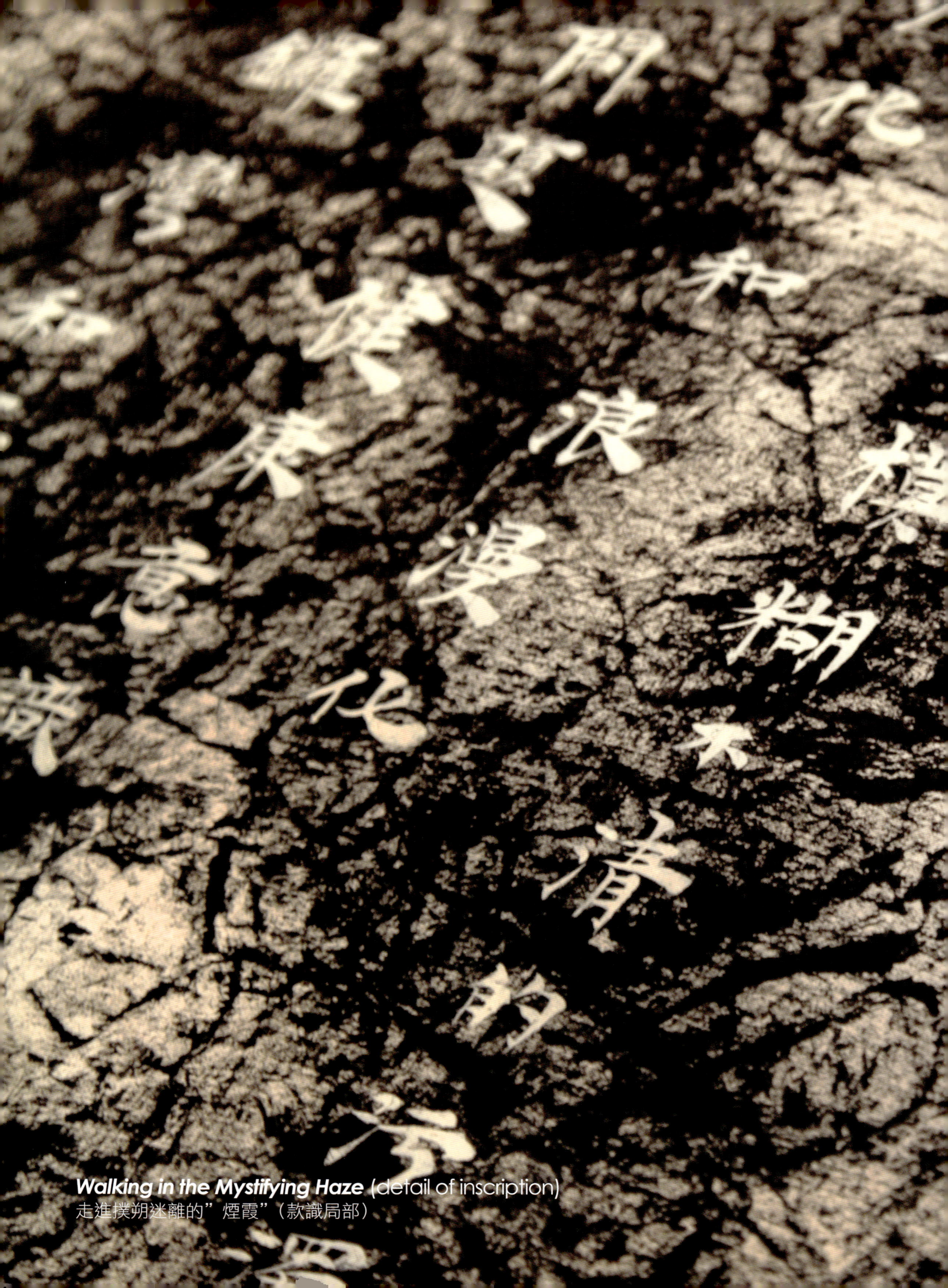

Walking in the Mystifying Haze (detail of inscription)
走進撲朔迷離的”煙霞”（款識局部）

崢嶸嶺上有
煙霞
讚嘆不已
煙霞

Walking in the Mystifying Haze (Detail)
走進撲朔迷離的“煙霞”（局部）

1/F, Koo Ming Kown Exhibition Gallery
Communication and Visual Arts Buliding
Hong Kong Baptist University
香港浸會大學傳理視藝大樓顧明均展覽廳一樓

Walking in the Mystifying Haze (Detail)
走進撲朔迷離的“煙霞”（局部）

1/F, Koo Ming Kown Exhibition Gallery
Communication and Visual Arts Buliding
Hong Kong Baptist University
香港浸會大學傳理視藝大樓顧明均展覽廳一樓

23 *Louis Vuitton & Porsche* | *LV* 與波子

Seal script
Ink and watercolor on canvas,
92 X 92 cm (each)
2010

篆書
布本水墨水彩
各92 x 92厘米
2010年

Transliteration:
Between heaven and earth, LV is the most expensive.
Amidst the busy city, Porsche is genuinely showy.

釋文：
天地間 L V最貴
鬧市中波子真威

1/F, Koo Ming Kown Exhibition Gallery
Communication and Visual Arts Buliding
Hong Kong Baptist University
香港浸會大學傳理視藝大樓顧明均展覽廳一樓

24 *Service for Renminbi (People's Currency)*

為人民幣服務

Semi-cursive script
Acrylic on canvas
91 X 61cm (each)
2010

行書
布本膠彩
各91x 61厘米
2010年

Transliteration:
Service for renminbi
(literally people's currency)

釋文：
為人民幣服務

考

施与受

CHAPTER 2/ 第二章

Give
&
Receive

Inheritance and Innovation : Daniel Chak kwong Lau's Exploration into Seal Engraving[1]

Vincent K. T. Tong
Associate Professor
The Chinese University of Hong Kong

The earliest record on seal-engraving in Hong Kong can be traced back to around 1872, but it is not until the establishment of the Republic that the art of seal-engraving in Hong Kong began to develop rapidly. Its development can roughly be divided into three periods, each of them thirty years long. The economic and cultural progress of Hong Kong was closely related to the migration wave from mainland China. The art of seal-engraving was no exception. The political incidents that occurred during the three periods, including the establishment of the Republic, the Second Sino-Japanese War and the liberation of China, all caused a large number of seal-engravers to move southward to Hong Kong, and thus formed the backbone for the development of seal-engraving here. Most of these seal-engravers were Cantonese due to the geographical proximity between Guangdong and Hong Kong. They created ceaselessly and put much effort in passing on their skills to new generations of seal-engravers, thus bringing the art of seal-engraving in Hong Kong to one climax after another.

In the 1980s, the Chinese Economic Reform was implemented and the mainland economy started to take off. Many seal-engravers migrated to Hong Kong and to some extent influenced the local seal-engraving art. The advent of the 21st century generally saw a period of stability and prosperity in our adjacent regions. Without the influence of migration, and with the decease of senior seal-engravers, the art of seal-engraving in Hong Kong was apparently declining. The most obvious phenomenon was that the seal-engravers' creative passion dropped sharply, very few books of seal impressions (yinpu) were published, and many seal-engraving classes could not be run due to a lack of students. We can say that seal-engraving in Hong Kong was in recession. 2009 is a year to rejoice in. Several months ago I received the yinpu of the experienced seal-engraver Chen Liyuan. Not long after that I wrote a preface for the seal-engraving publication of my student Pau Mo-ching. And recently I was informed that my friend Daniel Chak-kwong Lau will also publish his seal-engraving catalogue. The latter two in particular are Hong Kong's locally born and bred young seal-engravers. It seems that the art of seal-engraving in Hong Kong is being revitalized, ushering in some new progress.

I have known Daniel for almost twenty years. At that time he was working as a teacher. At leisure Daniel learnt calligraphy and Chinese painting from the eminent calligrapher Han Yunshan (1923-2010) and painter Long Ziduo (1915-2008). Later he wrote his Master's Thesis under the supervision of Professor Wan Qingli. After that he furthered his study at University of California and obtained his Doctor of Philosophy. He then started teaching at the Academy of Visual Arts, Hong Kong Baptist University in 2006.

Daniel devoted himself mainly to calligraphy in his early years. Later he started to learn seal-engraving in the 1990s to pursue the state of "Three Perfections" (in calligraphy, painting and seal-engraving). At the beginning he had no teacher. The over a hundred seals engraved by senior masters for his teacher Mr. Han hence became Daniel's model for learning. Many of these seal-engravers are the aforementioned Cantonese masters who had migrated to Hong Kong, including Feng Kanghou (1901-1983), Lu Dinggong (1903-1979), Rong Geng

1 A version of this essay was published in: Daniel C.K. Lau ed. *Impression: Seals Engraved by Daniel Chak-kwong Lau*. Hong Kong: Academy of Visual Arts, Hong Kong Baptist University, 2009, pp. 8-10.

(1894-1983), Shang Chengzuo (1902-1991), Lin Qianshi (1918-1990), Zhang Xiangning (1911-1958), and Qiu Siming (1925-1994). These seals are most suitable for comparative learning when different masters carved upon similar subject matters. Additionally one can have the opportunity to touch the original seal stone and gain a better insight into the use of the blade. With these seals, it can be said that Daniel has reaped no little benefit.

In the early days, seal-engraving in Hong Kong was really dominated by Cantonese seal-engravers. Most of these seal-engravers were influenced by the style of Huang Mufu (1849-1908), and they were labelled "the Cantonese School". Daniel mainly consults the works by these seal-engravers, but he has his own thoughts on the use of the blade. Rather than the thrusting knife method popular among the Cantonese seal-engravers, Daniel usually employs the "blade method of short cutting" (碎切刀法) of the Zhe School. Master seal-engraver Ding Jing (1695-1765), the head of the Eight Masters of Xiling, is much admired by Daniel. This master seal-engraver is exactly the research focus in Daniel's Ph.D. thesis, so no wonder Daniel's blade methods are much influenced by him. Moreover, Daniel is also fond of the "black-tiger" calligraphy of the calligrapher and seal-engraver Luo Shuzhong (1898-1969). This kind of calligraphy is done by blotting to achieve the effect of stele rubbing, so that the works look mottled and jagged. When applied in seal-engraving, the "blade method of short cutting" makes it easier to attain the effect of roughness.

Inheritance and innovation have been the issues faced by the artists. Because of the history and its uniqueness, the art of seal-engraving can be considered a rather self-sufficient art form. Unlike painting and calligraphy, the impact of Western contemporary art trend on seal-engraving is much milder. Some describe seal-engraving as a kind of art that "dances with shackles on". Perhaps its charm lies precisely in the opening-up of a universe under a great deal of limitations. Undoubtedly, the art of seal-engraving has its special nature, but seal-engravers still need to discover ways of innovation, so that this art form can be carried on from the past and pave the way for future generations.

Daniel has done much exploration on this topic. It can generally be classified into two aspects. One is the aspect of content. Daniel uses Cantonese and slangs in his seals which keeps the art of seal-engraving abreast with the times and society. The other is the aspect of the type of script. Apart from seal scripts, he largely uses different types of script in his seals, including standard script, xiejing ti (Buddhist Sutra script), Han jian (bamboo slip inscriptions of Han Dynasty), bafen (one of the various forms of the clerical script), draft-cursive, and even the English alphabet. Among these, the styles Daniel uses most often are Ni Zan's (1306-1374) small-character standard script, Han jian and bafen. Daniel has inherited these few types of script from his teacher Master Han, and he can easily and naturally incorporate them into his seals. There are a number of predecessors that created fine seals in scripts other than seal script, like Luo Shuzhong's clerical-script seal, Jian Qinzhai's (1888-1950) seal in the style of stele inscriptions of the Six Dynasties period, and Tan Yuese's (1891-1976) shoujin ti ("slender gold", or "slender tendon" script) seals. But they only made these seals occasionally, much less than what Daniel has done. This of course has become one of the characteristics of Daniel's seal-engraving.

The development of the art of seal-engraving in Hong Kong relies on the seal-engravers' creation and exploration. More important is that, in relation to training, the young people should especially be targeted for cultivation. The traditional mentor-mentee teaching and learning does have its value. Meanwhile, institutional training can better fulfil the needs of the time for its comprehensive and focused course design. This also explains why tertiary art education is significant. The Department of Fine Arts, Chinese University of Hong Kong started delivering seal-engraving courses in 1957. But this can hardly satisfy the great demands for cultivating seal-engraving talents. In recent years, the Academy of Visual Arts, Hong Kong Baptist University has been established, and seal-engraving courses are offered. Under the guidance of Daniel, who is well-versed in both artistic creation and historical research, I believe the training of seal-engraving talents in Hong Kong will certainly be enhanced. May I encourage and work hard with Daniel, for prospering the art of seal engraving in Hong Kong!

繼承與創新：
劉澤光篆刻探索[1]

唐錦騰
香港中文大學副教授

有關香港篆刻的資料最早約可追溯至1872年左右，然而香港篆刻藝術有長足發展則在民國以後，其發展大致可分為三個時期，每一時期約為三十年。香港經濟文化的發展，與國內來港的移民潮息息相關，篆刻藝術也不例外，三個時期所發生的政治事件，包括民國成立、抗日戰爭、中國解放等，都帶動了大批印人南來，並建構香港篆刻藝術發展的骨幹。廣東與香港毗鄰，因此這些印人又以粵籍佔多數，他們創作不絕外，更致力傳授印藝，培養了不少印人，使香港篆刻藝術發展經歷一次又一次的高峰。

八十年代中國改革開放，經濟起飛，也有不少印人移居香港，同樣對香港篆刻藝術發揮了一定的影響力。進入二十一世紀，海內外安定昇平，沒有移民因素的影響，加上老一輩印人相繼謝世，香港篆刻藝術似有萎縮的情況。最明顯的現象是印人創作熱情鋭降，印譜出版甚少，不少篆刻班因收生不足而未能開課，可以説，香港篆刻藝術正處於低潮之中。二〇〇九年是值得欣喜的一年，數月前收到資深印人陳禮源社兄的印譜，個多月前剛為學生鮑慕貞印集作序，而日前又得知硯友劉澤光亦將出版其印集；尤其後二者均為香港土生土長的年青印人，似乎可以看到香港篆刻藝術正在煥發生機，迎來了新的發展。

與澤光相識已差不多二十年了，那時他正從事教育工作，課餘隨名宿韓雲山（1923-2010）及龍子鐸（1915-2008）兩位前輩研習書畫，其後又在萬青屴教授指導下撰寫碩士論文，畢業後更負笈美國加州大學深造，並取得博士學位。二〇〇六年起任教於浸會大學視覺藝術院。

澤光早年致力研習書法，後因探求書、畫、印「三絕」融通之理，於九十年代亦開始學習篆刻，起初並無師承，其師韓老所珍藏的百多方前輩印人為其所治印石，遂成為澤光的學習範本。這些印人不少為前述移居香港的粵籍名手，包括馮康 （1901-1983）、盧鼎公（1903-1979）、容庚（1894-1983）、商承祚（1902-1991）、林千石（1918-1990）、張祥凝（1911-1958）、丘思明（1925-1994）等。不同名家鑄刻相類似的題材，最宜比較學習，加上有機會摩挲原石，對於用刀的正側虛實，可以有更深入的瞭解。澤光透過這批印章，可謂獲益匪淺。

香港篆刻早期確是以粵籍印人為主，當中又以受黃牧甫（1849-1908）流風影響的佔多數，這些印人有被冠以「粵派」之名。澤光兄雖以參考這些印人作品為主，但在用刀方面，卻有自己的想法，較少使用粵派印人常用的衝刀，反而更多是浙派的碎切刀法。西泠八家之首的丁敬（1695-1765）是澤光所敬服的篆刻宗匠，澤光的博士論文即是以之為中心的研究，故其篆刻刀法肯定受到很大的影響。此外，澤光亦醉心於前輩書法篆刻家羅叔重（1898-1969）的「黑老虎」書法創作。這種書法以墨漬法仿效碑拓效果，追求斑駁剝落之趣，運用於篆刻時，碎切刀自然較容易達到蒼莽效果。

繼承與創新一直是藝術家們不斷面對的課題。篆刻藝術因為歷史及其獨特性，可説是一門較自足的藝術，它面對西方當代藝術思潮而承受的衝擊，遠遠不及繪畫和書法那麼強烈。有人形容篆刻是一種「帶着鐐銬跳舞」的藝術，或許它的魅力就是要在諸多的限制中，開拓一片廣闊的天地。雖然篆刻藝術有其獨特的本質，然而在這個大前提下，印人還是需要有所開拓創新，使這門藝術可以繼往開來。

澤光在這個課題上亦有不少探索，這大概可分為兩個方面。其一是在內容方面，以廣東話或俚語入印，使印章藝術更能貼近時代和社會。其次，是在用字方面，即篆文以外，大量運用不同書體入印，包括楷書、寫經體、漢簡、八分、章草，以至英文字母。其中又以倪瓚（1306-1374）風格的小楷、漢簡和八分運用得最多，這幾種正是澤光得自韓老真傳的書體，自然駕輕就熟，最為合作。前輩印人亦有不少以非篆體入印的佳構，如羅叔重的隸書印、簡琴齋的六朝碑體印和談月色的瘦金體印等，但他們都只是偶一為之而已，在印作比例上遠沒有澤光使用得那麼多。這自然成為澤光個人篆刻特點之一了。

1　本文曾發表於劉澤光編，《印象：劉澤光篆刻》，香港：香港浸會大學視覺藝術院，2009年，頁11-12。

香港篆刻藝術的發展，端賴印人們努力創作探求，而更為重要的是在人材培養方面，尤其是年青一代，理應成為重要培育對象。傳統師徒式的教學有其存在的價值，而學院式的訓練，因課程設計全面且具針對性，更能切合時代需要，這也是大專藝術教育有其重要性的原因。香港中文大學藝術系於一九五七年便開設有篆刻課程，然而這遠遠不能滿足對培養篆刻人材的廣大需求。近年浸會大學視覺藝術院成立，亦開設了篆刻課，在創作和史論兼修的澤光兄教導下，相信香港篆刻人材的培養會有一定的提高。願與澤光兄共勉，為繁榮香港篆刻藝術一同努力！

The Bond between the Giver and Recipient in the Practice of Seals as Gifts: A New Approach to Integration between Creative Work and Scholarly Research[1] ◣

Daniel C.K. Lau
Assistant Professor
Hong Kong Baptist University

A Cross between Production of Artworks and Art Historical Research

This project is a pioneering endeavor that examines the synergy between art-historical research and the creative practice of Chinese seal engraving, which are essentially two completely different fields of study and inquiry. Consisting of a scholarly writing titled "Seals as Artistic Expression, Projection of Self-Image and Token of Like-Mindedness" and the ninety-five works of seal engraving selected from the author's oeuvre completed in the past decade, this chapter presents the results of an in-depth interdisciplinary study on the theories and practice of Chinese seal engraving, offering a new approach of integrated undertaking of scholarly research and creative work in the same project by the same author.[1]

Impression — From Seal to Symbol

Impression (cat. no. 62) is a seal-engraving draft that embodies multi-faceted meanings —— a rectangular seal impression showing the intaglio image of the great-seal-script (*dazhuan* 大篆 or *jinwen* 金文) character *xiang* (象),[2] which primarily means "elephant" and, when joined with a prefix or suffix, has multiple extended meanings such as, image (*xingxiang* 形象) and symbol (*xiangzheng* 象徵). In fact, the adoption of the Chinese character *xiang* in this work unfolds the overall objective of treating seals as visual images, self-images and symbols in the artist's practice of seal engraving.

The Chinese term that conveys the meaning of "impression" comprises the two characters *yin* (印) and *xiang* (象), which means "seal" and "elephant" respectively before joining together to form the new meaning of "impression". Hence, the rectangular "seal" impression, which enfolds the hieroglyphic character of "elephant", seeks to deconstruct the Chinese term of "impression" in a pictorial manner, eventually highlighting the primordial elements of the word in a daringly fresh artistic context.

The symbolism embodied in a seal intriguingly transforms the visual image of a seal impression into abstract concepts. This supposed mental process naturally involves the audience's power of imagination. Imagination is indeed one of the key factors pertinent to the effectiveness of art production and consumption, as this can be especially enlightened by the art of seal engraving which essentially involves symbolism. A seal, by its very nature, is a functional object that symbolizes the seal owner. From the perspective of the art producer, a seal and its impression are intended to symbolically represent the seal owner, whereas from the perspective of the audience (i.e. the consumer of art), a seal impression reminds the viewer of the seal owner as a person. Apparently, the whole idea of the personification of seals is a covert mental process that requires both the producer and consumer of art to exercise their power of imagination beyond their

1 A version of this essay was published in: Daniel C.K. Lau ed. *Impression: Seals Engraved by Daniel Chak-kwong Lau*. Hong Kong: Academy of Visual Arts, Hong Kong Baptist University, 2009, pp. 13-15.

2 This hieroglyph of the character *xiang* (象) is adopted from the inscription of the character on *Xiangqiexin Ding* of Shang Dynasty (ca. 1600-ca.1100 B.C.). The original rubbing of the inscription was published in Liu, Tizhi (1879-1963) (ed.), *Xiaojiaojingge jinshi wenzi: yinde ben* (小校經閣金石文字：引得本), (Taipei: Datong shuju, 1979). For the reproduced image of the original rubbing, see "Digital Archives of Bronze Images and Inscriptions", The Institute of History and Philology, Academia Sinica, http://www.ihp.sinica.edu.tw/~bronze, (item no.: 01512). Also see Rong, Geng (容庚) (ed.), *Jinwen bian* (The Compilation of Bronze Inscriptions) (金文編) (Beijing: Zhonghua shuju, 1985), p. 673.

perception of seals as merely artworks. Consequently, a seal impression that bears the owner's name serves as symbols signifying one's commitment in such situations as authorship of a piece of artwork or literary composition, or credibility and responsibility in legal agreements and other types of covenants.

Jireh, Idle Cloud and *Little Friend of the Ox-shed*: Sobriquet Seals as Self-Images

Beyond the primary category of seals bearing the owners' names, seal impressions that bear the owner' sobriquets vividly sublimate their self-images and convey self-referential ideas that suggest the seal owners' personality, temperament, aspirations, hobbies, special life experience, other attributes like personal values, cultural and sub-cultural identifications, and religious beliefs and commitments.

All produced by the author of this book, the ninety-five works of seal engraving selected in this chapter are categorized by a special principle highlighting the sobriquets of three ultimate seal owners: The first group includes the seals that the author engraved for himself (cat. nos. 25 - 78); the second group consists of the seals that the author engraved for his calligraphy teacher Mr. Han Yunshan (cat. nos. 79 - 105) and the third group comprises the seals that the author engraved for his academic mentor Professor Wan Qingli (cat. nos. 106 - 120):

1. Jireh —— Seals Often used by Dr. Daniel C. K. Lau
2. Idle Cloud —— Seals Often used by Mr. Han Yunshan
3. Little Friend of the Ox-Shed —— Seals Often used by Professor Wan Qingli

Jireh 以勒 is the author's sobriquet adapted from the biblical expression "Yahweh-jireh", meaning "Yahweh will provide". The author engraved *Jireh* 以勒 (cat. no. 37) as his sobriquet seal to commemorate his transient sojourn in Santa Barbara, California from 2000 to 2006, during which he experienced God's abundant provision in times of need.

The two seals reading "*Lanyun*"(嬾雲), or "Idle Cloud" (cat. nos. 87 and 88) are sobriquet seals the author engraved for his calligraphy teacher Mr. Han Yunshan (1923-2010). Han uses the word *lan* (嬾), or "idle" to identify with Ni Zan (倪瓚, 1301-1374), one of the groups of Chinese painters later known as the Four Masters of the Yuan Dynasty (1206–1368), who previously used the same word "*lan*" in his sobriquet "*Lan zan*" (嬾瓚). Han Yunshan is a reclusive artist who has been working in Hong Kong for more than half a century. The redolent connotation of idleness or laziness in Han's sobriquet well suggests his reclusive temperament in the masquerade of a self-sarcastic tone. Apart from being a calligrapher, Han also holds multiple identities of a poet, a philologist, a paleographer of Chinese and a connoisseur collecting paintings, works of calligraphy, seals, rubbings from ancient steles, ancient coins, jade, porcelains, antique inkstones and teapots.[3]

Produced also by the author, the sobriquet seals reading "*Little Friend of the Ox-Shed*" 小棚友 (cat. nos. 110, 111 and 112), are used by Professor Wan Qingli to commemorate his sojourn in the ox-shed in a political movement where he unexpectedly and luckily met his teacher Li Keran李可染 (1907-1989) and other artists. Well known as both art historian and painter, Professor Wan is Chair Professor and Director of the Academy of Visual Arts, Hong Kong Baptist University.

In a sense, the above mentioned sobriquet seals shed light on how the three individuals see themselves as people struggling in various important aspects of their life. Therefore, using the three individuals' sobriquets to categorize even all other non-sobriquet seals, which the author produced and subsequently collected in this chapter, significantly accentuates the whole idea of seals as self-images.

The Bond between the Giver and Recipient

All the seals, as produced by the author and eventually given to his two teachers, signify how like-minded people, especially those who are passionate and study traditional Chinese painting and calligraphy, maintain friendship by giving and receiving seals. For this circle, seals in a sense serve as a symbolic token of like-mindedness between the giver and the recipient of the seal. The giver and recipient mutually embrace the shared values expressed through the literary content of the seals. Eventually, a sense of in-group identity is gradually established.

---

3 On Han's biographical accounts and an approach of appreciation of his calligraphy, see Lau Chak-kwong, "The Recluse-Artist Han Yunshan and an Approach of Appreciation of His Art of Chinese Calligraphy," in *Besides: A Journal of Art History and Criticism*. 2001, vol. 3, 51-67; and *Hong Kong Calligraphy: Collection of Hong Kong Museum of Art* (Hong Kong: Urban Council, Hong Kong, 1990), 44.

以印為禮的實踐體現贈者與受者間之凝聚力：創作與學術研究結合的新途徑[1]

劉澤光
香港浸會大學助理教授

跨越藝術創作及藝術史

是項先驅計劃結合藝術史研究與中國篆刻創作，以圖從兩個截然不同領域吸取養分，探討當代篆刻的新方向。本章以英文論文“Seals as Artistic Expression, Projection of Self-Image & Token of Like-Mindedness”(作為藝術表現、自我形象投射及同道信物的印章)為本，並從筆者近十年來的創作選出95件篆刻作品，以跨領域的視野探究中國篆刻藝術理論及創作，以發展創作和學術研究並行的新途徑。

印象：從“印”章到“象”徵

名為《印象》(*Impression*)的印稿（展品62）是一富有多重含義的作品一長方形的“印”以縷空的方式書寫出金文“象”字。[2]這象形的“象”字可引申作“圖象”或“形象”解。有趣的是，這也暗合英文“image”一字包含“圖象”和“形象”的雙重解釋。此外，“象”字也可引申作“象徵”，意指用具體事物表示抽象概念或思想感情。這正是英文字“symbolism”的含義。“印象”也有語帶雙關的含義：一方面指印章蓋在物體表面上所留下的“視覺圖象”(visual image).——即“印拓”(英文“seal impression”)；另一方面指“自我形象”，包含“象徵”或“象徵主義”等有關概念。印章中蘊含的“象徵主義”將“視覺圖象”(即印拓) 轉化為抽象的概念。

想像力乃決定藝術生產與消費能否交通交融的關鍵，而與象徵主義息息相關的篆刻藝術正是其例子。印章有代表擁有者的功能。就藝術生產者的角度而言，印章和印拓以代表印章主人為要；從觀者（即藝術消費者）看來，印章俾人「見印如見人」。顯然，印章人格化是潛藏的思想過程，端賴藝術生產者和消費者發揮想像力賞玩其中意涵，而不是把印章抬舉為高不可攀的藝術品。所以，姓名印可用來象徵印章擁有者所許下的承諾，諸如其藝術或文學作品創作人的身分，或在法律合同與其他契約中的信用和責任。

《以勒》、《嬾雲》和《小棚友》：作為自我形象的別號印

印章除了姓名印外，以別號為內容者更可將印章主人的自我形象昇華，並傳達自我指涉的意念，暗示印章主人的性情、抱負、嗜好、特別的人生經驗，以及價值觀、文化及次文化身份認同和宗教信仰等個人信念。

本章收錄的95件印章及印稿作品全部由本書作者創作，以三位主要印章主人的別號分類：第一組印是作者為自己所刻的“自用印”(展品25-78)；第二組印是作者為其書法老師韓雲山先生（1923-2010）所刻的常用印 （展品79-105)；第三組印是作者為其學術導師萬青屴教授所刻的常用印(展品106-120)，並以三人的別號作分類標題：

1. 以勒——劉澤光博士自用印
2. 嬾雲——韓雲山先生常用印
3. 小棚友——萬青屴教授常用印

「以勒」是作者從聖經中「耶和華必預備」的「耶和華以勒」一語擷取而來的別號。筆者刻此《以勒》別號印（作品37）紀念2000至2006年旅居美國加州聖芭芭拉數年間，雖然貧困，卻得以經歷神豐足的供應。

兩方以「嬾雲」為文的印章（作品87、88）是筆者為其書法老師韓雲山先生（1923-2010）所刻的別號印。「元朝四大家」之一的倪瓚（1301-1374）以「嬾瓚」為別號，韓氏亦在別號中套用此「懶」的本字——「嬾」，自比倪雲林。韓雲山在香港從事藝術工作逾半個世紀，既是書法家，亦是詞人、語文學家、中國古文字學家，以及書畫、印章、碑拓、古錢、玉器、瓷器、古董硯石和茶壺收藏鑑賞家。[3]其

1　本文大部份內容曾發表於劉澤光編，《印象：劉澤光篆刻》，香港：香港浸會大學視覺藝術院，2009年，頁16-17。。

2　這象形文的“象”字是筆者參考商代（約西元前16世紀初-約西元前11世紀）《象且辛鼎》銘文中的“象”字。銘文原拓片收錄於劉體智（1879-1963）主編：《小校經閣金石文字：引得本》（台北市：大通書局, 1979）。銘文原拓片的圖像複製，參考中央研究院歷史語言研究所金文工作室製作之『殷周金文暨青銅器資料庫』(http://www.ihp.sinica.edu.tw/~bronze)，（器號:01512）。另參考容庚編著：《金文編》（北京：中華書局，1985），頁673。

3 有關韓雲山的生平及欣賞其書法的方法，見Lau Chak-kwong, " The Recluse-Artist HanYunshan and an Approach of Appreciation of His Art of Chinese Calligraphy", 載於《左右》, 2001,vol.3,51-67;及《香港書法：香港藝術館藏品》(香港：香港市政局, 1990)，頁44.

以懶閒為號正於自我嘲諷中突顯隱逸淡泊的作風。

同樣是筆者本人刻製的《小棚友》（作品110、111和112）是萬青屴教授的別號印。萬教授為著名藝術史學家及畫家，現為香港浸會大學視覺藝術院講座教授及建院總監。文革期間，萬教授竟然得以與老師李可染（1907-1989）和其他藝術家相遇。而他的別號印用以紀念其牛棚生涯這一段難得的遇合。

在某種意義上，上述的別號印顯示三位印章主人對自己人生種種奮鬥所作出的反思。因此，以三位的別號為綱領，將筆者收錄於本章的其他“非別號印章”分類，正突顯印章作為自我形象的意念。

贈者與受者間之凝聚力

所有作者刻後贈予其兩位老師的印章意味著志同道合的人(尤其是熱愛及研究傳統中國書畫者)，如何透過印章的惠贈及接受，維繫彼此間的情誼，並藉彼此認同印章內容所表達出的思想，以擁抱共同價值觀，並在不知不覺間建構內群體身份認同。

Seals as Artistic Expression, Projection of Self-Image and Token of Like-Mindedness[1]

Daniel C.K. Lau
Assistant Professor
Hong Kong Baptist University

Symbolic Presence: Seal Impression as Self Impression

Seal engraving is a highly developed yet much understudied form of Chinese art.[2] Few people have any idea how to appreciate the beauty of a seal's imprinted image, let alone grasp the subtlety and complexity of these multi-faceted objects.[3] More than simply tools used to imprint one's presence (commonly authorship or ownership) on a painting or work of calligraphy, seals are carefully designed works of art that express a variety of cultural and personal values.[4] What renders seals even more to look at than artworks is that seals can be sent as gifts and eventually used by the recipients, who are the new seal owners, and the act of impressing the seals embodies an extra sense of symbolic significance that alludes to the relationship between the seal-engraver and the new seal owner. Indeed, seals and other works of art have long been used as objects for social exchange among like-minded individuals, especially in various literati circles in both traditional and contemporary Chinese societies.

Predominantly appearing in red-against-white imageries, seal impressions are vivid expression that tellingly alludes to the different aspects of seal owners. Primarily, seal impressions bearing the names of the owners can be viewed as symbolic imposition of the seal owners' presence, hence compensating for one's actual physical absence. In this light, a seal impression that bears the owner's name serves as a reinforcement of one's signature, reiterating one's commitment in such situations as authorship of a piece of artwork or literary composition, ownership of an artwork, or credibility and responsibility in legal agreements and other types of covenants. On the other hand, a seal impression that bears literary content other than the seal owner's name can convey self-referential ideas in such disguise as style names (*zi* 字), pennames, studio names and literary allusions that suggest the seal owners' personality, temperament, aspirations, hobbies, special life experience, other attributes like personal values, cultural and sub-cultural identifications, and religious beliefs and commitments. Moreover, a "larger-self" can be projected through the practice of "seal-as-gift," a practice which serves as a semi-private vehicle to signify the intimate bond as well as the common aspirations and values that the sender shares with the recipient of seals.

---

1 A version of this essay was published in: Daniel C.K. Lau ed. *Impression: Seals Engraved by Daniel Chak-kwong Lau* (Hong Kong: Academy of Visual Arts, Hong Kong Baptist University, 2009), pp. 18-38.

2 Examples of preliminary studies on the historical development of Chinese seal engraving and the relevant issues of techniques, styles and schools of seal engraving include: Sha Menghai 沙孟海, *Yinxue shi* 印學史 (The History of Studies in Seals) (Hangzhou: Xiling yinshe 西泠印社, 1999);Ye Yiwei 葉一葦, *Zhuanke xue* 篆刻學 (The Study of Seal Engraving) (Hangzhou: Xiling yinshe 西泠印社, 2003.); Qian Juntao 錢君匋 and Ye Luyuan 葉潞淵, *Xiyin yuanliu* (The Origin and Development of Seals) (Beijing: Beijing chubanshe北京出版社, 1998); Sun Weizu 孫慰祖, *Sun Weizu lunyin wengao* 孫慰祖論印文稿 (Shanghai: Shanghai shudian chubanshe 上海書店出版社, 1999); Sun Weizu, *Yinzhang* 印章 (Seals) (Shanghai: Shanghai renmin meishu chubanshe, 1998); and Jason C. Kuo, *Word As Image: The Art of Chinese Seal Engraving* (New York: China House Gallery, China Institute In America, 1992).

3 For a study of the aesthetics of seal engraving, see Liu Jiang 劉江, *Zhuangke meixue* 篆刻美學 (The Aesthetics of Seal Engraving) (Hangzhou: Zhongguo meishu xueyuan chubanshe 中國美術學院出版社, 1994). In a sense, the subtlety and complexity of seals can be partially reflected by the existence of a large corpus of treatises on seal engraving. See for example, Huang Dun 黃惇, *Zhongguo gudai yinlun shi* 中國古代印論史 (A History of Chinese Ancient Treaties on Seal Engraving) (Shanghai: Shanghai shuhua chubanshe上海書畫出版社, 1994).

4 For a study of collector's seals, other types of seals stamped on Chinese painting and works of calligraphy, and the connoisseurship of seals, see Robert H.Van Gulik, *Chinese Pictorial Art as Viewed by the Connoisseur* (Original edition published by INSTITUTO ITALIANO PER IL MEDIO ED ESTREMO ORIENTE, Roma, 1958. Reprinted by SMC Publishing Inc., Taipei, 1993), 417-457.

The purpose of this paper is to examine how seals have been produced and used as vehicles of artistic expression, projection of self-image and token of like-mindedness in traditional and contemporary Chinese societies. More specifically, selected examples of seals engraved by major seal-engravers in the past and myself will be investigated in an attempt to unfold the intriguing artistic phenomenon in which the production and use of seals is interwoven with the assertion of personal value and the adhering power of "seal-as-gift" in social and scholarly exchanges.[5]

Seals as Artistic Expression

Seal engraving is a unique form of Chinese art that fundamentally encompasses the act of engraving Chinese characters or pictorial representations on the surface of three-dimensional objects (stone seals have been largely used by Chinese seal-engravers in the last few centuries and bronze seals were relatively more popular in earlier tradition). These three-dimensional objects are a product of the color and texture of natural material, man-made sculptural forms and the correlated craftsmanship; and although their appearance is undoubtedly one aspect for appreciation, the essence of the art of seal engraving tends to culminate in the impressions of seals. Appearing in the form of a two-dimensional imagery, seal impressions are imprinted images that are mostly intended to perform certain functions. For instance, an artist's seal, appearing as an eye-catching red impression onto the surface of a painting or work of calligraphy, can be utilized as an integral part of the whole artistic composition.

Perhaps due to the inherent functionality of seals, which is especially noticeable in other cases of non-artistic activities such as endorsing a commercial contract, seal engraving had not been treated as a form of fine arts for a prolonged period of time in most parts of traditional China, hence the identity of the seal-engravers remained anonymous in most cases. It was not until the Yuan (1271-1368) and Ming (1368-1644) Dynasties when the literati were earnestly exploring the aesthetic and expressive potentials of seals that seal engraving was seriously considered an art form that was comparable with calligraphy and painting. Some seal engravers were then treated as venerable artists, and hence their social status was uplifted to an unprecedented level. He Zhen 何震 (1535-1604), for example, enjoyed an unrivaled reputation as a seal-engraver in his time. He is considered in several literatures as the founder of the Hui School 徽派, or Wan 皖 (Anhui 安徽) School of Seal Engraving[6]. The seventeenth-century scholar Xu Shipu 徐世溥 (1608-1658) even compared He Zhen's accomplishments in seal engraving to those of his well-known contemporaries and counterparts such as the calligraphy and painting of Dong Qichang董其昌 (1555-1636), the astronomy of Xu Guangqi徐光啟 (1562-1633) and Matteo Ricci (1552-1610), and the pharmacology of Li Shizhen 李時珍(1518-1593)[7].

Beyond the already recognized perception of seal engraving as a form of visual arts, seal engraving is in fact a truly interdisciplinary form of art because this artistic practice requires the knowledge and skills from diverged artistic, literary and academic fields. Throughout the whole process from seeking inspirations from a variety of literary and artistic references to designing and carving a seal, the practice of seal engraving essentially involves the intriguing synergy achieved by the intrinsic requirement of the versatile mastery

5 My previous scholarly endeavor of examining how seals had been produced and used as vehicles of artistic expression, projection of self-image and token of like-mindedness in traditional Chinese societies culminated in my Ph.D. dissertation: Chak Kwong Lau, "Ding Jing (1695-1765)—Art, Hangzhou, and the Foundation of the Xiling Identity" (Ph.D. dissertation, University of California, Santa Barbara, 2006). This work centers on Ding Jing 丁敬 and largely focuses on seal engraving both as a form of Chinese art and as a signifier of social and cultural discourse. Ding Jing was considered the head of the Eight Masters of Xiling. My dissertation is the first in-depth study of how his identity emerged and his lineage developed. My work particularly highlights how Ding Jing utilized both the styles and the literary content of his seals to construct an idea of his own self-image as a scholar of epigraphy who was resolved not to pursue an official career. At the same time, the work also examines how a "larger-self" is projected through Ding's practice of "seal-as-gift," a practice which signified the common aspirations and values he shared with the recipients of his seals.

6 For instance, Kong Yunbai 孔云白, Fang Quji 方去疾 and Jason Kuo has treated He Zhen as the leader of the Hui school. See Kong Yunbai, *Zhuanke rumen* 篆刻入門 (Shanghai: Shanghai shudian 上海書店, 1979), 96; Fang Quji, *Ming-Qing zhuanke liupai yinpu* 明清篆刻流派印譜 (Shanghai: Shanghai shuhua chubanshe上海書店出版社, 1980), 2; and Jason Kuo, *Word as Image: The Art of Seal Engraving*, 31. For a detailed study of the emergence and the different developmental stages of the Hui school and the transformation of styles within the school, see Zhang Yuming 張郁明, "Lun Huizong zhi goucheng ji qi yishu fengge zhi shanbian" 論徽宗之構成及其藝術風格之嬗變, in *Qing-dai huizong yinfeng* 清代徽宗印風, edited by Huang Dun and Zhang Yuming (Chongqing : Chongqing chubanshe重慶出版社, 1999), 1-55.

7 Li Chu-tsing, James Cahill, and Ho Wai-kam, eds. *Artists and Patrons: Some Social and Economic Aspects of Chinese Painting* (Seattle: University of Washington Press, 1991), 184.

of carving or engraving techniques, basic principles of design, calligraphy, and the knowledge of philology, etymology and literature. Through conscious manipulation of various elements from the aforementioned fields and their flexible application in the production of seals, seal-engravers are able to effectively communicate ideas through the literary content and the styles and other formal qualities of the artworks. No wonder in his preface to *Yincun chuji* 印存初集 of 1661 (compiled by Hu Zhengyan 胡正言), the late-Ming-dynasty writer Wu Qi 吳奇 comments on how the expressive sentiment conveyed in a seal impression can be enhanced by the synergistic effect originated from the union between the artistic and literary content of a seal:

> Although a seal is small, no longer than a finger, and no larger than two square inches, it contains development and structure and, in its sweep and profundity, can be as satisfactory as a fine work of literary art. Furthermore, it can make oneself feel leisurely and calm, but it can also suddenly stir up emotions sometimes as [strong as] dragons and sometimes as [convoluted as] snakes; it cannot be regarded merely as a literary composition[8].

Focusing on the artistic content of a seal, seals can be analyzed in terms of styles emanating from studies of previous styles of seal engraving and personal interpretations and touches. A tentative examination of my repertoire reveals how I as a seal-engraver, on the one hand, actively work in styles modeled after a wide array of ancient models of seal engraving and calligraphy, and on the other hand also learn from a variety of sources including the works by the seal-engravers of the Qing Dynasty (1644-1911) and the twentieth century and newly excavated ancient works of calligraphy:

The Full-White Mode

Never-Ending Joy 樂未央 (cat. no. 51) and *Han Yunshan's Seal* 韓雲山印 (cat. no. 80) are two examples of work executed in a mode known as the "*manbai*" 滿白, which literally means "full-white." Widely adopted in the seals of the Han Dynasty (206 BC- AD 220), this mode is characterized by the extremely bold white strokes against the red background space in the impression of intaglio (*baiwen* 白文) seal. In a similar manner, *Lau Chak-kwong* 劉澤光 (cat. no. 28) is an intaglio seal employing the same stylistic principle of expanding the white areas and minimizing the red areas. The square character structure of the seal-script writings in this seal is modified from the standard *xiaozhuan* (小篆), or lesser seal script, to fit into the shape of a square seal. Meanwhile, I injected enormous vitality into this work with a strong personal touch as shown by the modulated character strokes, which tellingly remind the viewers that they are looking at an imprinted image of natural handwriting as opposed to abstract or mechanical patterns. Hence, this work is a fresh and lively interpretation of the "full-white" mode of the Han seal.

Sinuous Seal Script & Broken Knifing and Short Cutting

Miaozhuan (繆篆), or sinuous seal script, is another mode of Han seal that serves as one of the other sources of my inspiration. As exemplified by *Lau Chak-kwong* 劉澤光 (cat. no. 27) this mode is distinguished by the repeated angular turns within the square-shaped characters. Executed in the mode of relief legend (*zhuwen* 朱文) in sinuous seal script, my adaptation of the Han seal element in this case embodies an additional innovation inspired by the major eighteenth-century artist Ding Jing's丁敬 (1695-1765) seal-engraving technique known as the method of "broken knifing and short cutting" (*suidao duanqie* 碎刀短切), by which the contour lines of a stroke are carved in a consecutive and short chop-and-lift motion of the blade. The painstaking effort involved in creating a deceptively simple line is noticeable in the coarse and oscillating contours and frequent breaks in the strokes. These vivid marks of the blade, in a sense, enable the audience to relive every motion in the artist's seal engraving process, thus epitomizing the self-expressive aspect of my seals.

Alternating Red and White Legends

In the two seals *Chak-kwong* 澤光 (cat. no. 30) and The Seal of Lau Chak-kwong 劉澤光印 (cat. no. 32), I adopt a mode known as "alternating red and white legends" (*zhubai wen xiangjian* 朱

8 Quoted in Han Tianheng 韓天衡ed., Lidai yinxue lunwenxuan 歷代印學論文選 (Hangzhou: Xiling yinshe 西泠印社, 1999), 2: 611-12.Tanslation by Jason C. Kuo in Word As Image, 45.

白文相間) that was widely utilized in the private and official seals (*siyin* 私印and *guanyin* 官印) of the Han Dynasty. Distinguished by the harmonious intermingling between the red and white legends, the two characters (i.e. *guang* 光 carved in relief on the left, and *ze* 澤 carved in intaglio on the right) in the seal *Chak-kwong* magically form an integral and perfect composition as expressed in a well structured yet illusionist maze-like imagery. Consciously detouring from my Han Dynasty predecessor, I attempted to create some stylistic difference in that the conventionally neat and smooth character strokes that appeared in the impressions of the Han Dynasty cast bronze seals are substituted by my extremely coarse and jerky marks of incision executed with Ding Jing's hallmark carving technique—"broken knifing and short cutting". These two seals exemplify my personal approach of borrowing the ancient seal engraving traditions initially, and then somehow roaming in my own path until eventually finding various ways to express my own aesthetic language.

Small Seal in Relief Legends

A considerable portion of works from my oeuvre reveals my indebtedness to a form of ancient seal from the Warring States Period (480-221 BC) which is commonly referred to as "small seal in relief legends" (*zhuwen xiaoxi* 朱文小璽).[9] Small in size, the imprints of this type of seal are usually no larger than 1.5 cm by 1.5cm. To describe this type in terms of design and style of writing, the archaic seal-script writing, consisting of variable-size characters, are executed in fine strokes and enclosed in the four contrastingly broad rims. On the basis of the general principle of this specific type of seal, I engraved *Chao'an* 潮安 (cat. no. 38) and *Yunshan's Seal* 雲山之鉩 (cat. no. 83). In the case of Yunshan's Seal, it is obvious that I purposefully subvert the small-size tradition of the zhuwen xiaoxi, to create a large design of 1.9 cm by 1.9 cm. The resulting seal imprint accordingly has a fairly spacious composition. The relatively ample void space, as background, generates a nice contrast with the tightly structured seal-script writing, eventually causing the four characters to stand out sharply against the void. This seal's idea of playing around with the "sparse-and-dense" principles (*shu-mi* 疏密) is further intensified in the other seal Chao'an. Packing all the strokes of the two fine-line characters closely together leaves two seemingly excessive spaces in the lower-right and lower-left corner of the composition. My act of stretching the very limits of the "sparse-and-dense" principles renders the two characters enthrallingly dynamic. Yet at the same time the work is filled with an extra sense of archaic aura because of the jerky rims.

Inspirations from Non-Seal-Script Sources

Apart from adopting relatively more conventional seal script as a rudimentary element for my design of seals, I use different types of script conspicuously in my seals, which truly marks the major difference between myself and most of my predecessors and contemporaries. The wide spectrum of non-seal-script sources includes clerical script (*lishu* 隸書), standard script (*kaishu* 楷書), draft-cursive script (*zhangcao* 章草), the Buddhist sutra script (*xiejing ti*, 寫經體), bamboo slip inscriptions of Han Dynasty (*Han jian* 漢簡, original hand-written works of clerical-script calligraphy characterized by generally more spontaneous and rough brushwork), and even the English alphabet.

For instance, *Academy of Visual Arts, HKBU* 浸會大學視覺藝術院 (cat. no. 77) and *How Can Landscape be Priced?* 山水豈可論價？ (cat. no. 118) are executed in small-character standard script (*xiaokai* 小楷) reminiscent of the style of the eminent Yuan Dynasty painter *Ni Zan* (倪瓚, 1301-1374). The former is the draft of a seal (*yingao* 印稿) rendered in a freshly articulate brushwork that is pure yet emphatic (*qingjing* 清勁). A visually pleasing contrast is created between the fluent and refined character strokes and the four mottled and jagged borders of the seal. This approach of counterbalancing the graceful and elegant brushwork of small-character standard script with more powerful and masculine elements is further intensified in the latter work. Upon a closer inspection, the variation of brushwork in the latter work (*How Can Landscape be Priced?*) is achieved by employing the carving technique of "broken knifing and short cutting" to create a strong suggestion of ruggedness to counterbalance the

9 On Chinese naming of this type of seals, see, for example, Qian Juntao and Ye Luyuan, *Xiyin yuanliu*, 32. On dating and authenticating of ancient seals, see Sun Weizu, *Kezhai lunyin xingao* 可齋論印新稿 (Shanghai: Shanghai cishu chubanshe上海辭書出版社, 2003), 38-9; 61-77; and 156-96.

graceful air of the originally ethereal brushstrokes. This exemplifies a strong sense of my personal touch, reinterpreting the enigmatic aesthetics of "archaic elegance" (*guxiu*古秀).

Last but not least, *Zau Kam Hall* 就咁堂 (cat. no. 92) is a work rendered in the Buddhist sutra script. Distinguished by the speedy execution of one dramatically long and showy horizontal stroke with pointed beginning and the exaggeratedly heavy finishing, the overall brushwork witnesses the stylistic transition from clerical to standard scripts. The draft of this seal is executed with an agile brush technique that emphasizes the rhythm of the "lifting" and "pressing" of the brush tip (*ti'an* 提按), and hence the rich visual effect consisting of variations between "light" and "heavy" strokes. Meanwhile, by using a hard and sharp seal-engraving knife to carve the ironically pliant brushstrokes, I fully explore the reciprocity of my calligraphic brush and carving knife to achieve a style that captures the original fluent brushwork and the crisp and sharp knife work.

Balance between Deliberation and Spontaneity

While the cast bronze seals of the Han Dynasty was characterized by the well structured legends and neat styles that bespeak a high degree of deliberation, the "general seals" (*jiangjun yin* 將軍印) were often executed in a hasty and spontaneous manner immediately after the swift appointment of a general so as to empower him to command in an instant battle.[10] Parallel to this dichotomy of deliberation and spontaneity that exists in the repertoire of the Han Dynasty seals, my seal engraving also embraces this bipolar stylistic decision as evident in my existing oeuvre that comprises thoughtful designs and painstaking effort in knife work on the one hand, and seemingly unplanned composition and experimental effects on the other hand.

In his two poetic lines, Ding Jing likens the aesthetically unintentional spirit in seal engraving to the special practice of improvisation in a musical performance: "Upon engraving a stone seal instantaneously, the stone emits radiance; just like plucking the crimson strings in an improvisational manner."[11] Ding Jing raises the issue of unpremeditated creativity in the above lines as he suggests that brilliant music stems from the natural genius of the performer who plays the music at his or her own discretion without rigidly following a score. By the same token, some of my seals, as exemplified by impulsive composition and the use of speedy and more expressive knife work in *The Broken Stone Studio* 殘石齋 (cat. no. 40), *Without Due Care* 草草 (cat. no. 57) and *Faith, Hope, Love* 信 望 愛 (cat. no. 61), reveal the flexible state of my mind in the midst of the instantaneous process of creativity. The overall whimsical knife work and natural aura present a sharp contrast to such work as *Everlasting Love* 恩愛偕老 (cat. no. 35) which is apparently a product of high degree of deliberation of composition and attention to details in knife work.

Archaism, Personal Interpretation & Self-Expressiveness

In summary, the artistic aspect of my seal engraving can be understood from several perspectives. First, my fascination with archaism leads me to embark on a keen study of a wide range of previous models including those from the Warring States Period to the twentieth century. In this light, the major points of significant development of seal engraving through the ages relive in my oeuvre through the lens of my own interpretation. In fact, the highly diversified nature of my aesthetic vocabularies emanates not only from my ability to assimilate the techniques and spirit of the ancients as an integral portion of my repertoire but also from my cognizant endeavor to transform the various forms and genres of the earlier models to suit my own purposes in new situations.

My fascination with the ancient seal-engraving styles and my cross-referencing approach to artwork production renders my overall style of seal engraving a kaleidoscopic facade. Consequently, the pluralistic references of style in fact undermine the emergence of a straightforwardly personal style. Therefore, it is generally difficult for the audience to identify my work at first glance. Nevertheless, upon careful observation, my unique hallmark approach to seal engraving can be distinguished first by my novel adoption of a wide spectrum of non-seal-script calligraphy in my compositions, and second by the transformed

10 On *jiangjun yin*, see Qian Juntao and Ye Luyuan, *Xiyin yuanliu*, 49-52.

11 See the side inscription that Ding Jing carved on his seal reading "Zhili" (芝里). For reproduction of this work, see Yu Zheng 余正 ed. *Qingdai Zhepai yinfeng shang* 清代浙派印風上 (Chongqing: Chongqing chubanshe重慶出版社, 1999), 46.

brushwork achieved by the renewed interpretation and application of the carving technique known as "broken knifing and short cutting"— which creates not only a nostalgically archaic aura but also a strong personal touch in my seals.

Perhaps my practice of making references to earlier stylistic sources in the history of seal engraving bespeaks my other identity as an art historian who has a strong awareness of the general development of art through the ages and the earlier Chinese literati theories of the arts. In this light, the evasive notion of self-expressiveness is instinctively featured in my seals. In short, my seal engraving embodies a strong sense of a constant internal process of negotiation between archaism, eclecticism, and self-expression.

Projection of Self-Image in Seal

Undeniably, seals are artworks that sublimate seal-engravers' artistic intuition, and seal impressions are recognized as aesthetically pleasing imagery resulting from seal engravers' multitalented mastery of calligraphic, carving and literary skills. Parallel to this intrinsically artistic significance, a seal impression that bears literary content other than the seal owner's name can convey self-referential ideas in such disguise as style names, pennames, studio names and literary allusions that suggest the seal owners' personality, temperament, aspirations, hobbies, special life experience, other attributes like personal values, cultural and sub-cultural identifications and religious beliefs and commitments.

For instance, a seal created by the eighteenth-century seal-engraver Ding Jing, reading "*Longhong waishi Ding Jingshen yinji*" 龍泓外史丁敬身印記 ("the seal of the External Secretary called Longhong, Ding Jingshen"), tellingly manifests Ding Jing's self-image (Fig. 1).

Fig. 1. Ding Jing, *Longhong waishi Ding Jingshen yinji* 龍泓外史丁敬身印記. Impression of a stone seal. 2.1 x 2 cm.

This seal is a perfect example of how Ding endeavored to monumentalize his self-image by pronouncing his style names in the form of tangible images. First, he adopted the sobriquet Longhong to identify himself with the famous Tang dynasty scholar-recluse Ding Fei 丁飛, a native of Hangzhou who was recorded to have lived close to the Longhong Grotto 龍泓洞.[12] Anyone in the literary world ever since the Tang dynasty would certainly associate the name Longhong to Ding Fei's reclusive image because the well-known Tang scholar-poet Lu Guimeng 陸龜蒙 (?-ca. 881), a failed candidate of the Metropolitan Examination (*jinshi*) who led a reclusive life, wrote "Ding yinjun ge" (丁隱君歌), or "The Eulogy of the Reclusive Gentleman Ding," not only to pay tribute to Ding Fei but also to suggest Lu Guimeng's own reclusive persona in a self-referential allusion.[13]

On the other hand, the Longhong Grotto was famous for the ancient writings inscribed all around the site.[14] Ding Jing, as a scholar of epigraphy, carefully studied these inscriptions and documented them by providing full accounts of their physical conditions and appearances in his scholarly writing on epigraphy *Records of Metallic and Stone Monuments in Hangzhou*. For instance, he wrote:

> The three large characters "*Long-hong dong*" (Longhong Grotto), measuring seven by seven *cun* [inches], now weathered and illegible..... [The monument described] on the right is a *moyai*, or cliff carving. Its height measures three *chi* [feet], and its width is one *chi* and eight *cun*. To its right, there is an [inscribed] five-character writing "*Jinhua Wang Ting su*" (the writing by Wang Ting from Jinhua, [Zhejiang province]), [with each character] measuring one *cun* and five *fen* [i.e. one tenth of *cun*]. To the right of this writing, there is also another [inscribed] writing, reading "the Yuan dynasty Buddhist general of the Jiang-huai region has traveled to this place. Written by Guo [an unidentified character], each character measuring two *cun*." [15]

龍泓洞三大字，字大七寸，今已漫漶…右摩崖，縱

12 For a biography of Ding Fei, see Qian Shouyou 潛説友, *Xianchun Lin'an zhi* 咸淳臨安志, *juan* 69, 5a-5b.

13 Lu Gui Meng, "Ding Yinjun ge," in his *Fuli Ji* 甫里集, *Jingyin Wenyuange Siku quanshu* 景印文淵閣四庫全書 ed. (Taipei: Taiwan shangwu yinshuguan, 1983-1986, hereafter SKQS ed.), *juan* 17, 9a-10b.

14 See for example those documented in Ni Tao倪濤, *Liuyi zhiyi lu* 六藝之一錄, SKQS ed., *juan* 110.

15 Ding Jing, *Wulin jinshiji* 武林金石記, *Xuxiu Siku quanshu* 續修四庫全書 ed. (Shanghai: Shanghai Guji chubanshe上海古籍出版社, 1995-2002), *shibu jinshi lei* 史部金石類 no. 910, *juan* 8, 8b-9a.

三尺，橫一尺八寸，右有金華王庭書五字，徑一寸五分，其右又有元江淮釋教都總所經歷郭 口 書字，徑二寸。

In order to record the above observations with precise data of the dimensions of the different parts of the monument and other relevant descriptions, Ding Jing must have conducted an on-site study, and presumably made a rubbing from the cliff carving. By adopting the name of this specific monument as his own sobriquet, Ding Jing implicitly revealed himself as both a recluse and a scholar of epigraphy.

In fact, Ding Jing was a major epigrapher of his time in the Zhejiang province. Unlike his friend Quan Zuwang's 全祖望 (1705-1755) approach to studying epigraphical material on the biographies of historical figures, Ding Jing's primary scholarly interest was in epigraphy concerning local monuments in the city of Hangzhou. He spent extended periods of time throughout his entire life visiting the numerous ancient monuments and archaeological sites within Hangzhou to conduct field investigations, make rubbings from stelae, collect data and research for his scholarly writing *Wulin jinshi lu* 武林金石錄 (Records of Metals and Stones in *Wulin*). This work is a systematic study recording and examining the physical conditions of some three hundred relics as well as the inscriptions attached to ancient metallic and stone monuments, dating from the Tang dynasties (618-907) to the first half of the Qing dynasty, and located all over the city of Hangzhou.[16]

Employing the empirical methods widely used in *kaozhengxue* (考證學), or "evidential research", Ding Jing compared the epigraphical material he obtained with relevant existing textual records to examine a wide range of subjects including history, language, customs and calligraphy. Ding Jing was particularly interested in the local history of Hangzhou, so he sought to scout out the ancient texts preserved in the monuments located in the city so as to study those incidents that were either absent from or understudied in official history. To conduct thorough on-site investigation and to acquire first-hand material for this epigrahical research (*jinshi xue* 金石學), Ding Jing like other major epigraphers practiced stele visiting and traveled to remote places to examine and to make rubbings from artifacts housed at various historical sites, ancient monuments and temples. The eminent historian Quan Zuwang reports Ding Jing's painstaking effort of stele visiting and his diligent attitude towards epigraphy, remarking that "[Ding Jing] sometimes traveled alone among mountains" and he "copied the newly acquired material at night."[17]

Apart from revealing himself as both a recluse and a scholar of epigraphy through the literary allusion of the name Longhong (龍泓), Ding Jing adopted the official title "External Secretary" (*waishi* 外史) as an integral part of his long sobriquet— "*Longhong waishi Ding Jingshen*" (龍泓外史丁敬身).[18] According to the *Zhouli* 周禮— one of the Confucian classics that describes the official system of the Zhou dynasty, External Secretary (waishi 外史) was one of the four subcategories of the official historians under the Spring Official (*chunguan* 春官). External Secretary was specifically responsible for collecting and recording information regarding vernacular writings and records as well as local customs, legends, ancient tales and mythologies. In Confucian thoughts, it was believed that the recording of local customs and nonofficial history was beneficial to the implementation of a moralized and humanized rule.[19]

By adopting the title of "External Secretary" used in the Zhou Dynasty, Ding Jing saw himself as an unofficial historian in his time, working in his hometown, scouting out the epigraphical material found in the archaeological sites, ancient ruins and monuments located in Hangzhou, and recording them in his scholarly writing. Ding Jing played an extremely significant role not only in recreating Hangzhou's glorious past but also in seriously and honestly constructing the local history of Hangzhou that is beyond the reach of the conventional official histories and records. In a sense, Ding Jing took great pride in engraving his nine-character sobriquet on this seal, and his act of cutting this seal signifies his extraordinary conscious effort to create his own public image because before he cut the seal, he must have been well aware that each impression of this seal

16 This book was renamed *Wulin jinshi ji* 武林金石記 and printed in 1916 by an epigrapher and seal-engraver in the late nineteenth and early twentieth century, Wu Yin 吳隱 (1886-1942), who was one of the founders of the Xiling Seal Engraving Society and the founder of its branch in Shanghai. See ibid.

17 Quan Zuwang, *Jieqiting ji* 鮚埼亭集 (1804), in *Mingqing shiliao huibian* 明清史料彙編, edited by Shen Yunlong 沈雲龍 (Taipei, Wenhai 文海, 1969), *juan* 26, 3b. For a more detailed discussion on Ding Jing as an epigrapher, see Chapter Three of my Ph.D. dissertation.

18 The official title "*waishi*" is translated as External Secretary in Charles O. Hucker, *A Dictionary of Official Titles in Imperial China* (Stanford, Calif.: Stanford University Press, 1985), 7604.

19 *Wang Zhaoyu* 王昭禹, *Zhouli xiangjie* 周禮詳解, SKQS ed., *juan* 24, 3a-b.

on his work of calligraphy, letter or poetic draft, well represents his own proclamation of his multi-faceted identity as a recluse, scholar of the epigraphical study and historian.

In fact, this powerful process of externalization of Ding Jing's self-image is achieved by the literary content of the seal, and is further intensified by the austere graphic effects of the writings, as one can see in the seal impression. Heedless of fine details, the overall knife work is spontaneous, wild and forceful, imitating the rough and natural appearance of the eroded cliff-side inscriptions (*moyai keshi* 摩崖刻石) and the weathered stelae, as this is particularly noticeable in the natural breaks in the brushstrokes and the notable crack deliberately created at the lower-left corner. All these strikingly and powerfully rough graphic effects not only bespeak the strong impact of Ding Jing's long-term exposure to epigraphical material and antiquarian objects on his seal engraving, but also incisively remind the audience of Ding Jing's identity as an epigrapher and antiquarian.

In short, this nine-character seal engraved with Ding Jing's sobriquet epitomizes his most significant achievement in the art of seal engraving—namely the creation of aesthetically pleasing images as well as his own self-image. The compelling image created in this case well represents a microcosm of nearly every aspect of Ding Jing's whole life—his reclusive public persona, his lifelong pursuits of epigraphy, antiquarian study, and seal engraving.[20]

By the same token, contemporary seal-engravers also create seals that project the self-images of themselves and the recipients of their seals. For instance, the two seals reading "*Lanyun*" (嬾雲), or "Idle Cloud" (cat. nos. 87 and 88) are sobriquet seals I engraved for my calligraphy teacher Mr. Han Yunshan. Mr. Han uses the word *lan* (嬾), or "idle" to identify with Ni Zan (倪瓚, 1301-1374), one of the group of Chinese painters later known as the Four Masters of the Yuan Dynasty (1206–1368), who used the same word "lan" in his sobriquet "*Lan zan*" (嬾瓚). Ni was born to a wealthy family in Jiangsu Province, yet he chose not to serve the foreign Mongol regime but instead lived a life of reclusion and cultivated the scholarly arts of poetry, painting and calligraphy. The redolent connotation of idleness or laziness in Ni Zan's sobriquet well suggests his reclusive temperament in the masquerade of a self-sarcastic tone. Mr. Han is very much fascinated with Ni Zan as a cultural pillar and legendary figure in historical and cultural contexts. Like many other literati artists in the past, Mr. Han imitates the pure yet emphatic style of Ni Zan's calligraphy to symbolically associate with Ni. Beyond Mr. Han's conscious creation of this observable stylistic connection with Ni Zan, Han, through impressing his sobriquet seal reading "Idle Cloud", suggests his identification with not only the cultural undertone originated from the legacy of Ni Zan, but also Ni's reclusive persona and temperament.[21]

Other self-referential content can also be found in the seals I engraved for Mr. Han Yunshan. For example, *Obsession with Coins* 泉癖 (cat. no. 102) is a straightforward self-statement that reveals Mr. Han's great passion for collecting ancient coins. Appearing in the shape of an ancient coin, which is a flat circular disc with a square opening in the center, this work visually epitomizes Mr. Han's identity as an antiquarian and collector of cultural relics.

The seals I engraved for my academic mentor Professor Wan Qingli also reflect a high degree of his own self-image and various unforgettable aspects in his special life experience. The seals reading "*Little Friend of the Ox-Shed*" 小棚友 (cat. nos. 110, 111 and 112), are used by Professor Wan to commemorate his sojourn in the ox-shed where he unexpectedly and luckily met his teacher Li Keran李可染 (1907-1989) and other artists. This is apparently a critical point in Professor Wan's artistic career, thus he takes pride in stamping these seals on his paintings, tracing the unexpected move in his path of learning Chinese painting.

In a similar vein, the sobriquet seals I engraved for myself also personify a variety of aspects of myself in both my secular and religious lives. *Jireh* 以勒 (cat. no. 37), for example, signifies a special religious experience in my life. The biblical expression "Yahweh-jireh" originates from Chapter 22 of the Book of Genesis, meaning "Yahweh will provide". In this sobriquet seal, I adopt "Jireh" as my style name to commemorate my transient sojourn in Santa Barbara, California from 2000 to 2006, during which I experienced God's abundant provision and peace of mind bestowed by God in times of need. My other sobriquet seals convey not

20 The above discussion on Ding Jing seal reading "Longhong waishi Ding Jingshen" is adapted from my Ph.D. dissertation, 55-59.

21 For a pioneering study of the relationship between Han Yunshan's reclusive temperament and his art of calligraphy, see my article "The Recluse-Artist Han Yunshan and an Approach of Appreciation of His Art of Chinese Calligraphy," in *Besides: A Journal of Art History and Criticism*. 2001, vol. 3, 51-67.

only self-referential ideas but also my personal values, attitudes and projection of my idealized lifestyle. Looking at my seal reading *The Woodcutter called Broken Stone* 殘石山樵 (cat. no. 39), for example, it is easy for the audience to note my own expression of an idealized lifestyle of reclusion in the mountains where I can leisurely appreciate rubbings from the broken ancient stone steles in my spare time without any worry about fulfilling responsibilities in the hustle and bustle of city life. Although I am literally living in the mountains in Sha Tin now, the busy routine of my responsibilities as an academic at university makes it hard for me to live in a "genuine" hermitage and enjoy the "real" leisure in the mountains.

Other self-referential works, including *Emmanuel* 以馬內利 (cat. no. 32 and *Alleluia (Hallelujah)* 阿利路亞 (cat. no. 63) are reflections of my Christian faith. Both are Hebrew expressions conveying a strong religious sentiment. While the former means "God is with us", the latter is referred to as "praise Yahweh". Furthermore, *Give Thanks in All Circumstances* 凡事謝恩 (cat. no. 64), *Do Not Be Anxious About Anything* 一無掛慮 (cat. no. 65), and *Each Day Has Enough Trouble of Its Own* 一天的難處一天當就夠了(cat. no. 66) are verses taken from the bible that serve as not only axioms but also spiritual guidance in my daily secular life.

Initially inspired by famous Chinese literary works, my other seals are often finished with reinterpretations of famous lines that eventually embody myself as a person struggling with such issues as aging, physical appearance and health. *Sitting by Idly and Growing Old* 等閒，白了少年頭 (cat. no. 67) is a self-sarcasm adapted from the original line "So do not sit by idly, or young men will grow old in regret" in the renowned Song Dynasty general Yue Fei's 岳飛 (1103-1142) lyric titled "The Entirely Reddened River" (Man Jiang Hong 滿江紅). In another self-sarcasm, *I Grow Plumper than the Plumpest Cucumber* 人比黃瓜肥 (cat. no. 68), I twist the original line "I grow frailer than the frailest yellow flowers" 人比黃花瘦 in a Song Dynasty female lyric composer Li Qingzhao's李清照 (1084-1155) lyric "Intoxicated under the Shadow of Flowers" (Zui Hua Yin 醉花陰), to express a conscious awareness of my own substantial weight gain that is warningly noticeable in my own cucumber-like belly. Designed with the squat clerical-script (*lishu* 隸書) characters contained in the boundary lines forming the shape of a chunky cucumber, the appearance of this seal engraving draft serves as an admonition against the lack of exercise, in spite of the ironically softened expression as evidenced in the light-hearted literary humor and the ethereal brushwork of the clerical-script characters.

Last but not least, *Jump Shot* (cat. no. 74) is the draft of a pictorial seal that visually enlightens not only my strong passion for basketball but also my personal perception of the correspondences between this specific type of sports and the artistic practice of calligraphy:

> I have a strong passion for basketball. More than just a physical form of competition, basketball is a game of skill, determination, teamwork and creativity. I enjoy learning the game, which essentially involves various techniques of shooting, passing and dribbling, as well as offensive and defensive tactics. In a sense, the repetitious practice of special skills, the physicality of body movements and the application of strategy in the game coincide with the inherent spirit of my Chinese calligraphy practice. I believe the traces of ink on my calligraphic works are vivid clues to the dynamism of the physical act of writing. My wielding of the brush embodies a strong sense of strategy and eventually transforms into a configuration of strokes, which emphasize speed, fluidity, rhythm and spontaneity.[22]

I have spent a tremendous amount of time on playing basketball and practicing calligraphy. In this light, this seal draft tellingly suggests my dual identity as a basketball player and calligrapher.

In summary, seal impressions can be viewed as images liberated from the traditional calligraphic concerns of brush and ink effects and carving techniques. By looking instead at the verbal content of the seals, one is able to understand the art form both as a conscious projection of self-image and as an indication of different social discourses emerging in different eras.

Seals as Token of Like-Mindedness

For many years, works of art had been exchanged among like-minded individuals in various literati circles in

22 Lau Chak-kwong Daniel,"The Ball and the Brush," in Michael Lee and Cornelia Erdmann eds., *Preoccupations: Things Artists Do Anyway* (Hong Kong: Studio Bibliotheque, 2008), 108-109.

Chinese society. For instance, the renowned sixteenth-century literati artists in Suzhou such as Shen Zhou 沈周 (1427-1506), Wen Zhengming 文徵明(1470-1559), and Tang Yin 唐寅 (1470-1523) are known to have exchanged their literary compositions, paintings and works of calligraphy among themselves and close circles of like-minded associates. For these men of letters, works of art served not only as tokens of friendship in social exchanges but also as vehicles confirming the shared values and the honorable social identity mutually embraced among themselves.[23] Craig Clunas views the artworks produced by the Ming literati artists as products of "social actions," and asserts that "painting was one of the major sites of affirmation of multiple fields of age, rank, gender, region, fame, clientage, and subjecthood in which the social actor was situated."[24] The study of the social function of art reveals that works of art take on much more profound cultural meanings and value once they become the cultural elites' objects of social exchange. Decisions of the literati artists throughout the processes of art making and their giving away of artworks as gifts to certain recipients can be informed by a number of factors as exemplified by both the artists' and the recipients' aesthetic choices, artistic philosophies, social backgrounds, intellectual interests, specific types of scholarly endeavors, and political standpoints. The study of the exchange of artworks thus unfolds the specificities of the society and culture in which the object is exchanged.[25]

According to the eighteenth-century Hangzhou scholar official Hang Shijun 杭世駿 (1696-1773), Ding Jing created works of art exclusively for his best friends because "[if you are] not his close friend, [you] cannot obtain one single word from him"[26] Unlike many other contemporary professional seal-engravers, Ding Jing seldom engaged in the sale of his works of seal engraving. He actually treasured his own works so much that he saw them as a part of himself or his life which he would not easily share with others. The pride and self-confidence embodied in Ding Jing's seals, in fact, functioned as an obvious signal, telling the people around him that his gesture of seal-as-gift was an indication of his acceptance of like-minded friends to enter a social circle headed by himself. Therefore, more than simply tokens of friendship, Ding Jing's seals convey a sense of shared values embraced by him and the recipients of his seals. In this light, the corpus of Ding Jing's seal engraving is indeed a microcosm of his social and cultural life against the backdrop of the intellectual circle in eighteenth-century Hangzhou.

Ding Jing's self-image as a hermit and scholar of epigraphy, as projected in the aforementioned sobriquet seal, was particularly cherished by his associates who were basically a group of elite frustrated with pursuing an official career initially and yet finally capable of securing solace in scholarly research, poetry and art. Li E 厲鶚 (1692-1752) and Hang Shijun, for example, were two such recipients of Ding Jing's works of seal engraving. The seal reading "Taihong" 太鴻 (Li E's style name) was a work dedicated to Li E while the one reading "Dazong" 大宗 (Hang's style name), was to Hang Shijun. Both of the said two friends of Ding Jing were capable of assuming a high degree of focus on their scholarly and poetic pursuits only after their detachment from their dismal official career paths. Therefore, Ding Jing, as a close friend in their native place who earned his success and prestige exclusively by scholarly, literary and artistic pursuits as opposed to the more conventional official track, was a true soul-mate to them. It is not surprising that both Li E and Hang Shijun repeatedly showed deep admiration to Ding as a recluse and scholar in their literary works. Unquestionably, the shared values within Ding Jing's circle were the primary force that motivated him to create such a kind of seals-as-gifts. Used by the recipients in a number of different circumstances such as stamping it right after their signatures on paintings, calligraphic works or letters, the seal created by Ding Jing in turn confirms these individuals' identification with Ding Jing's self-image and personal values and aspirations.

Another perfect example that shows a sense of shared value embraced by Ding Jing and the recipient of his seal is the seal engraved with two poetic lines by the late fourth-century and early fifth-century cultural figure Tao Yuanming 陶淵明 (AD 365-427) that Ding Jing

23 Shan Guolin, "Wumen huapai zongshu," 吳門畫派綜述 in *Zhongguo meishu quanji— huihua bian 7* 中國美術全集—繪畫編7 (The Complete Works of Fine Arts of China: Painting Volume 7), edited by Zhongguo meishu quanji bianji weiyuanhui 中國美術全集編輯委員會 (Shanghai: Shanghai shuhua Chubanshe 上海書畫出版社 and Shanghai renmin meishu chubanshe 上海人民美術出版社, 1989, 1-26; Craig Clunas, *Elegant Debts: The Social Art of Wen Zhengming* (1470-1559) (London : Reaktion, 2004.).

24 Craig Clunas, "Social History of Art," in *Critical Terms for Art History*, edited by Robert S. Nelson and Richard Shiff (Chicago and London: The University of Chicago Press, 1996), 475.

25 The above discussion on the social aspect of artworks is adapted from my Ph.D. dissertation, 9-11.

26 Hang Shijun, "Ding yinjun zhuan," 丁隱君傳 in *Yanlin shiji* 硯林詩集 (Yanlin's Anthology), *Xiling wu buyi yizhu* 西泠五布衣遺著 ed., compiled by Ding Bing 丁丙, Yangzhou, 1873, zhuan, 1b.

created for his poetry student Bao Fen 包芬. Reading "As I pluck chrysanthemums beneath the eastern fence, I distantly see the South Mountain" 采菊東籬下，悠然見南山 — the legends of this seal are engraved in intaglio, distributed in three vertical columns that are meant to be read from right to left, and from top to bottom.[27] The two characters cai, or "to pluck" (first character in the first column), and nan, or "south" (second character in the last column) in the two five-character line verses (*"cai-ju dong-li xia, and you-ran jian nan-shan"*) are in fact the same two characters that Bao Fen, the recipient of this seal, adopted as his style name. In the side inscription of this seal, Ding Jing straightforwardly states that the reason for him to engrave this seal was that the two characters *cai* and *nan* in Tao Yuanming's lines perfectly match Bao Fen's style name.[28] More than simply an idea of playing with words, this seal embodies deeper personal values and broader cultural implications. In fact, the men of letters in traditional China were very conscious of creating their self-image in the form of their style names. Therefore, the meanings conveyed by style names were usually far more significant than those of the original names. A style name usually reflects personal temperaments and aspirations and certain self-referential ideas.

In order to obtain a better understanding of how this seal serves as a personification of Bao Fen, an investigation into Tao Yuanming and his poem is of utmost importance. Also known as Tao Qian 陶潛, Tao Yuanming is one of the greatest pastoral poets in the history of Chinese literature. He was well known for his embracing the idea of political eremitism, especially in the second half of his life. Tao was born into an impoverished family. From the age of twenty-nine to forty-one, he held various public offices including those of army secretary and magistrate. He however encountered repeated frustrations in the course of his official career. Time after time, he was humiliated in his positions, so he was very disillusioned with the government. He finally decided to resign from his office and go back to the country. Then he lived in retirement, working as a farmer until his death at sixty-three. In the fullness of time, Tao Yuanming became a role model for people following and identifying with the idea of political eremitism.

Engraved on a stone seal by Ding Jing, Tao Yuanming's two lines, reading "As I pluck chrysanthemums beneath the eastern fence, I distantly see the southern mountains," portray an idealistic pastoral life that Tao Yuanming was enjoying during his retired life. These lines are indeed all about escape, being true to oneself, and more importantly, the idea of political eremitism. These two lines are taken from the fifth of Tao Qian's Twenty Poems on Drinking Wine. Although Tao Yuanming mentions in the preface to this series of twenty poems that these "impromptu verses" were composed to "amuse" himself when he was drinking wine, these poems are not entirely about drinking.[29] Beyond the face value of these poems is the manifestation of Tao Yuanming's political eremitism. Albert David incisively suggests that the "wine" that Tao Yuanming wrote about alludes to a broader socio-political phenomenon, as he wrote:

> The word [wine] seems to be used as a symbol of political world, or to put it in another way, the world within which the scholar-official determines his personal course of action. Judging from Drinking Wine it is an imprecise symbol, including both positive and negative aspects. For Chinese conceptualization runs readily in paired opposites—"going or staying", "serving or retiring", the false and the true aspect of any state. Drinking Wine thus serves as a title for the poet's anguished brooding on the true course for the Confucian scholar-official in an age where the Way has been lost.[30]

Unquestionably, Tao Yuanming's two lines under examination embody a strong sense of eremitism, especially when they were chanted by Ding Jing who saw himself as a recluse. By engraving Tao Yuanming's lines on a seal, and eventually presenting the seal as a gift to his student Bao Fen, Ding Jing seemed to commend Bao Fen's persona as a recluse too. In fact, little is known about Bao Fen's life. His biography is not included in *The Gazetteer of Hangzhou*, and this suggests that he did not hold any official title. Therefore, it is quite safe to state that Bao Fen was a commoner (*buyi*布衣), just like Ding Jing. Fortunately, sporadic accounts about Bao Fen are found in some other sources. For instance, several places in Ding Jing's *Yanlin shiji* 硯林詩集 (*Anthology of Yanlin*) record that Bao Fen was an active participant of the gatherings of the Nanping Poetry Society. Also, the

27 Tao Qian, Tao Yuanming ji 陶淵明集, SKQS ed., *juan* 3, 11a. Translation adopted from Albert Davis, *T'ao Yüan-ming, His Works and Their Meaning*, vol. 1, 96.

28 For the reproduction of the seal impression and the rubbing from the side inscription, see Yu Zheng ed., 71.

29 Tao Qian, *Tao Yuanming ji*, *juan* 3, 9a.

30 Albert Davis, vol. 1, 105.

Compilation of the Poetry by Poets from the County of Hanzhou in the Qing Dynasty has a brief biographical account of Bao Fen:

> [Bao Fen's poetic talent was] highly appreciated by the reclusive gentleman Longhong [Ding Jing]. Since Bao loved plum blossoms, the front and the back of his house were planted with plum blossoms. When the plum blossoms were flowering, he stayed in his house for months. [31] 為龍泓隱君所激賞，性喜梅，屋前后罔不 植梅。當花放時，輒累月不外出。

Apparently, Bao Fen is remembered both as a talented local poet and as a recluse in this local record regarding the poets and poetry of Hangzhou in the Qing dynasty. In fact, in traditional Chinese culture, the beauty of plum blossoms is associated with moral purity and resilience. Plum blossoms are thus a symbol for recluse. Lin Bu 林逋 (967 - 1028) was one quintessential figure of scholarly reclusion, and he was famous for his admiration of the plum blossoms. He refused an official position at court, choosing instead to live in seclusion in Hangzhou. He did not marry or have children, and is said to have considered plum trees his wife and pet cranes his children. One of his nicknames—"Fleeing Immortal" (Buxian 逋仙) bespeaks both his self-image and public persona as a recluse. Based on this understanding, Bao Fen seemed to proclaim his identification with the ancient recluse through his act of physically encircling himself with plum blossoms and immersing himself into the beauty of the flowers.

Ding Jing, both as Bao Fen's poetry teacher and as a recluse, presumably not only appreciated Bao Fen's poetic talent but also his reclusive temperament. The reason for Bao Fen to adopt the two characters *cai* and *nan* as his style name remains unknown because Bao Fen never mentioned whether his adoption of this style name was due to his fascination with Tao Yuanming's lines or some other reasons. Nevertheless, judging from the tone of the side inscription of the seal that Ding Jing dedicated to Bao Fen, we know for sure that Ding deliberately imposed an arbitrary relationship between Tao Qian's lines and the alleged, symbolic meaning of Bao Fen's style name. In his inscription, Ding Jing mentions that this seal, bearing Tao Yuanming's two five-character lines, could be used by Bao Fen as a "seal of style name" (*ziyin* 字印). As mentioned above, style names were a vehicle for men of letters in traditional societies to project their self-image. A "seal of style name" is habitually stamped right after a "seal of personal name" (*mingyin* 名印) on a painting or work of calligraphy to further accentuate the author's symbolic presence. In this light, Ding Jing's subjective intention to treat Tao Yuanming's two five-character lines as Bao Fen's style name suggests that in Ding Jing's eyes, Bao Fen was really a recluse.

Moreover, the eremitic connotation of the seal is further enhanced by Ding Jing's mention of another line by Tao Yuanming in the side inscription: "Chrysanthemums may arrest declining years" 菊為制頹齡 .[32] This line and the preceding line: "Wine can drive out manifold cares" 酒能祛百慮 are taken from Tao Yuanming's famous poem "*Jiuri xiangju*" 九日閒居, or "Living in Retirement on the Ninth Day," which dwells on how Tao enjoyed his pastoral life in his retirement.[33] In short, the seal Ding Jing sent to Bao Fen evocatively signifies not only Bao Fen's persona as a recluse but also the notion of eremitism commonly embraced by the seal maker and the recipient of the seal. This is a case that clearly demonstrates how a seal engraved by Ding Jing conveyed not only far-reaching personal and cultural values but also the cohering power of seals as signifier of shared values embraced by like-minded individuals.[34]

In the contemporary world, seals can also be a powerful signifier of like-mindedness. For instance, the two seals reading "Wonders of Nature" 嘆世界 (cat. nos. 116 and 117), that I engraved for Professor Wan Qingli, signify our shared value as expressed in our intensified admiration of the wonders of nature. In the face of the greatness of nature, as embodied in the awestruck natural objects and phenomena, both of us (i.e. the seal engraver and the recipient of his seals) show an awareness of the beauty of nature, which without doubt overwhelms the transitory nature of man's life. Interestingly, the Chinese title "*tan shi jie*" (嘆世界), when being read as a Cantonese slang, can be roughly translated as "to relax and enjoy life". This

---

31 Wu Hao 吳顥, comp. *Guochao Hangjun shiji* 國朝向杭郡詩輯(The Compilation of the Poetry by Poets from the Country of Hangzhou in the Qing Dynasty), Shouduntang 守惇堂ed., 1800, *juan* 8, 4a.

32 *Tao Qian, juan* 2, 3a. Translation adopted from Albert Davis, vol. 1, 44.
33 Ibid.
34 The above discussion on Ding Jing's seals as signifier of shared values is adapted from my Ph.D. dissertation, 197-204.

colloquial interpretation of the original meaning of the expression "wonders of nature" can be understood as the seemingly cynical yet healthy attitude commonly embraced by the seal engraver and the recipient of his seals in the midst of their busy academic career and the hectic city life.

Last but not least, the seal reading "How Can Landscape be Priced?" 山水豈可論價？ (cat. no. 118) that I engraved for Professor Wan Qingli alludes to not only our common attitude of cherishing the awesome and enchanting landscape but also our common identity as landscape painter. Undoubtedly, the real landscape in nature is priceless. By the same token, the landscape paintings sublimating both landscape painters' artistic and academic careers are personification of the painters themselves, and hence beyond price. In a sense, both of us believe that the embodied value of landscape paintings transcends the face value of landscape paintings as commodities for sale.

Conclusion

The above-mentioned examples of seals produced by the author of this book and his predecessor Ding Jing illustrate that seals can be viewed as aesthetically pleasing objects and embodiments of self-images. Through the seal-engravers' practice of "seals-as-gifts," seals can additionally serve as vehicle to signify the common aspirations and values the seal-engravers share with the recipients of their seals.

25-78
以勒——劉澤光博士自用印
Jireh —— Seals Often used by Dr. Daniel C. K. Lau

25 "Chak", "Kwong" "澤"、"光"
26 The Seal of Lau Chak-kwong 劉澤光印
27 Lau Chak-kwong 劉澤光
28 Lau Chak-kwong 劉澤光
29 The Seal of Lau Chak-kwong 劉澤光印
30 Chak-kwong 澤光
31 "Chak", "Kwong" "澤"、"光"
32 "Emmanuel", "The Seal of Lau Chak-kwong" "以馬內利"、"劉澤光印"
33 Ah Kwong 阿光
34 Kit-ming 潔明
35 Everlasting Love 恩愛偕老
36 DAN
37 Jireh 以勒
38 Chao'an 潮安
39 The Woodcutter called Broken Stone 殘石山樵
40 The Broken Stone Studio 殘石齋
41 The Thatched Hut (Studio) Called Cultivating Clouds 耕雲草廬
42 The Living Stone 活石
43 At Ease 自在
44 Looking Around the World 看世界
45 One Who Has Sailed the Seven Seas 曾經滄海
46 Auspicious Always 常吉
47 Safe and Auspicious 安且吉兮
48 Impression 印象
49 Wealthy and Prosperous 富昌
50 Stay Joyful 常樂
51 Never-ending Joy 樂未央
52 Ten Thousand Years 萬秋
53 Be Under Favourable Auspices wherever One Goes 出入大利
54 Especially Fond of the Stele of Hao Dawang 尤好好大王
55 Assemblage of Words from the Diamond Sutra of Mount Tai 集北齊泰山金剛經字
56 There She is, Where Lanterns Are Few and Far Between 那人正在燈火闌珊處
57 Without Due Care 草草
58 Benevolent Heart 仁心
59 Peace 平安
60 The Living Stone 活石
61 "Faith", "Hope", "Love" "信"、"望"、"愛"
62 Impression 印象
63 Alleluia (Hallelujah) 阿利路亞（哈利路亞）
64 Give Thanks in All Circumstances 凡事謝恩
65 Do Not Be Anxious About Anything 一無掛慮
66 Each Day Has Enough Trouble of Its Own 一天的難處一天當就夠了
67 Sitting by Idly and Growing Old 等閒，白了少年頭
68 I Grow Plumper Than the Plumpest Cucumber 人比黃瓜肥
69 Chak 澤
70 Lau Chak-kwong 劉澤光
71 Extraordinary 不常
72 Polo 馬球
73 Hermès 赫密士
74 Jump Shot (Basketball Shooting Technique) 跳投
75 Rhapsody 狂想曲
76 The Living Stone 活石
77 HKBU Academy of Visual Arts 浸會大學視覺藝術院
78 Lau Chak-kwong's Collection of Books 劉澤光藏書

79-105
嬾雲——韓雲山先生常用印
Idle Cloud —— Seals Often used by Mr. Han Yunshan

79 Han Yunshan 韓雲山
80 Han Yunshan's Seal 韓雲山印
81 Han Yunshan's Seal 韓雲山印
82 Yunshan's Seal 雲山之鉨
83 Yunshan's Seal 雲山之鉨
84 Han's | 韓氏
85 Yunshan | 雲山
86 Yunshan's Private Seal 雲山私印
87 Lanyun(Idle Cloud) 嬾雲
88 Lanyun (Idle Cloud) 嬾雲
89 Yunshan the Lay Buddhist 雲山居士
90 Nanhai | 南海
91 The Cloister of the Imagery of Dreams 夢影盦
92 Zau Gam Hall 就咁堂
93 The Hall of No Regret 終不悔堂
94 The Hall of No Regret 終不悔堂
95 The Frost Red Lyric House 霜紅詞館
96 Composed by Yunshan after the Age of Seventy 雲山七十後作
97 Composed by Yunshan after the Age of Eighty 雲山八十後作
98 Calligraphy by Yunshan after the Age of Eighty 雲山八十後書
99 Calligraphy by Yunshan after the Age of Eighty 雲山八十後書
100 Calligraphy by Yunshan after the Age of Eighty 雲山八十後書
101 Calligraphy by Yunshan after the Age of Eighty-five 雲山八十五後書
102 Obsession with Coins 泉癖
103 May Yunshan Live Long 雲山長壽
104 Yunshan with Palms Together 雲山合十
105 The Zen of Acquiring Freedom 得自在禪

106-120
小棚友——萬青屴教授常用印
Little Friend of the Ox-Shed —— Seals Often used by Professor Wan Qingli

106 "Wan", "Qingli" "萬"、"青屴"
107 Wan Qingli 萬青力
108 WAN
109 QL (i.e. Qingli)
110 Little Friend of the Ox-Shed 小棚友
111 Little Friend of the Ox-Shed 小棚友
112 Little Friend of the Ox-Shed 小棚友
113 Wanshan | 萬山 (Ten Thousand Mountains)
114 Qingli's Memory 青屴存念
115 Qingli's Memory 青屴存念
116 Wonders of Nature 嘆世界
117 Wonders of Nature 嘆世界
118 How Can Landscape be Priced? 山水豈可論價？
119 Completed After the Eye Disease 目疾後作
120 Global Man 地球人也

25-78
以勒——劉澤光博士自用印
Jireh —— Seals Often used by Dr. Daniel C. K. Lau

25 *"Chak", "Kwong"* |
"澤"、"光"

Red and white legends
(relief and intaglio)
Impressions of a two-sided
stone seal
Each 7.8 x 7.8 cm
2010

朱文及白文
石章(兩面印)印拓
各7.8 x 7.8 厘米
2010 年

26 ***The Seal of Lau Chak-kwong*** | 劉澤光印

Red legend (relief)
Impression of a stone seal
4.9 x 4.9 cm
2009

朱文
石印印拓
4.9 x 4.9 厘米
2009

Artist's inscription:
The four cells are drawn with lines imitating the brick inscriptions of Han Dynasty (206 B.C. - A.D. 220).

按：
用漢磚線條畫四字格

27 ***Lau Chak-kwong*** | 劉澤光

Red legend (relief)
Impression of a stone seal
2.6 x 2.6 cm
2003

朱文
石章印拓
2.6 x 2.6 厘米
2003

28 ***Lau Chak-kwong*** | 劉澤光

White legend (intaglio)
Impression of a stone seal
1.2 x 1.2 cm
2003

白文
石印印拓
1.2 x 1.2 厘米
2003

29 ***The Seal of Lau Chak-kwong*** | 劉澤光印

Red legend (relief)
Impression of a stone seal
1.8 x 1.8 cm
2003

朱文
石印印拓
1.8 x 1.8 厘米
2003

30 ***Chak-kwong*** | 澤光

Alternating red and white legends
(alternating relief and intaglio)
Impression of a stone seal
1.7 x 1.7 cm
2003

朱白文相間
石印印拓
1.7 x 1.7 厘米
2003

31 ***"Chak", "Kwong"*** |
"澤"、"光"

Red and white legends
(relief and intaglio)
Impressions of 2 stone seals
1 x 1 & 1 x 1 cm
2003

朱文及白文
石印印拓 x 2
各1 x 1 厘米
2003

32 ***"Emmanuel", "The Seal of Lau Chak-kwong"***
"以馬內利"、"劉澤光印"

White legend (intaglio), and
alternating red and white legends
(alternating relief and intaglio)
Impression of a two-sided stone seal
Each 1.9 x 1.9 cm
2009

白文及朱白文相間
石章(兩面印)印拓
各1.9 x 1.9 厘米
2009

Emmanuel: Hebrew; meaning "God is with us"
以馬內利： 希伯來文；意謂「上帝與我們同在」

33 *Ah Kwong* | 阿光

White legend (intaglio)
Impression of a stone seal
1.6 x 1.2 cm
2003

白文
石印印拓
1.6 x 1.2 厘米
2003

34 *Kit-ming* | 潔明

Red legend (relief)
Impression of a stone seal
1.8 x 1.1 cm
2003

朱文
石印印拓
1.8 x 1.1 厘米
2003

Artist's inscription:
It is neither clerical script nor standard script.

按：
非隸非楷

35 *Everlasting Love* | 恩愛偕老

Red legend (relief)
Impression of a stone seal
4.3 x 1.1 cm
2009

朱文
石印印拓
4.3 x 1.1 厘米
2009

Artist's inscription/ 題識：
With the compositional strategy of the brick inscriptions of Han Dynasty (206 B.C. - A.D. 220)
用漢磚布白

36 ***DAN*** I

Red legend (relief)
Impression of a stone seal
6.3 x 6 cm
2008

朱文
石章印拓
6.3 x 6 厘米
2008

37 ***Jireh*** | 以勒

Red legend (relief)
Impression of a stone seal
2.5 x 1.4
2009

朱文
石章印拓
2.5 x 1.4 厘米
2009

Note: Yahweh-jireh originates from Chapter 22 of the Book of Genesis, meaning "Yahweh will provide". The artist adopts Jireh as his style name to commemorate his sojourn in Santa Barbara, California from 2000 to 2006, during which he experienced God's abundan provision.

按:耶和華以勒一詞源於舊約聖經《創世記》第22章，意即「耶和華必預備」。作者借此為別號, 以紀念他旅居美國加州聖芭芭拉數年間 (2000-2006) 所經歷神豐足的供應。

38 ***Chao'an*** | 潮安

Red legend (relief)
Impression of a stone seal
1.5 x 1.4 cm
2009

朱文
石章印拓
1.5 x 1.4 厘米
2009

Artist's inscription:
In the style of the small seals of the Warring States Period (ca.470 - 221 B.C.)

按：
仿戰國小璽

39 ***The Woodcutter called Broken Stone*** | 殘石山樵

White legend (intaglio)
Impression of a stone seal
2.9 x 2.8 cm
2003

白文
石章印拓
2.9 x 2.8 厘米
2003

40 ***The Broken Stone Studio*** | 殘石齋

White legend (intaglio)
Impression of a stone seal
2.9 x 2.7 cm
2009

白文
石章印拓
2.9 x 2.7 厘米
2009

41 ***The Thatched Hut (Studio) Called Cultivating Clouds*** | 耕雲草廬

Red legend (relief)
Impression of a stone seal
10.3 x 2 cm
2008

朱文
石章印拓
10.3 x 2 厘米
2008

42 ***The Living Stone*** | 活石

Red legend (relief)
Impression of a stone seal
1.5 x 1 cm
2009

朱文
石章印拓
1.5 x 1 厘米
2009

43 ***At Ease*** | 自在

Red legend (relief)
Impression of a stone seal
8 x 4 cm
2008

朱文
石章印拓
8 x 4 厘米
2008

44 ***Looking Around the World*** | 看世界

Red legend (relief)
Impression of a stone seal
5.4 x 2 cm
2008

朱文
石章印拓
5.4 x 2 厘米
2008

45 ***One Who Has Sailed the Seven Seas*** | 曾經滄海

White legend (intaglio)
Impression of a stone seal
5.9 x 5.8 cm
2009

白文
石章印拓
5.9 x 5.8 厘米
2009

46 ***Auspicious Always*** | 常吉

Red legend (relief)
Impression of a stone seal
5.6 x 5.9 cm
2003

朱文
石章印拓
5.6 x 5.9 厘米
2003

47 ***Safe and Auspicious*** | 安且吉兮

White legend (intaglio)
Impression of a stone seal
4.8 x 4.8 cm
2009

白文
石章印拓
4.8 x 4.8 厘米
2009

Artist's inscription/ 按：
In the style of the white legend seals of Mr. Luo Shuzhong
仿羅叔重先生白文印

48 ***Impression*** |
印象

Red legend (relief)
Impression of a synthetic ivory seal
1.9 cm diameter
2009

朱文
人造象牙
直徑 1.9 厘米
2009

49 ***Wealthy and Prosperous*** | 富昌

Red legend (relief)
Impression of a stone seal
1.4 x 0.5 cm
2009

朱文
石章印拓
1.4 x 0.5 厘米
2009

Artist's inscription/ 按：
In the style of the brick inscriptions of Han Dynasty (206 B.C. - A.D. 220)
用漢磚文筆意

50 ***Stay Joyful*** | 常樂

White legend (intaglio)
Impression of a stone seal
1.4 x 0.6 cm
2009

白文
石章印拓
1.4 x 0.6 厘米
2009

51 ***Never-ending Joy*** | 樂未央

White legend (intaglio)
Impression of a stone seal
1.5 cm diameter
2009

白文
石章印拓
直徑 1.5 厘米
2009

52 ***Ten Thousand Years*** |
萬秋

Red legend (relief)
Impression of a stone seal
4.5 cm diameter
2003

朱文
石章印拓
直徑 4.5 厘米
2003

Artist's inscription:
Imitation of the tile ends of Han Dynasty (206 B.C. - A.D. 220), with a grasp of the spirit of the seal script at that time

按：擬漢瓦當，頗得漢篆丰神

53 ***Be Under Favourable Auspices wherever One Goes*** |
出入大利

White legend (intaglio)
Impression of a stone seal
1.2 x 1.1 cm
2009

白文
石章印拓
1.2 x 1.1 厘米
2009

Artist's inscription:
Imitation of the white legend seals of Han Dynasty
(206 B.C. - A.D. 220)

按：摹漢白文印

54 ***Especially Fond of the Stele of Hao Dawang***
尤好好大王

Red legend (relief)
Impression of a stone seal
2.7 x 2.5 cm
2009

朱文
石章印拓
2.7 x 2.5 厘米
2009

55 ***Assemblage of Words from the Diamond Sutra of Mount Tai***
集北齊泰山金剛經字

Red legend (relief)
Impression of a stone seal
3 x 3 cm
2009

朱文
石章印拓
3 x 3 厘米
2009

56 ***There She is, Where Lanterns Are Few and Far Between*** | 那人正在燈火闌珊處

White legend (intaglio)
Impression of a stone seal
2 x 2 cm
2009

白文
石章印拓
2 x 2 厘米
2009

57 ***Without Due Care*** | 草草

Red legend (relief)
Impression of a stone seal
2.5 x 2.5 cm
2008

朱文
石章印拓
2.5 x 2.5 厘米
2008

58 ***Benevolent Heart*** | 仁心

Red legend (relief)
Impression of a stone seal
2.6 x 1.3 cm
2009

朱文
石章印拓
2.6 x 1.3 厘米
2009

59 ***Peace*** | 平安

Red legend (relief)
Impression of a stone seal
1.9 x 1.9 cm
2003

朱文
石章印拓
1.9 x 1.9 厘米
2003

60 ***The Living Stone*** |
活石

Red legend (relief)
Impression of a stone seal
5.5 x 3.8 cm
2009

朱文
石章印拓
5.5 x 3.8 厘米
2009

61 *"Faith", "Hope", "Love"*
"信"、"望"、"愛"

White legend (intaglio)
Impressions of 3 stone seals
Each 1.6 x 1.6 cm
2009

白文
石章印拓 x 3
各1.6 x 1.6 厘米
2009

And now these remain: faith, hope and love. But the greatest of these is love. (1 Corinthians 13:13)

如今常存的有信、有望、有愛，這三樣，其中最大的是愛。(哥林多前書 13:13)

62 ***Impression*** |
印象

Seal-engraving draft
Ink on paper
6 x 9 cm
2009

肖形印印稿
水墨紙本
6 x 9 厘米
2009

63 ***Alleluia (Hallelujah)*** |
阿利路亞（哈利路亞）

Seal-engraving draft
Ink on paper
3.3 x 3.9 cm
2009

印稿
水墨紙本
3.3 x 3.9 厘米
2009

Alleluia: Hebrew; meaning "praise Jehovah"
阿利路亞：希伯來文；意謂「讚美耶和華」

64 ***Give Thanks in All Circumstances*** |
凡事謝恩

Seal-engraving draft
Ink on paper
3.2 x 3.5 cm
2009

印稿
水墨紙本
3.2 x 3.5 厘米
2009

Be joyful always; pray continually; give thanks in all circumstances, for this is God's will for you in Christ Jesus. (1 Thessalonians 5:16-18)

要常常喜樂，不住的禱告，凡事謝恩，因為這是神在基督耶穌裡向你們所定的旨意。（帖撒羅尼迦前書 5:16-18）

65 ***Do Not Be Anxious About Anything*** |
一無掛慮

Seal-engraving draft
Ink on paper
4 x 4 cm
2009

印稿
水墨紙本
4 x 4 厘米
2009

Do not be anxious about anything, but in everything, by prayer and petition, with thanksgiving, present your requests to God. (Philippians 4:6)

應當一無掛慮，只要凡事藉著禱告、祈求、和感謝，將你們所要的告訴　神。(腓立比書 4:6)

66 ***Each Day Has Enough Trouble of Its Own*** | 一天的難處一天當就夠了

Seal-engraving draft
Ink on paper
10.1 x 5.1 cm
2009

印稿
水墨紙本
10.1 x 5.1 厘米
2009

Therefore do not worry about tomorrow, for tomorrow will worry about itself. Each day has enough trouble of its own. (Matthew 6:34)

所以不要為明天憂慮，因為明天自有明天的憂慮，一天的難處一天當就夠了。(馬太福音6:34)

67 ***Sitting by Idly and Growing Old*** | 等閒，白了少年頭

Seal-engraving draft
Ink on paper
5.8 x 6.1 cm
2009

印稿
水墨紙本
5.8 x 6.1 厘米
2009

Annotation:
Self-sarcasm adapted from the original line "So do not sit by idly, or young men will grow old in regret" in Yue Fei's lyric "The Entirely Reddened River" (Man Jiang Hong).

註： 自嘲句，語出岳飛《滿江紅》：「莫等閒，白了少年頭，空悲切。」

68 ***I Grow Plumper Than the Plumpest Cucumber*** | 人比黃瓜肥

Seal-engraving draft
Ink on paper
3.5 x 4.7 cm
2009

印稿
水墨紙本
3.5 x 4.7 厘米
2009

Annotation:
The artist's self-sarcasm about his own weight gain; modified from the original line "I grow frailer than the frailest yellow flowers" in Li Qingzhao's lyric "Intoxicated under the Shadow of Flowers" (Zui Hua Yin).

註： 自嘲句，改自李清照《醉花陰》句：「人比黃花瘦」

69 ***Chak*** | 澤

Seal-engraving draft
Ink on paper
7.8 x 7.8 cm
2009

印稿
水墨紙本
7.8 x 7.8 厘米
2009

70 ***Lau Chak-kwong*** |
劉澤光

Seal-engraving draft
Ink on paper
15 x 14.2 cm
2009

印稿
水墨紙本
15 x 14.2 厘米
2009

71 ***Extraordinary*** |
不常

Seal-engraving draft
Ink on paper
22 x 18 cm
2009

印稿
水墨紙本
22 x 18 厘米
2009

72 ***Polo*** |
馬球

Seal-engraving draft
of pictorial seal
Color ink on paper
7 x 4.5 cm
2009

肖形印印稿
彩墨紙本
7 x 4.5 厘米
2009

73 ***Hermès*** |
赫密士

Seal-engraving draft
of pictorial seal
Color ink on paper
8.3 x 8.5 cm
2009

肖形印印稿
彩墨紙本
8.3 x 8.5 厘米
2009

74 ***Jump Shot*** | 跳投
(Basketball Shooting Technique)

Seal-engraving draft of pictorial seal
Color ink on paper
3.3 x 3.3 cm
2009

肖形印印稿
彩墨紙本
3.3 x 3.3 厘米
2009

Artist's inscription/ 題識：
I have a strong passion for the game of basketball. More than just a physical form of competition, basketball is a game of skill, determination, teamwork and creativity. I enjoy learning the game, which essentially involves various techniques of shooting, passing and dribbling, as well as offensive and defensive tactics. In a sense, the repetitious practice of special skills, the physicality of body movements and the application of strategy in the game coincide with the inherent spirit of my Chinese calligraphy practice. I believe the traces of ink on my calligraphic works are vivid clues to the dynamism of the physical act of writing. My wielding of the brush embodies a strong sense of strategy and eventually transforms into a configuration of strokes, which emphasize speed, fluidity, rhythm and spontaneity.

("The Ball and the Brush," in Michael Lee and Cornelia Erdmann (eds.), Preoccupations: Things Artists Do Anyway. Hong Kong: Studio Bibliotheque, 2008, pp 108-109.)

我對籃球運動情有獨鍾。它不只是一項運動競技，更是一種集技術、意志力、團體合作和創意於一身的遊戲。我享受學習籃球的過程，當中主要是射籃、傳球和運球的技巧，還有進攻和防守的戰術。在某種意義上，籃球運動中對特別技巧的反覆練習、身體動作的形體性和策略的運用與我書法實踐中蘊含的精神不謀而合。我相信書法作品的墨跡是窺探書寫動作和力量的線索。毛筆的揮動包含着強烈的策略意味，最終轉化成強調速度、流動性、節奏和自發性的筆畫佈局。

75 ***Rhapsody*** |
狂想曲

Seal-engraving draft
Color ink on paper
17.1 x 7.9 cm
2009

印稿
彩墨紙本
17.1 x 7.9 厘米
2009

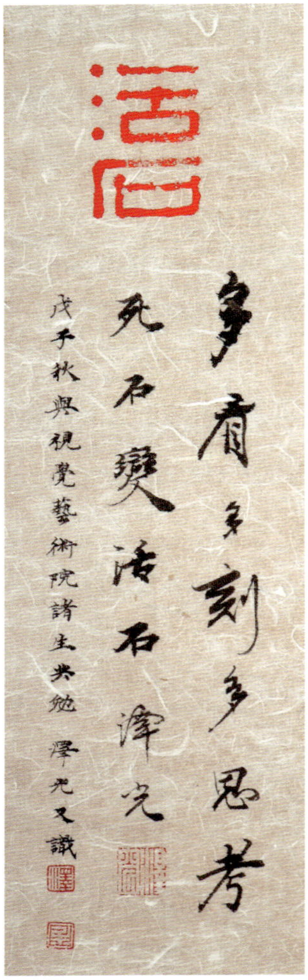

76 ***The Living Stone*** |
活石

Seal-engraving draft
Ink and colour on paper,
mounted on wood block
37 x 11 cm
2008

印稿
水墨、彩墨紙本
37 x 11 厘米
2008
Transliteration/ 釋文:
The Living Stone —— Observe widely, carve frequently and think thoroughly, the dead stone can be transformed into a living stone.
活石 —— 多看多刻多思考，死石變活石。

Artist's inscription/ 題識:
I share this with the students of the Academy of Visual Arts in the autumn of 2008.
戊子秋與視覺藝術院諸生共勉。

77 ***HKBU Academy of Visual Arts*** |
浸會大學視覺藝術院

Seal-engraving draft
Ink on paper
4.2 x 4.2 cm
2009

印稿
水墨紙本
4.2 x 4.2 厘米
2009

78 ***Lau Chak-kwong's Collection of Books*** |
劉澤光藏書

Red legend (relief)
Impression of a stone seal
4.9 x 4.9 cm
2009

朱文
石印印拓
4.9 x 4.9 厘米
2009

Artist's inscription:
The four cells are drawn with lines imitating the brick inscriptions of Han Dynasty (206 B.C. - A.D. 220).

按：
用漢磚線條畫四字格

79-105
嬾雲——韓雲山先生常用印
Idle Cloud —— Seals Often used by Mr. Han Yunshan

79 ***Han Yunshan*** | 韓雲山

Red legend (relief)
Impression of a stone seal
3 x 2.5 cm
2003

朱文
石章印拓
3 x 2.5 厘米
2003

Collection of Mr. Han Yunshan
韓雲山先生收藏

80 ***Han Yunshan's Seal*** | 韓雲山印

White legend (intaglio)
Impression of a stone seal
3.9 x 3.9 cm
2003

白文
石章印拓
3.9 x 3.9 厘米
2003

Collection of Mr. Han Yunshan
韓雲山先生收藏

81 ***Han Yunshan's Seal*** | 韓雲山印

White legend (intaglio)
Impression of a stone seal
4.6 x 4.6 cm
2003

白文
石章印拓
4.6 x 4.6 厘米
2003

Collection of Mr. Han Yunshan
韓雲山先生收藏

Artist's inscription:
In the style of cast seals of Han Dynasty (206 B.C. - A.D. 220), for my teacher Yunshan

按：為雲山師仿漢鑄印

82 ***Yunshan's Seal*** | 雲山之鉨

White legend (intaglio)
Impression of a stone seal
4.8 x 4.8 cm
2003

白文
石章印拓
4.8 x 4.8 厘米
2003

Collection of
Mr. Han Yunshan
韓雲山先生收藏

83 ***Yunshan's Seal*** | 雲山之鉨

Red legend (relief)
Impression of a stone seal
1.9 x 1.9 cm
2003

朱文
石章印拓
1.9 x 1.9 厘米
2003

Collection of
Mr. Han Yunshan
韓雲山先生收藏

84 ***Han's*** | 韓氏

Red legend (relief)
Impression of a stone seal
2 cm diameter
2009

朱文
石章印拓
直徑2 厘米
2009

Collection of
Mr. Han Yunshan
韓雲山先生收藏

85 ***Yunshan*** | 雲山

Red legend (relief)
Impression of a stone seal
2.7 x 2.8 cm
2009

朱文
石章印拓
2.7 x 2.8 厘米
2009

Collection of
Mr. Han Yunshan
韓雲山先生收藏

Artist's inscription/ 題識:
In the style of s ealing clay of Tang Dynasty (A.D. 618-907)

仿唐封泥

86 ***Yunshan's Private Seal*** | 雲山私印

Red legend (relief)
Impression of a stone seal
1.9 x 2.8 cm
2009

朱文
石章印拓
1.9 x 2.8 厘米
2009

Collection of
Mr. Han Yunshan
韓雲山先生收藏

Artist's inscription/ 題識:
In the style of sealing clay of Qin Dynasty (221-206 B.C.)

仿秦封泥

87 ***Lanyun(Idle Cloud)*** | 嬾雲

White legend (intaglio)
Impression of a stone seal
2.7 x 2.5 cm
2003

白文
石章印拓
2.7 x 2.5 厘米
2003

Collection of Mr. Han Yunshan
韓雲山先生收藏

Artist's inscription/ 題識:
In the style of pottery inscriptions of Han Dynasty (206 B.C. - A.D. 220)
仿漢陶文

88 ***Lanyun (Idle Cloud)*** | 嬾雲

White legend (intaglio)
Impression of a stone seal
2.4 x 2.4 cm
2003

白文
石章印拓
2.4 x 2.4 厘米
2003

Collection of Mr. Han Yunshan
韓雲山先生收藏

Artist's inscription/ 題識:
Such compositional strategy is common in the six-faced seals of Han Dynasty (206 B.C. - A.D. 220). The characters on the seal are designed with reference to the style of the inscriptions on the Jia standard measure of the Xin Dynasty (A.D. 9-24).

漢人六面印中多有此布白。
略參新莽嘉量筆意成之。

89 ***Yunshan the Lay Buddhist*** | 雲山居士

White legend (intaglio)
Impression of a stone seal
2.4 x 2.4 cm
2009

白文
石章印拓
2.4 x 2.4 厘米
2009

Collection of Mr. Han Yunshan
韓雲山先生收藏

Artist's inscription/ 題識:
In the style of the white legend seals of Huang Yi (1744-1802)

略參黃小松(黃易)(1744-1802)
白文印風

90 ***Nanhai*** | 南海

White legend (intaglio)
Impression of a stone seal
1 x 0.7 cm
2009

白文
石章印拓
1 x 0.7 厘米
2009

Collection of Mr. Han Yunshan
韓雲山先生收藏

91 ***The Cloister of the Imagery of Dreams*** | 夢影盦

Red legend (relief)
Impression of a stone seal
6.4 x 4.6 cm
2003

朱文
石章印拓
6.4 x 4.6 厘米
2003

Collection of Mr. Han Yunshan
韓雲山先生收藏

92 ***Zau Gam Hall*** | 就咁堂

Red legend (relief)
Impression of a stone seal
6.3 x 2.3 cm
2003

朱文
石章印拓
6.3 x 2.3 厘米
2003

Collection of Mr. Han Yunshan
韓雲山先生收藏

題識：
歐陽永叔撰《晝錦堂記》以述大丞相魏國公韓琦以昔人之所榮為戒，故能成社稷之臣。董其昌有「晝錦堂圖」卷，絹本青綠沒骨山水之作也。 雲山師則以廣東俗語諧音「就咁堂」戲而顏其居，以俚俗之趣一變古人雅集之暢敘幽情，頗過癮痛快也。余試以晉人寫經筆意為雲山師 此石，自覺略得古人率直天真、揮灑淋漓之快感。澤光並識。

93 ***The Hall of No Regret*** | 終不悔堂

Red legend (relief)
Impression of a stone seal
5.5 x 1.7 cm
2003

朱文
石章印拓
5.5 x 1.7 厘米
2003

Collection of Mr. Han Yunshan
韓雲山先生收藏

Artist's inscription:
In the style of the Cuan Baozi Stele Inscription

題識：
擬爨寶子

94 *The Hall of No Regret* | 終不悔堂

White legend (intaglio)
Impression of a stone seal
3 x 3 cm
2009

白文
石章印拓
3 x 3 厘米
2009

Collection of Mr. Han Yunshan
韓雲山先生收藏

95 *The Frost Red Lyric House* | 霜紅詞館

Red legend (relief)
Impression of a stone seal
2.6 x 2.9 cm
2009

朱文
石章印拓
2.6 x 2.9 厘米
2009

Collection of Mr. Han Yunshan
韓雲山先生收藏

Artist's inscription:
In the style of the remnant manuscripts of Jin Dynasty (A.D. 1115-1234), perceiving the transition from clerical script to standard script.

題識：
仿晉殘紙，窺隸楷過渡之理

96 *Composed by Yunshan after the Age of Seventy* | 雲山七十後作

Red legend (relief)
Impression of a stone seal
1.8 x 1.8 cm
2003

朱文
石章印拓
1.8 x 1.8 厘米
2003

Collection of Mr. Han Yunshan
韓雲山先生收藏

97 ***Composed by Yunshan after the Age of Eighty*** | 雲山八十後作

White legend (intaglio)
Impression of a stone seal
1.9 x 1.9 cm
2003

白文
石章印拓
1.9 x 1.9 厘米
2003

Collection of Mr. Han Yunshan
韓雲山先生收藏

98 ***Calligraphy by Yunshan after the Age of Eighty*** | 雲山八十後書

Red legend (relief)
Impression of a stone seal
6 x 3.8 cm
2003

朱文
石章印拓
6 x 3.8 厘米
2003

Collection of Mr. Han Yunshan
韓雲山先生收藏

99 ***Calligraphy by Yunshan after the Age of Eighty*** | 雲山八十後書

Red legend (relief)
Impression of a stone seal
2.3 x 2.2 cm
2003

朱文
石章印拓
2.3 x 2.2 厘米
2003

Collection of Mr. Han Yunshan
韓雲山先生收藏

100 ***Calligraphy by Yunshan after the Age of Eighty*** | 雲山八十後書

Red legend (relief)
Impression of a stone seal
1.7 x 1.6 cm
2003

朱文
石章印拓
1.7 x 1.6 厘米
2003

Collection of Mr. Han Yunshan
韓雲山先生收藏

101 ***Calligraphy by Yunshan after the Age of Eighty-five*** | 雲山八十五後書

Red legend (relief)
Impression of a stone seal
1.8 x 1.7 cm
2003

朱文
石章印拓
1.8 x 1.7 厘米
2003

Collection of
Mr. Han Yunshan
韓雲山先生收藏

102 ***Obsession with Coins*** | 泉癖

Red legend (relief)
Impression of a stone seal
2.2 cm diameter
2009

朱文
石章印拓
直徑 2.2 厘米
2009

Collection of
Mr. Han Yunshan
韓雲山先生收藏

103 ***May Yunshan Live Long*** | 雲山長壽

Red legend (relief)
Impression of a stone seal
4.8 x 4.8 cm
2003

朱文
石章印拓
4.8 x 4.8 厘米
2003

Collection of Mr. Han Yunshan
韓雲山先生收藏

Artist's inscription/ 題識：
Clerical script of Han Dynasty (206 B.C. - A.D. 220) is applied to the seal. The characters yun (cloud) and shou (longevity) are extracted from Ode to Fenglong Mountain.
漢隸入印，集封龍山頌「雲」、「壽」二字

104 ***Yunshan with Palms Together*** | 雲山合十

Red legend (relief)
Impression of a stone seal
1.5 x 1.5 cm
2009

朱文
石章印拓
1.5 x 1.5 厘米
2009

Collection of
Mr. Han Yunshan
韓雲山先生收藏

Artist's inscription:
There is such mode in ancient seals

題識：古鈢中有此形制

106-120
小棚友——萬青屴教授常用印
Little Friend of the Ox-Shed —— Seals Often used by Professor Wan Qingli

105 ***The Zen of Acquiring Freedom*** | 得自在禪

White legend (intaglio)
Impression of a stone seal
2.5 x 2.3 cm
2009

白文
石章印拓
2.5 x 2.3 厘米
2009

Collection of Mr. Han Yunshan
韓雲山先生收藏

Artist's inscription/ 題識：
Rough impression of Huang Yi (1744-1801)
黃小松(黃易)(1744-1801)大意

106 ***"Wan", "Qingli"*** | "萬"、"青屴"

Red legend (relief)

Impressions of 2 stone seals
1.8 x 1.8 cm & 3.4 x 1.6cm
2003

朱文
石章印拓 x 2
1.8 x 1.8 厘米及3.4 x 1.6 厘米
2003

Collection of Professor Wan Qingli
萬青屴教授收藏

107 ***Wan Qingli*** | 萬青力

Red legend (relief)
Impression of a stone seal
4.5 x 1.5 cm
2003

朱文
石章印拓
4.5 x 1.5 厘米
2003

Collection of Professor Wan Qingli
萬青屴教授收藏

108 ***WAN*** |

White legend (intaglio)
Impression of a stone seal
3.5 x 3.5 cm
2008

白文
石章印拓
3.5 x 3.5 厘米
2008

Collection of Professor Wan Qingli
萬青屴教授收藏

109 ***QL (i.e. Qingli)*** |

Red legend (relief)
Impression of a stone seal
3.9 x 3.2 cm
2008

朱文
石章印拓
3.9 x 3.2 厘米
2008

Collection of
Professor Wan Qingli
萬青屴教授收藏

110 ***Little Friend of the Ox-Shed*** |
小棚友

Red legend (relief)
Impression of a stone seal
3.4 x 2 cm
2008

朱文
石章印拓
3.4 x 2 厘米
2008

Collection of
Professor Wan Qingli
萬青屴教授收藏

111 ***Little Friend of the Ox-Shed*** |
小棚友

Portrait seal of Wan Qingli (upper) (engraved by Mancy Li)
萬青屴肖像印（上）（利雪玲刻）
Red legend (relief)/ 朱文
3 x 3 cm

Chinese character seal (lower)
(engraved by Daniel Lau)
小棚友印（下）（劉澤光刻）
White legend (intaglio)/ 白文
3 x 1.2 cm

Impression of a stone seal
石章印拓
2008

Collection of
Professor Wan Qingli
萬青屴教授收藏

112 ***Little Friend of the Ox-Shed*** |
小棚友

Red legend (relief)
Impression of a stone seal
4 x 2.4 cm
2008

朱文
石章印拓
4 x 2.4 厘米
2008

Collection of
Professor Wan Qingli
萬青屴教授收藏

113 ***Wanshan*** | 萬山
(Ten Thousand Mountains)

White legend (intaglio)
Impression of a stone seal
2.5 x 1.8 cm
2008

白文
石章印拓
2.5 x 1.8 厘米
2008

Collection of
Professor Wan Qingli
萬青艻教授收藏

114 ***Qingli's Memory*** |
青艻存念

Red legend (relief)
Impression of a
stone seal
3.1 x 0.8 cm
2008

朱文
石章印拓
3.1 x 0.8 厘米
2008

Collection of
Professor Wan Qingli
萬青艻教授收藏

115 ***Qingli's Memory*** |
青艻存念

Red legend (relief)
Impression of a
stone seal
4.5 x 0.5 cm
2008

朱文
石章印拓
4.5 x 0.5 厘米
2008

Collection of
Professor Wan Qingli
萬青艻教授收藏

116 ***Wonders of Nature*** |
嘆世界

Red legend (relief)
Impression
of a stone seal
10.5 x 3.4 cm
2008

朱文
石章印拓
10.5 x 3.4 厘米
2008

Collection of
Professor Wan Qingli
萬青艻教授收藏

117 ***Wonders of Nature*** |
嘆世界

Red legend (relief)
Impression of a stone seal
4.7 x 1.3 cm
2008

朱文
石章印拓
4.7 x 1.3 厘米
2008

Collection of
Professor Wan Qingli
萬青屴教授收藏

118 ***How Can Landscape be Priced?*** |
山水豈可論價？

Red legend (relief)
Impression of a stone seal
5 x 5 cm
2008

朱文
石章印拓
5 x 5 厘米
2008

Collection of
Professor Wan Qingli
萬青屴教授收藏

119 ***Completed After the Eye Disease*** |
目疾後作

Red legend (relief)
Impression of a stone seal
5.3 x 1.4 cm
2008

朱文
石章印拓
5.3 x 1.4 厘米
2008

Collection of
Professor Wan Qingli
萬青屴教授收藏

120 ***Global Man*** |
地球人也

Red legend (relief)
Impression of a stone seal
5 cm diameter
2008

朱文
石章印拓
直徑 5 厘米
2008

Collection of
Professor Wan Qingli
萬青屴教授收藏

黑与白

CHAPTER 3/第三章

Black & White

The Void-Solid Reciprocity or Designating the White When Applying the Black: Ink-Rubbing Calligraphy by Daniel Chak-kwong Lau[1]

Professor Peter Y. K. Lam
Director, Art Museum
The Chinese University of Hong Kong

"Void-solid reciprocity" is a structural characteristic of Chinese artistic conception. It is widely applied to the Chinese arts of literature, poetry, Chinese opera, music, painting, calligraphy, decorative arts, gardening and architecture. There are sayings like "taking the concrete as solid, the abstract as void" and "taking the limited as solid, and the infinite as void". In Chinese gardening, the synergy between elements is emphasized, whereas in Chinese painting, attention is paid to contrasts between the obscure and the obvious, the concealed and the revealed, the dynamic and the static, the subject and the object, the strong and the weak, the dense and the dilute, the crafted and the unadorned, the ample and the scarce, and the shallow and the deep. In calligraphy, we talk about "void-solid reciprocity", of which "solid" refers to the inked strokes on paper, and "void" refers to the unpainted blank space outside the strokes. The relationship between black and white must be well balanced and adjusted in order for them to complementarily set off each other, so that the focus stands out. In this exhibition, Dr. Daniel Chak-kwong Lau develops his ink-rubbing calligraphy as an example to explain the artistic conception of "void-solid reciprocity" in calligraphic expressions, thus opening up new domains of Chinese calligraphy.

Ink rubbing is one of the rubbing techniques. A rubbing, in general, is a pigment-on-paper reproduction of a surface – usually of objects made with stone, bronze or other materials – that is incised or sculptured with intaglio or relief texts and pictorial images. It is obtained by laying paper or similar materials over the object and rubbing it with ink, colours, crayon or dyes, with the help of some simple tools. In Europe, rubbings of epitaphs and inscriptions in churches are taken by laying an unmoistened sheet of paper onto the surface being copied and rubbing on it with crayons. Such rubbing technique is simple and convenient. But if the paper is thick, the surface is three-dimensional, or the inscriptions are high-relief, the results would unlikely be ideal.

In China, however, the traditional rubbing techniques are relatively more complex. The rubbing-artisans are very particular about the choice of paper. They prefer an absorbent, thin but strong paper like *mazhi* (hemp paper), mianzhi (paper made from paper mulberry), *jingpi* (bark paper), *mianlian* ("cotton-continuous" paper) and luowen (net-grain paper). They first paste a moistened paper onto the surface with a slightly glutinous solution of baiji (Latin: Bletilla bytacinthina) which is a tropical orchid. The paper is lightly tapped with a stiff brush so that it conforms to the relief features to be copied. When the paper is almost dry, its surface is either tapped again with an inked tampon of cotton and wool wrapped under layers of fine silk, or swiped with a coiled woollen flannel inking implement similar to a blackboard duster, so that the projecting areas of the surface become dark, and the indented areas remain white. The rubbing thus produced is an accurate reproduction of the original reliefs or inscriptions in a 1:1 scale. It differs from printmaking in that a rubbing follows the façade while a print is a laterally reversed impression. Also, rubbings can help with the identification and reading of textual inscriptions and the deciphering of pictorial reliefs, when the original stone or wood objects have suffered natural erosion as well as damages caused by the constant tapping of inking implements in rubbing-making, that the texts and images can no longer

1 A version of this essay was published in: Daniel C.K. Lau ed. *The Void-Solid Reciprocity: Black-Tiger Calligraphy by Daniel C.K. Lau.* Hong Kong: Academy of Visual Arts, Hong Kong Baptist University, 2009, pp. 7-12..

be recognized. Therefore, the method of rubbing still has its value even in the contemporary world of digital photography. Complete and realistic records of cultural relics can no doubt be produced by the methods of photography and drawing; but in rubbings the contrasts between black and white and between the positive and the negative are even sharper. Moreover, by the method of rubbing, carvings of a full 360-degree range on cylindrical objects like a brush pot can even be recorded as a panoramic rubbing. It can in no way be replaced by photographs, videos or diagrams.

For these reasons, ink rubbing is a crucial vehicle for ancient Chinese civilization. Since Tang (618-907) and Song Dynasties (960-1279), rubbings have preserved important documents and the arts of Chinese calligraphy and painting. They have also accomplished the history of bei and tie connoisseurship of more than a thousand years. *Bei* (stele calligraphy) and *tie* (model calligraphy) are two different kinds of textual ink rubbings. *Beike* are inscribed records of events, which include landscape carvings, stele, epitaphs, stupas, sutra pillars, statues, monumental gates, smoothed cliffs, title deeds for land, stone carvings of classics and sutras and inscriptions. *Beita* (stele rubbings) are original ink-rubbing sheets or the stitch-bound albums of such rubbings mounted to facilitate reading and copying. *Fatie* (calligraphy model) are rubbings of calligraphic works of renowned calligraphers copy-cut on stone or wood, which are used as model calligraphy for people to learn and imitate. Occasionally there are vermilion or coloured-ink rubbings, but mostly the rubbings are black in colour. Hence stele rubbings are commonly called *hei laohu* ("black tigers"). The ancient shrewd dealers produced fake rubbings by the methods of recutting, making up inscriptions, filling cracks with wax, dyeing to pretend early rubbings, and retouching the broken lines with ink. These counterfeit techniques pose difficulties for the connoisseurs and collectors. If not cautious enough one would be deceived by a carefully crafted counterfeit, as if being bitten by a tiger. This is to remind the collectors and connoisseurs to be well versed in the professional knowledge of calligraphy rubbings.

Rubbing is a very unique Chinese traditional art technique that integrates cultural and historical implications, artistic quality and technical processing. In the past, the rubbing-artisans did not have a social status in spite of their skilful craftsmanship. With the decline of the traditional culture, even the more successful rubbing-artisans in Hong Kong have completed their missions and gradually become history. The connoisseurship of *beitie* (stele rubbings) has become a skill that will soon be lost. Due to the popularization of printing, the *guben* (only extant rubbing) and *shanben* (rare rubbings) can be reproduced into thousands of copies easily. The ownership of and access to rare rubbings and quality copies are much easier now.

Things change. Traditional calligraphy is confronted with the crisis of decline with societal changes and the widespread use of computers. Contemporary calligraphers are facing the hardest challenge ever. Now the most urgent task for calligraphers is to modernize the art of calligraphy which is timeless and the most representative in Chinese art history, and enter the arena of contemporary conceptual art by employing Chinese handwriting as a special cultural symbol. In the face of such challenge, many Chinese artists incorporate other techniques into traditional brush-and-ink techniques in their modern art creations, for example: paper rubbing and wrinkling, collage, paper-fibre ripping, oil-adding, roll-printing、permeation, ink-rinsing, water-resisting, spray-dyeing, corrosion, absorption, precipitation, and batik. On the level of modern calligraphy techniques, some artists incorporate ink-and-wash techniques, movable-type printing, mirror image of texts, object graffiti, characters and symbols, repetitive writing, ink-splashing and colour-adding, and deconstructionist installation into their calligraphic artworks. Some of these experimentations have achieved great success, but many of them are shallow, superfluous and formalistic to stand the test of time.

In fact, traditional Chinese ink-rubbing techniques can also be applied to painting and calligraphy appropriately. The mottled, heavy and raw texture of rubbings somehow draws the viewers into reveries of the archaistic past. Dr. Daniel Chak-kwong Lau is an outstanding figure in the application of ink-rubbing form to calligraphic skill. He develops his ink-rubbing calligraphy artworks on the foundation of traditional calligraphy, seal-engraving and rubbing. His works are visually refreshing with his archaic, unadorned style and the traits of the era.

I first met Daniel in 2002, one year before the SARS outbreak in Hong Kong. He was a Ph.D. candidate of University of California, Santa Barbara supervised by Professor Peter Sturman. In that year the Art Museum, Chinese University of Hong Kong, organized the exhibition "Double Beauty: Qing Dynasty Couplets from the Lechangzai Xuan Collection". Daniel was one of the contributors for the catalogue entries. He completed the 36 bilingual entries very quickly in elegant Chinese and English, explaining the complex ideas in simple language comprehensible to a layman. Next year the couplet was open to the public. One of the accompanying events was a couplet calligraphy contest. Daniel took part, and his work was presented in the form of ink rubbing. At that time the judges had diverse opinions - one of them questioned whether Daniel's work could be considered calligraphy as it was different from the traditional calligraphic style done with a brush. After detailed discussions and assessments, most of the judges considered that it was not a problem to use ink rubbing as calligraphic expression and Daniel's entry was awarded a Merit Prize of the Open Section. I was present during the assessment. Although I did not participated in the adjudication, I was amazed at his dexterous ink-rubbing skills. Moreover, I appreciated his inscription on the side of the couplet written in small-character standard script in the style of Ni Zan (1306-1374). Later I found out that he is an artist as well as art historian who has received formal training in both fields. His M.Phil. thesis at the University of Hong Kong centres on the calligraphy theories of Kang Youwei (1858-1927), whereas his Ph.D. dissertation at University of California, Santa Barbara focuses on Ding Jing (1695-1765), one of the Eight Masters of Xiling. He has studied calligraphy and seal-engraving as artistic practices from Mr. Han Yunshan (1923-2010), and learnt Chinese painting from Mr. Long Ziduo (1915-2008). Hence, Daniel is genuinely a versatile young scholar-artist who is well versed in both scholarly and artistic pursuits.

Ink-rubbing calligraphy can show the aura of calligraphy as well as the interesting flavor of inscriptions on stele, bronze and stone. Daniel specializes in calligraphy. But more important is that he is also good at seal-engraving, where he can perfectly merge the aura of calligraphy and the "bronze-and-stone" flavor of rubbings. Traditional rubbings are inked with either coiled inking implement or inking tampon. But Daniel abandons these tools when creating calligraphic works with rubbing techniques. He does it with the brush, but he never outlines a draft, because he already has a design of the characters and the void and the solid in his mind. Hence he is able to write with spirit. Local calligrapher Mr. Luo Shuzhong (1898-1969) and his disciple Luo Xiaoshan have also created "black-tiger" calligraphy in imitation of rubbing from stone carvings. They formed characters directly by the application of dense ink, blurring the slightly dark ink traces to achieve the effect of rubbing that delineates shapes of natural erosion and flaking in stele inscriptions. Inspired by this unique approach to calligraphic practice, Daniel puts more emphasis on the application of the dry-brush technique to recreate the mottled and rough textural effect produced by the coiled inking implement and the inking tampon. He cleverly combines calligraphy, seal-engraving and ink-rubbing practice, reproducing the profoundly powerful, honest and austere style of the stele inscriptions of Han (206 B.C. – A.D. 220) and Wei Dynasties (386-535).

If we take "void-solid reciprocity" as a structural characteristic of artistic conception, Daniel's ink-rubbing calligraphy can be regarded as "void-solid inversion". He applies ink as the void, and leaves blank spaces as the solid, reversing the black and the white. This exactly proves true the theory of "void-solid reciprocity", which "the void can bring about the solid, and the solid can bring about the void". Qing calligrapher Deng Shiru (1743-1805) said, "The wonder of the calligraphy manifests as one designates the white when applying the black." The "white" means the inkless area, that is the void; the "black" means the inked area, that is the solid. In the treatment of calligraphy, one needs to "take the void as the solid, take the solid as the void", and also "see the solid in the void, see the void in the solid", so that the void and the solid are mutually complementary, and the spaces are properly arranged. Daniel's ink-rubbing calligraphy has attained the quality of "void-solid inversion". He does "designate the white space when applying the black ink". The spacings are in place, the artistic decisions are full of natural variations, and the lingering aura is lasting. Daniel is truly a talented expert in ink-rubbing calligraphy!

虛實相生、計白當黑 ：
劉澤光的墨拓書法[1] ◣

林業强教授
香港中文大學文物館館長

“虛實相生”是意境的結構特徵。中國文學、詩歌、戲曲、音樂、繪畫、書法、工藝、園林、建築技巧上，廣為應用。所謂形象為實，抽象為虛；有限為實，無限為虛等等。園林講究掩映，繪畫講究隱與顯、藏與露、動與靜、主與賓、強與弱、濃與淡、工與拙，少與多、淺與深等。書法章法講究“虛實相生”：“實”指紙上的點畫，即落墨的地方，“虛”指紙上點畫以外的空白，即無墨的留白。在書法上最重要是要調配好黑白之間的關係，能夠做到相輔相成，形成渲染烘托，從而突出中心重點。在這次展覽中，劉澤光博士以墨拓書法為例，闡釋書法表現中“虛實相生”的意境，開展書法新領域。

墨拓是傳拓技法的一種。廣義的傳拓是指用紙或其他的軟薄物料，覆蓋在石頭、銅器或各式物料的器物上，以墨、顏料、蠟筆、染料等，再加上一些簡單傳拓工具，捶印其凹凸浮雕或線刻文字和圖像後，所得到的拓印本。歐洲拓印墓碑、教堂銘刻，將乾紙用膠紙黏貼在要拓印的器物上，用蠟筆擦拓。這樣的平塗擦拓（英文稱之為Rubbing），技法簡易方便，但也有它的局限，例如用紙較厚，只適用於較光滑的平面器物，如果文字或圖像為高浮雕，效果不會很理想。

中國傳統墨拓技術，技巧較複雜。拓工講究用紙，他們多選擇紙質薄、韌性好的麻紙、綿紙、淨皮、棉連、羅紋紙等。刷輕膠性的白芨水上紙，將輕微濕潤的紙張貼附於器物表面。利用打刷等捶打工具，使薄紙緊貼器物上的紋路或文字，凹凸刻劃顯露分明。再用沾墨的擦子（細毛氈卷成）或用撲包（布或綢緞包棉花）輕輕擦、撲其上，使器物紋飾或銘文呈現紙上。凸出的地方沾墨成黑色，凹下處則沒有沾墨，成為黑白分明的拓本。拓本是原器物文字圖像一比一原大的真確傳移，它與版畫印刷不同，文字圖形是由器物本身正面傳拓出來，並沒有經過反面印刷，所以圖形並非左右顛倒。此外，原本器物上的文字圖像經過日久磨損，用肉眼往往不能辨識，但拓印卻黑白分明，可以協助文字的辨識閱讀和圖像紋飾的解讀。所以，即使在攝影技術出現以後，數碼攝影普及的今天，傳拓技法仍有它存在的價值。攝影、繪圖技術雖然能夠完整寫實的將文物實況清晰的記錄下來，但拓本凹凸有致、黑白對比鮮明，傳拓又能夠將圓筒物體（如筆筒）上360度立體花紋化為手卷式的的通景圖畫，這絕非平面照片、錄像、線圖所能夠取代。

因此之故，墨拓印本是中華古代文明的重要載體，自唐宋以來，拓本保存了重要的文獻資料和豐富多彩的書法、繪畫藝術，也造就了長達千餘年的碑帖鑒藏歷史。碑帖是指兩種不同的文字墨拓本。碑刻是記述人物與事件的石刻文字總稱，包括刻石、碑碣、墓誌、塔銘、經幢、造像、石闕、摩崖、[illegible]、石經、題刻等。碑拓便是將這些石刻文字傳拓留傳於世的墨拓單張，或是剪裝成冊、以便觀賞臨摹的拓冊。法帖拓本則是將前人墨蹟摹刻上石或上木，傳拓後供人們效法臨習書法的範本。碑帖俗稱“黑老虎”，因為拓本雖然偶有朱拓或彩墨拓，但一般顏色仍多為黑色。古代碑帖商賈作偽做假，如重刻、翻刻、偽刻、嵌蠟填補、染色充舊、塗墨描補等手段，防不勝防，鑑定不易，稍一疏忽，就會上當，就似被老虎咬了一口，這是要告誡鑒藏碑帖者要有足夠的專業知識。

傳拓是一種有文化歷史內涵，又有藝術品位和工藝加工三者相結合的中國獨有的傳統藝術技法。以前傳拓工匠，雖然身懷絕技，但社會地位低微。面對傳統文化逐漸沒落，香港現在能做得比較好的拓工，也逐漸完成其使命，淡出歷史舞台。碑帖鑒藏成為十分冷門的絕學，因為印刷普及，以前的孤本善本碑帖，很容易便化身千萬。善本碑帖、下真跡一等複印本的擁有、臨摹，比過去容易得多了。

時移世易，隨著社會的轉變，電腦的流行和普及，傳統書法面臨沒落。現代書法家所要面對的課題，所要面對的挑戰，比以前嚴峻得多。書法家當前急務在於怎樣把中國藝術史上最具歷史跨步、最富民族特性的書法藝術現代化，將漢字書寫作為獨特的文化符號，進入當代觀念藝術。面對挑戰，在現代藝術創作中，不少中國藝術家在傳統筆墨技法中糅入了其他技巧，如：揉紮紙張、拼貼挖補、抽撕紙筋、加油、滾印、滲透、沖墨、讓水、噴染、腐蝕、吸收、沉澱、蠟染等。在現代書法技巧上，也有人將水墨技法、活字印刷、文字鏡像、器物塗

1 本文曾發表於劉澤光編，《虛實相生：劉澤光黑老虎書法》，（香港：香港浸會大學視覺藝術院，2009年），頁13-16。

鴉、文字符號、重複書寫、潑墨加彩、解構裝置等，糅入書法創作中。有些利用這些技巧的嘗試，很有成就，但也有不少，淺薄浮躁，畫蛇添足，流於表面形式，經不起時間考驗。

中國傳統墨拓技術，其實也可以適當地應用在繪畫、書法上。墨拓斑駁、厚重、粗糙的肌理，往往容易使人不經意的墜入歷史時空的遐想。將墨拓模式應用在書法技巧上，劉澤光博士是其中的表表者。澤光在傳統書法篆刻傳拓的基礎上，發展墨拓書法作品，風格古樸渾厚，極具時代特色，使觀者視覺一新。

初識澤光是在二零零二年，香港"SARS（非典）"肆虐的前一年。當時他正於加州大學聖地巴巴拉分校，在石曼教授指導下攻讀博士學位。香港中文大學文物館籌辦"合璧聯珠：樂常在軒藏清代楹聯展覽"，澤光參加了其中部分楹聯條目的撰寫。他很快便完成任務，三十多條中英文雙語的説明，文字儒雅，內容深入淺出。第二年楹聯展覽開幕，一連串配合活動之一，是楹聯書法比賽，他也參加了，作品就是以墨拓技術表現。當時有評審提出不同意見，認為墨拓技術有異於以毛筆書寫的傳統作品，究竟算不算書法，值得斟酌。經過詳細討論比評之後，大多數評審認為以墨拓作為書法表現，並無不妥，而且還將澤光的作品評為公開組的優異獎。評審的時候，本人在場，雖然我沒有參與審議評分，但我驚訝於他的墨拓技法，運用純熟，更欣賞他在聯文旁邊的倪雲林（1306-1374）風格小楷題識。稍後我才知道他是藝術家，也是藝術史學者，在兩個領域中都受過正規訓練。他的香港大學藝術史碩士論文是研究康有為（1858-1927）的書論，而他的加州大學博士論文則以西泠八家之一的丁敬（1695-1765）為中心。他的書法、篆刻師事韓雲山先生（1923-2010），國畫則問藝於龍子鐸先生（1915-2008），是名副其實的文武雙全、學藝兼修的年青學者藝術家。

墨拓書法既能展示書法的韻味，又能彰顯碑刻金石趣味特質。澤光擅書，不過更重要的，是他也懂篆刻，將書法的韻味與拓片的金石趣味完美結合在一起。傳統墨拓以擦子或拓包上墨，但澤光在運用墨拓技法來創作書法作品的時候，屏棄這些工具，仍以毛筆為之，也不用線描草稿，而是心中早有腹稿，虛實早已了然於胸，故此下筆有神。香港前輩書法家羅叔重先生（1898-1969）和他的弟子駱曉山，也曾創作過"黑老虎"仿拓碑體書法，他們以墨漬法直接成字，利用微沉的墨痕，暈化而成拓本效果，寫出天然的剝蝕形狀。澤光一脈相承，不過他更注重以乾筆重現傳拓工具和墨擦、拓包的斑駁、粗糙肌理效果，巧妙的糅合書法、篆刻、傳拓，重現漢魏碑文的厚重、樸拙風格。

如果説"虛實相生"是意境結構特徵的話，澤光的墨拓書法則是"虛實倒置"。他點墨為虛，留白作實，黑白相反，正好印證了"虛可生實，實可生虛"——"虛實相生"的道理。清朝書法家鄧石如（1743-1805）説："常計白以當黑，奇趣乃出。"白指無墨處，即虛空處，黑指有墨處，即實處。在書法的處理上，要"虛者實之"，"實者虛之"，虛中有實，實中有虛，互補互生，空間調配得當，縝密無間。澤光墨拓書法作品"虛實倒置"，"計白當黑"，疏密得宜，上下呼應，變化自然，韻味無窮，不愧是箇中高手！

The Void-Solid Reciprocity – A Conversation Between Lines and Inkwork : Black-Tiger Calligraphy Exhibition of Daniel Chak-kwong Lau[1]

Dr. Vivian Wing-yan Ting
Assistant Professor
Hong Kong Baptist University

In 'Fits for Emperors and Kings (Ying Diwang)', Zhuangzi, the Taoist philosopher, tells an intriguing story:

> Hundun [lit. Chaos] was the emperor of the central region. Occasionally, Shu, the emperor of the South Sea, and Hu, the emperor of the North Sea, gathered in the central region and Hundun treated them very generously. Shu and Hu discussed how they could repay his kindness. 'Everyone', they said, 'has seven openings through which they can see, hear, eat, and breathe. But Hundun alone doesn't have any. Let's bore some on him!' Every day, they bored a hole on Hundun, and on the seventh day he died.[2]

Taoists, suggesting that one should follow the natural flow of life, blamed Shu and Hu for the death of Chaos in ignoring the true nature of his being. Generally, philosophers teach an esoteric notion that 'when nothing is done, nothing is left undone' in an attempt to free one from the limitations of the sensational world. The concept seems unfathomable, but for artists who give form to feeling and thought, the fable can be interpreted differently.

Like Chaos, the artist's muse hides in the shadows, but once in a while, this mysterious spirit presents itself like a sudden flash of light; immediately, the artist picks up a brush to create form from what was previously just a shapeless thought. Would this form of 'art' highlight technical consummation to portray the beauty of the sensational world but obliterate the true nature of Chaos? Or would the form be liberated from any formal elements and skills in illuminating the vigorous spirit of Chaos?

For thousands of years, Chinese artists have questioned how art can be created and yet remain true to the essence of Chaos. Inspired by nature, they have honed their skills to observe the inner spirit of a phenomenon and portray it using their personal vision and infinite imagination. In the art of calligraphy, the characters are vessels that embrace pictographs, ideographs, and phonetic compounds to communicate. It is this multi-faceted means of establishment and development of Chinese characters that endow the very nature of the dichotomy between the communicative function of these linguistic symbols and the abstract beauty of calligraphic art. The task of the calligrapher, therefore, is to explore the aesthetics of lines and ink without distorting the true nature of Chaos, to give a work its lingering sensibility. By the harmonious union of personal experience with the materiality of ink and brushes, the calligrapher unfolds the essence of the characters.

Rooted in traditions and learnt from contemporary avant-gardes, Dr. Daniel Chak-kwong Lau's calligraphy embodies the aesthetics of void and solid through spaatial arrangement, rhythmic lines, and tonal variants of ink. The works in this exhibition are unique blends of grace and uniformity inspired by seal script. They are firm and organic in their composition, and geometric in structure, re-enacting the archaic simplicity of ink rubbing. Lau does not content to be nostalgic in echoing the ancient art, but conveys his

1 A version of this essay was published in: Daniel C.K. Lau ed. *The Void-Solid Reciprocity: Black-Tiger Calligraphy by Daniel C.K. Lau*. Hong Kong: Academy of Visual Arts, Hong Kong Baptist University, 2009, pp. 17-23.
2 Burton Watson, trans., *Chuang Tzu: Basic Writings* (New York: Columbia University Press, 1964), 95.

daring experimentation, using the black-tiger style, where the void is filled with ink and the characters are left blank. With various densities of composition, light and heavy strokes, broken and flowing lines, the still image has a dynamic quality. Viewers would feel drawn into a bustling market place… bang… dong… dong… a peal of monastery music sends a refreshing sensation – unexpectedly, the simple movement of lines becomes more interesting, even captivating.

What brings Lau's art close to people's hearts is the diverse sources of content that come from traditional literature, touching on sentiments of friendship and mentorship, and personal remarks of the Christian faith. Viewers could easily slip into a more familiar world with a poetic perspective, relishing on how traditional artistry is fused with contemporary ideas. The calligrapher seems to be wandering between the ink and lines gracefully. Is it imaginary or perhaps real?

The vicissitudes of life embodied in the content of calligraphy is, in fact, another dimension of the void-solid contrast that encourages viewers to feel the richness of Chinese characters from different perspectives. Nevertheless, Lau's creation does not merely dwell on simulation, but it magnifies formal qualities of calligraphy in creating a lingering aesthetics that oscillates between the imaginary and the real, with both emptiness and fullness. The sophisticated design is built from organic spacing, and multi-layered effects of ink, with cadence and a sensitive movement of lines that creates exquisite tension between void and solid. Viewers enter the realm of literal meanings and proudly begin seeing their formal significance. There, sits Chaos, the pristine man of naïveté and candor. Faceless, he is revealed in all his might.

Looking at the brushwork of Lau's characters in detail, no momentum of flipping or obvious changes in the degree of thickness of the brushstrokes are apparent. Strengthened with a seemingly loose yet actually compact character structure, the round and bold brushstrokes present a profound and natural outlook. Like the movements of a Tai Chi master, the brushstrokes appear to be soft and slow, and yet their inner strengths are tenacious and stable. The posture is sometimes succinct, like counterworks, infused with vigor and charm, like blossoms that flourish in a spring breeze. The construction is meticulously treated with individual character that echoes every aspect. Overall, the work shows a balanced beauty of dynamics within stillness.

For example, in the work, *In the Beginning Was the Word* (*tai chu you dao*, cat. no. 124), Lau deliberately adjusts the styles of seal and clerical script into a square and thick typeface. The lines are geometric and the structure is tight. The posture of the characters resembles archaic fossils that might have stood erect for billions of years, as witness to the long process of evolution. The design ingeniously discloses the mysterious beginning of the world. The character '*tai*' (太) is tiny, suggesting the formation of the cosmic universe, when God uncloaked the darkness and allowed a beam of light to shine through. The characters '*chu*' (初) and '*you*' (有) are given equal space, while their postures are interlocked. '*Chu*' assumes a vertical appearance as an outline, like a giant tree that almost touches the sky; '*you*' takes a horizontal form, as the gist, like a cloud with a majestic presence above mother earth. '*Dao*' (道) is the character taking up the prominent position, with a structure that seems loose but having parts with different strokes that correspond to the other three characters. Indistinctly, the focal point suggests that the anarchic cosmos can only be adjusted by the Dao of God in granting the order for the world. Obviously, spatial composition plays a significant role in Lau's void-solid aesthetics, conveying the rhythm of characters and presenting calligraphy's inner beauty of balance.

Void is everything but form, and only through the expressive qualities of lines and ink does Lau's aesthetic of void-solid render a motionless beauty in the calligraphy. Interestingly, the black-tiger series is not confined to only a visual antithesis with contrasting elements of void and solid. Instead, the works explore possibilities for magnifying solid with void and for transforming void into solid, thus creating an artistic world for viewers to get in touch with, and wonder about. Void is not a quiet world with a vast expanse of blankness, but is a landscape of mountains and waters in the translucent ripples of ink.

Although little space is left blank, the white writing looks simplistic and carefree. The '*Prologue*,

Romance of the Three Kingdoms' (cat. no. 131) is an example of more blacks than whites. The blacks are densely packed in the rubbed brushwork, while the white lines are melodic, articulating the reserved but stylish posture of the characters. The blacks and whites confine the conflict within, eventually complementing each other, to create a random pattern derived from the texture of aging material. Temporality, therefore, is infused into the two-dimensional art of calligraphy, according to the artist's movement. It is not difficult to imagine that these dancing strokes are slow, but come with a tremendous momentum as if they could move mountains and rivers. In this work of art, Lau's calligraphy has transformed a pictorial design of dots, lines, and planes into a symphony of cosmic evolution, as the harmonious interplay between void and solid.

Lau's creations, embracing the aesthetics of void and solid, return to the unnamed land of Chaos, where expressions are liberated from ink and brushes. One of the experimental works of calligraphy, *Void* (cat. no. 127), reflects Lau's free wielding of brushes to reveal the formal significance of character that goes beyond a superficial appearance of lines and dots. At first glance, the work is a landscape painting in splash-ink. Viewers can see steep mountains rising abruptly from the bottom right corner, and strolling up the slope, viewers would nose into an enigmatic home of immortals enshrouded by a drizzle of mist. While catching their breath, viewers might feel a peculiar cool sensation creeping up from their feet, with a murmuring brook that seems to thread its way down the hill. From a distance, viewers would realize that the character '*xu*' (虛), or "void" (i.e. the negative/white spaces that suggest the configuration of strokes of the character xu in cursive script) is veiled in the quiet sea of clouds. According to *Shuowen Jiezi (Book of Chinese Characters and Phrases* – the first comprehensive Chinese dictionary), the character, 'void', is defined as a gorgeous mountain. Lau feeds the itinerant lines with sweeps of ink to magnify the character. The calligraphy is void in outlining any tangible form of the character, but sufficiently solid to reveal its aesthetic significance. The juxtaposition of void and solid releases a free expression of ink and brushes in conveying a sense of simplicity. It opens up a world with infinite aesthetic imaginations where Chaos can be found within an inner peace.

Liberated from lines and ink, Lau's artworks integrate elements of Chinese painting with the art of calligraphy to push a new boundary of penmanship. In an attempt to explore the meaning of calligraphy and the essence of writing, he uses a new means of writing in his experimentation. *Emptiness* (cat. no. 128), one of his latest works, draws inspiration from the form of seal script to create an artistic interpretation of the meaning of the word. By splashing, sweeping, and dripping ink onto the glassy silk chiffon, Lau applies strokes dashingly to reveal an amazing fusion of intricate sensitivity and strength. The character, "*kong*" (空), or 'emptiness', is represented as a gorgeous mountain from South China that is exposed in the pouring rain and whirling blast. The work is mounted on a rough wooden stand to present its three-dimensionality. The light passes through dreamily, and the ink landscape is crisscrossed with the surrounding scene, creating both an illusionary and realistic field. The work allows viewers to see through the glamorous phenomena and reflects upon the essence of the character, 'emptiness', in its complete vanity.

Working from a flat representation to a three-dimensional installation, Lau's aesthetics of void and solid extend the means of calligraphy. Thus, the writing embodies the notion of solid, whereas the technique of penmanship refers to the void. In a pair of sculptures, *A Deep and Tranquil Mountain* (cat. no. 5) and *An Endless Stream* (cat. no. 4), Lau uses glass and wood, respectively, to articulate the characters of 'mountain' (山) and 'stream' (川). Interestingly, the majesty of the mountain is portrayed with a fluid form of glass and its serenity, while a gnarly trunk of wood shapes the movement of running water. Looking at A Deep and Tranquil Mountain, the obscure and transparent facets of glass create a fair show of greenery with a touch of sparkling sunshine. Its gentle and smooth form is reminiscent of the Creator's hand – nurturing and miraculous – giving the hill a breath of life. Through the interplay of glass material and graceful form, Lau represents the 'mountain' character in a cursive script that resonates with the natural landscape, and embraces the wilderness with poetic sensibilities. In contrast, in 'An Endless Stream', Lau uses a trunk of rosewood (*huanghuali* wood) as the paper and a carving knife as the brush to reveal the restlessness of water. With a careful design and artistic processing, the form of the character is carved out of a natural tree trunk, conforming to the original wood pattern. The rhythmic form and wavy texture of the material resembles the swift lines and delicate inkwork to capture a tumbling current rushing across the view. The character is not the turbulent flow, but its formal significance is identical to the subject. Obviously, this group of experimental works by Lau does not resemble writing, but as calligraphy, the fully sculptured volume and rich relief make material the essence of the character. Such a fertile vocabulary of form and texture is also suggestive of the Confucian saying: 'The wise delight in water, but the humane delight in mountains. For although the wise are active; the humane are at rest'.[3] Hovering between formal significance and cultural reference, Lau invites viewers to explore the multi-layered interpretations of the characters. Ultimately, the richness of Chinese characters allow for an outpouring of personal expression without limits, as might occur with unconventional writing methods. Thus, Chaos is revealed directly from a simplistic vision.

Is calligraphy just a technique of wielding ink and brushes, or is it about the aesthetic significance of writing? In reviewing Lau's creations, calligraphy appears to be an eternal dialogue between formal significance, personal expression, and the essence of characters. A work of calligraphy is meaningful if it seeks resonance from a wider audience to enrich our aesthetic sensibilities. To achieve this, viewers must also be co-creators, to join in the dialogue with their individual perspectives. Moreover, to facilitate a meaningful dialogue, the interpretive text from an exhibition or catalogue must also offer a point of entry into calligraphy's world of art. No one knows exactly where the art of Chaos is located, but by recognizing the characters, and appreciating the artistic arrangement of writing, viewers can be invited to enter its realm.

---

3 Raymond Dawson, trans., *The Analects* (Oxford: Oxford University Press, 1993), 6:23, 22.

虛實相生：
筆墨、線條的對話 — 劉澤光黑老虎書法展[1] ◣

丁穎茵博士
香港浸會大學助理教授

傳說南海之帝名儵，北海之帝名忽，渾沌則為中央之帝。儵、忽常常相會於渾沌的國土，屢蒙渾沌款待，二人有意報其恩德。他們鑑於人有七竅，用作視、聽、食、呼吸，唯獨渾沌卻一竅不通，乃動工為渾沌穿鑿竅孔。豈料他們一日開鑿一竅，七日而七竅俱全的渾沌卻不幸身亡。

這個耐人尋味的故事見於《莊子》·〈應帝王〉篇。道家主張人生貴乎自然自適，怪罪儵、忽以人工強開渾沌耳目，大違其稟性，反累其無辜身死。哲人講求不拘於聲色，無為而無不為，未免高深莫測。不過，對於以形相為心聲的藝術家來說，這寓言卻別有一番解說。

作者心聲有如渾沌，藏於蒙昧昏暗間無形無跡。偶爾才思併發，作者乘興運腕提筆，無相無形的心思方才著了痕跡。這樣的「藝術品」究竟是以人工斧鑿之巧，展示七竅之美，而抹殺渾沌的性靈？還是順從渾沌本性，呈現不拘形跡卻又神氣生動的中央之帝？千百以來，中國藝術家一直思考如何以筆墨所得避免渾沌之死，成全其象外之意。他們提出師法自然氣韻，藉以觀照內心本質，探索呼應自然天性的藝術形式。其中書法藝術以文字為載體，文字涵蓋象形、指事、形聲等種種面相，並負起交流思想的實際功能，正反映這門藝術既抽象又具體的特質。書法家為求胸中渾沌得享天年，更必須追求主觀情思與筆墨意趣的諧協，以盡得文字之生意而不為形質所礙。

立足於傳統技藝，放眼於當今思潮，劉澤光博士的書法從「虛實相生」的美學入手，透過空間配置、線條律動、落墨敷色…包攬其所思所感的大千世界。是次展覽的書法線條吸收篆籀「橫平豎直」的筆意，章法疏拓而節奏感強，重現漢魏碑體的樸拙。然而，這絕非一味沉溺於傳統文化的餘緒。劉氏「黑老虎」書法擦墨為虛，留白作實，使明暗凹凸參差曲扭，畫面雖定而動態尤全。觀者仿如在紛紛嚷嚷的鬧市中，忽聞陣陣暮鼓晨鐘一呯…噹…噹…頓然發現周遭事物一橫一豎的意趣。讓人可親可感的是，書法的內容既來自詩詞歌賦，也取自師友交誼、宗教體驗及日常俚語等生活點滴，觀眾不經意溜進時空交錯的角度，細味傳統技藝如何與當代氣息相融。驀然回首，又見書者從字裡行間信步走來，幻耶？真耶？

書法內容引發今昔時空的對照，俾觀眾細味宜古宜今的文字，此略見劉氏把玩虛實相映的端倪。然而，其創作更於書法形式結構落墨，創造一種亦幻亦真、似虛還實的美感。從留白到落墨的分吋、設色濃淡厚薄、線條曲直頓挫、下筆動靜緩速…無不蘊藏虛實互濟的微妙張力，引領觀眾出入文義的廳堂，昂昂然步入書法形式美的居室。內裡端坐著淳淳然如化外之民的渾沌，此君雖然一竅不通，卻又無時無刻不飽含靜若深淵的生命力。

細看劉氏一筆一劃既無翻挑之勢，也乏明顯的粗細變化，形態寬博，筆勢圓渾，每個字外弛內歛，筋肉豐腴而神氣不墜。似是太極拳高手，動作既柔且慢，轉身運勁卻又韌又穩，全身隱隱有一股氣勢迴流，凜然不可侵犯。字體時而凝鍊似列陣對壘，蓄勢待發；偶爾團團熙熙如沐春風。字與字之間互相接應，若森森重巒得紫霞相伴，法度工整，通篇表現出靜中有動的平衡美。如題為《太初有道》（展品 124）的作品，劉氏特意以篆刻刀法入書，字體又方又厚，筆劃提按小卻結構緊歛，形態就如目睹滄海桑田，歷億萬年而屹立不倒的化石。作者處理手法甚見巧思，「太」字寫得小，彷彿天地初開，上帝雙手擘開昏暗，始見一絲光明。「初」跟「有」二字平分空間，卻又縱橫交錯，「初」字以縱為綱，只見幢幢參天巨木高聳入雲；而「有」字以橫為領，大有排雲浩浩蕩蕩駕臨大地的氣勢。「道」字所佔空間最廣，結構鬆散，但筆劃的不同部份卻又與其餘三字互相呼應，隱然成為全局領軍，點出太初蒙蒙混混，唯有「道」撥亂歸正，使天地萬物秩序井然。顯然，劉氏的虛實美學首要在於掌握空間布局，尋找筆劃線條的律動，表現出書法內在的平衡美。

虛空本無物，唯借線條、墨跡相襯，造就劉氏書法如千年磐石、萬里山巒般的靜態美。然而，「黑老虎」系列的作品並不自限於書法元素一收一放的對立，更力求以虛御實、化虛為實的意趣，創造層次豐富，讓人可親可遊可思的意境。書面上，虛空並非白茫茫的清靜世間，反而是墨光瑩潤的山水境地。

1 本文曾發表於劉澤光編，《虛實相生：劉澤光黑老虎書法》，（香港：香港浸會大學視覺藝術院，2009年），頁24-27。

留白處儘管少之又少，卻益發顯得字體閒散疏落，直是散髮弄扁舟，世事不縈懷抱的山人。是次展出「《三國演義》卷首語」（展品 131）的四聯立軸便是其中一例。是篇布局黑多白少，黑處幾近密不透風，白處卻又疏宕得如落木肅肅。劉氏以黑御白，使得全局黑白錯落有致，而字體更見方潤，棱角圓轉，線條稚拙平整。有意無意間留白處卻又逸出筆劃的規矩，看似石碑隨年月增長而留下的殘跡蝕痕，盡得天然野趣。由此平面的書法藝術融合了時間的元素在其中，不難想象筆墨騰舞雖緩，卻又往往挾山河變化之勢，流露世情無常的動態。劉氏書法走筆至此，字體已經轉化為圖案似的點、線、面，譜出滄滄茫茫的樂府曲。

沉醉於筆觸墨舞虛實交映間，劉氏的創作又另開一虛實渾然相融，回歸渾沌不開一竅，而萬事俱足的境界。如以《虛》（展品 127）為題的實驗書法，正反映劉氏揮毫自由自在不礙於線條、墨點，卻又突顯文意。乍看是篇作品彷如一幅潑墨山水，崢嶸山岳自右下角隆隆崛起，信目遊走至中境，山勢卻為冥冥雲海所遮蔽，旦見遠處雲煙隨隨而上，唯有稍事休息再一鼓登山，豈料腳下涼沁沁的，低頭又見潺潺泉水湲湲流過。細觀通篇似虛還實、濃淡調和，倒似是人跡荒絕的仙人山居。登臨遠眺，才發覺雲海杳然間原來有一個「虛」字在（留白的空間隱約形成了「虛」字的草書筆劃）。《説文解字》謂「虛」作大山解，而劉氏正以淋漓的墨色、流動的線條點染出文字的「玄虛」。這是抽象寫意的書法，也是接近中國山水畫的具象書法。亦虛亦實，書法回歸到單純講究筆墨的表現力，開拓了一片自由的想像天地，大抵也就是渾沌怡然自得的所在罷。

劉氏拋開線條、墨跡的規矩，以書為畫開拓了書法的新領域。得魚忘荃，他進一步不以傳統書法工具入書，追尋所謂「書法」、「書寫」之意何在。《空》（展品　128）是劉氏另一創新的實驗書法。是作取篆書「空」字的寫法，以暢快淋漓的筆墨在雪紡表面上潑出那觸不著、摸不透的空明。墨舞佻達達的在雪紡輕透的物料上圓轉流瀉，有如風馳雨驟的南國山水，奇雄卻又不失空靈。作品鑲成屏風式，配上材質粗獷的框架及腳座，亭亭而立。光線輕透雪紡書面，與四周事物交映出虛虛實實的空空世間。觀眾隔紗觀字彷如霧裡看花，一切疑幻似真，直指「空」的本義 — 世事空花夢一場，捕風捉影何為?

由平面而立體，從紙張筆墨到組件裝置，劉氏虛實相生的美學也引申到以書意為實、章法規矩、甚或書寫工具皆虛的境地。他的書法雕塑《山深杳杳》（展品5）、「川流不息」（展品4）以玻璃、木材將「山」、「川」二字入書，並置成立體對聯狀。有趣的是，山勢安固，所用的媒材竟是流動感強的玻璃；水周流不止，卻以堅實的木材為書。「山深杳杳」唯見磨砂玻璃溶濛、透光玻璃瑩徹，交映出山色一片澄靜。極目遠眺，層巒起伏如創物主的手掌般卷舒自如。山脈逶迤正以媒材為筆為紙，用行書書意描寫出「山野」悠然自得之趣。而「川流不息」則以花梨木為紙、雕刻刀作筆，按木材的天然紋理、色質疏理出流水滾滾的「川」字。天然、人工巧合，激發水流湍慄，波濤涌動，大有書法線條起伏的節奏、墨色層次的明快。一山一水跳脱傳統書法的形式，以意御「筆」表現山光水色，也隱含仁者樂山之寧定、智者好水之奔流的對比，大大豐富了觀賞作品的層次。物非物，書非書，卻見書法窮極變化而象由心生，留下渾沌撲拙的翻滾痕跡。

究竟何謂書法？傳統筆墨技藝固然是書法的一部份，但觸物生情，委情於文字書寫，書法意韻顯然不盡在筆墨，而在作者胸懷妙思。那末，書寫意韻又何處可尋？從是次展覽的作品觀之，書法創造了形式美，也傳達了文字的意趣、書者的心聲，顯然書寫之意在乎以美感尋求共鳴，激發弦外之音、象外之思。這就有賴觀眾的投入，使得書法作品完成於作者手中，再由觀眾的想像而重現靈光一閃、作品由無而有的剎那。為此書法必須從文字入手，利用展場資料或圖錄的題識，拉近觀眾與書法家、作品的距離。從實而虛，觀眾得以從認字入手，欣賞文字的藝術安排，走進書者虛實相生的藝術世界，飽覽筆觸墨舞。沒有人能清楚道出渾沌身處何方，但透過題識，欣賞劉氏的書法，一步一步走入既實亦虛的筆墨境界，説不定可以超脱七竅感官，以心傳心與渾沌神交於文字之間。

From Black Tigers to Black-Tiger Calligraphy[1]

Daniel Chak-kwong Lau
Assistant Professor
Hong Kong Baptist University

Black Tigers

Hei laohu (黑老虎), or "black tigers", is a jargon commonly adopted by connoisseurs as Chinese ink rubbings. A rubbing is "a reproduction of the texture of an incised or sculptured surface, created by laying paper or similar material over it and rubbing with crayon, wax, chalk, graphite or various forms of blotted and rolled ink" (Fig. 1). [2] Traditional Chinese rubbings from steles and stone carvings mostly bear the uniquely eye-catching imagery of engraved strokes of the white-legend Chinese characters set off against the "black" background of a rubbing, albeit there are occasional vermilion or coloured-ink rubbings. This predominantly white-against-black appearance is the primary reason for the common adoption of the name "black tigers" for Chinese ink rubbings (Fig. 2). Meanwhile, the connoisseurship of these cultural and historical objects, which takes account of such specialized issues as dating and determination of the quality of different versions of rubbings from the same original stone carving, is considered one of the most complicated and difficult tasks for experts because of the existence of thousands of "fake" rubbings masqueraded as ancient originals.[3] This is exactly the second reason for the prevailing adoption of the lingo "black tigers", which seemingly accentuates its inherently incisive warning tone, as Peter Lam insightfully notes: "they are considered to be as unpredictable and 'ferocious' as tigers — and many a collector has sustained a painful bite from a carefully crafted fake."[4]

The Centrality of Stone Carvings and Ink Rubbings in Chinese Culture and History

Chinese ink rubbings are invaluable cultural relics that document mostly public records of great historical, social, political, cultural and religious significance. For instance, the *Stone Slabs Canon of Filial Piety* (石台孝經), engraved in the 4th year of Emperor Xuanzong's (玄宗) reign (745C.E.) of the Tang Dynasty (618-907), is a public monument that incurs great political and cultural implications (Fig. 3). More than only a literary piece, this work of calligraphy was rendered, prefaced and annotated by Emperor Xuanzong. Explicating the Confucian virtue of filial piety, the literary content of this work gives an account of the conversation between Confucius and his disciple Zeng Shen (曾參). The *Canon* was executed in the emperors' handsome and luxuriant penmanship in clerical script. Engraved on four stone blocks that originally appeared in public, the *Canon* not only serves the purpose of showcasing the emperor's calligraphic talents but also deceptively presents the emperor as a role model who follows the teaching of Confucius.

Beyond the boundary of imperial household, Confucianism has been profoundly ingrained in every walk of life in traditional Chinese culture and customs. This can be illustrated by *Stone Tablet of*

1 A version of this essay was published in: Daniel C.K. Lau ed. *The Void-Solid Reciprocity: Black-Tiger Calligraphy by Daniel C.K. Lau*. Hong Kong: Academy of Visual Arts, Hong Kong Baptist University, 2009, pp. 28-37.

2 Peter Y. K. Lam, "Black Tigers: The Bei Shan Tang Gift of Chinese Calligraphic Rubbings to the Art Museum, The Chinese University of Hong Kong," *Orientations*, vol. 38, no. 7, Oct 2007, pp. 81-87. Peter Lam also presents in this publication a comparison between the Chinese traditional rubbing techniques and the Western ones.

3 For connoisseurship of Chinese rubbings, see for example Fang Rou (方若), *Jiaobei Suibi* (校碑隨筆) (Shanghai: Huazhang shuju華璋書局, 1923) and Wang Zhuanghong (王壯弘), *Zengbu Jiaobei suibi* (增補校碑隨筆) (Shanghai: Shanghai shuhua上海書畫, 1981).

4 Lam, p. 82. For the adoption of the term "black tigers", see also Kenneth Starr, *Black Tigers* (Seattle and London: University of Washington Press, 2008), p. 50. Wang Chi-chen uses a different term "ink tigers" in *Reproductions of Chinese Rubbings Taken from Inscriptions Cut in Stone, Wood, and Also from Bronzes, Monuments and Other Bas-reliefs* (NewYork: Huxley House, 1938). Interpretations of "black tigers" and "ink tigers" also comes from scholars and collectors in Hong Kong and Mainland China as well as specialists at such institutions as the Xi'an Beilin (Forest of Steles) in Xi'an, the Palace Museum in Beijing and the National Palace Museum in Taipei.

Yan Family Shrine (顏氏家廟碑, 780 C.E.), an important work of calligraphy by Yan Zhenqing (顏真卿) who is well known as a righteous official of Tang Dynasty (Fig. 4). Rendered in his mature style of calligraphy, which is characterized by the articulate and powerful brushwork and tinged with an extraordinary sense of upright air, this work presents a verbal content that documents the official careers of Yan's ancestors and his clan. Parallel to the idea of filial piety in the aforementioned *Canon*, Yan's accentuation of family glory through a public work of calligraphy bespeaks not only a strong Confucian overtone that emphasizes familial continuity but also the underlying patriarchal value and the social phenomenon of male dominance in traditional China. The two stone carvings discussed above represent two quintessential examples among thousands of similar works that mark the significance of stone carvings and ink rubbings in Chinese culture and history. Hence, it is not surprising that Peter Lam asserts that "no civilization has been as consistent as Chinese in utilizing carved stone inscriptions as a means of preserving record of history and culture."[5]

Bei (碑) & *Tie* (帖)

More than only historical and cultural relics, ink rubbings are well known for their distinctive function as transmitters of ancient calligraphic art. Taking the role of preserving and circulating important works of calligraphy through the ages, rubbings have been one of the major sources of inspiration for Chinese artists in both traditional society and the contemporary world. However, most people do not have an idea that the concept of the ink rubbing is not exactly equivalent to the commonly used Chinese term *beitie* (碑帖). In fact, bei and tie refer to two different schools or traditions in both artistic and scholarly pursuits.

Literally, *bei* means stone tablet or stele with monumental inscriptions. In a broader sense, it also refers to the calligraphic inscriptions engraved on other stones and specific sites in landscapes like cliffs.[6] Usually, seal (篆書), clerical (隸書) and standard (楷書) are the predominant types of script used for such epigraphic purposes.[7] As early as the Qin (221-207 B.C.) and Han (206 B.C.-220 A.D.) dynasties, aesthetic attention has been focusing on the *beike shufa* 碑刻書法 (calligraphy engraved on steles), although the original purpose of establishing steles was a political one, commemorating and legitimising the imperial authority.[8] These early calligraphic works are widely known and relatively well preserved in the form of rubbings.[9]

As for *tie*, it refers to the small pieces of handwritten works on paper and silk which were mostly personal letters or notes by eminent people and calligraphers. Originally, the writers of *tie* merely wrote some short paragraphs for trivial functions, and they probably did not mean to create works of calligraphy. Therefore, the cursive script and the semi-cursive script were being widely used for such casual purposes of writing.[10] It was not until the Six dynasties period that more and more people began to attach importance to the aesthetic value of these small pieces of writing. Consequently, the bei, or epigraphical calligraphy of the Qin and Han dynasty, was no longer the sole orthodoxy.[11]

There is a secondary or extended definition for *tie* in the later era. It refers to a compilation of duplicates of the celebrated works of the great masters that were adopted as models for learners to follow. Hence, tie has also been known as *fatie* 法帖 (model calligraphy or writings)[12] over a long period of time even until now.[13] In view of the distinctive difference between *bei* and *tie*, *tiexue* 帖學 (school based on *tie*) and *beixue* 碑學 (school based on *bei*) are treated as two completely different calligraphic traditions which prevailed independently and also coexisted throughout different phases in the history of calligraphy.[14]

5 Ibid.

6 For an in-depth and insightful study on ancient stone inscriptions amongst Chinese landscapes, see Robert Harrist, *The Landscape of Words: Stone Inscriptions from Early and Medieval China* (Seattle and London: The University of Washington Press, 2008)

7 Ledderose, p. 11.

8 Lothar Ledderose offers some early examples of *bei*. "The earliest known examples are the stones erected between 219 B.C. and 210 B.C. by Ch'in Shih-huang-ti [Qin Shihuangdi秦始皇帝] to commemorate his unification of the empire." (Lothar Ledderose, *Mi Fu and the Classical Tradition of Chinese Calligraphy* (Princeton: Princeton University Press, 1979), p. 11.)

9 ibid.

10 bid., pp. 10-11.

11 Ibid., p. 10.

12 Tseng Yuho provides a definition for *fatie*: '"*fa*" [法] means "law" or "method," and *t'ieh* [*tie*] is an inscribed sheet. *Fa-t'ieh* [*fatie*] is understood to be a facsimile copy of a calligraphic masterpiece that is used by students as a model.' (Tseng Yuho, *A History of Chinese Calligraphy* (Hong Kong: The Chinese University Press, 1993), p. 196.)

13 As early as the Song dynasty (960-1279), the term "*fatie*" was already in use. A Song literati-scholar, Qin Guan 秦觀 wrote, "...during the reign of [Song] Emperor Taizong, special officials were ordered to collect and make copies of the works of calligraphy of the previous dynasties. Such calligraphic works are engraved in woodblock [which are eventually for the sake of reproduction]. These subsequent duplicates formed a compilation of ten *juans* ... (a copy of such duplicates were bestowed as an honor upon individual high ranking official). Such duplicates are known as *fatie*" 法帖者，太宗皇帝時，遣使購摹前代法書，集為十卷，刻於木版，藏之業中，大臣初登二府者，詔以一本賜之，其後不復賜，世號法帖。" (Qin Guan, *Fatie tongjie* 法帖通解, in *Fatie kao*法帖考 (Textual Study on Model Calligraphy) (Taipei: Shijie shuju世界書局, 1962), p. 1.

14 My discussion of *bei* and *tie* in this section is primarily based on Chapter One of my M.Phil. thesis "A Study of Kang Youwei's (1858-1927) *Guang yizhou shuangji*" (The University of Hong Kong, 2000) with minor changes. For a study of the contrast of *beixue* and *tiexue* traditions, see the same chapter in this thesis.

The Embodiment of The Void – Solid Reciprocity in Black-Tiger Calligraphy

The age-old traditional Chinese ink-rubbing techniques can also be applied to the production of works of calligraphy in modern era. The visual effect of the mottled, heavy and raw texture of rubbings from stones and natural sites gradually becomes an inspiration for many modern calligraphers like Luo Shuzhong(羅叔重), Luo Xiaoshan(駱曉山) and myself. In the application of the ink-rubbing form to calligraphic skill, I develop my black-tiger calligraphy by combining techniques of traditional calligraphy, seal-engraving and rubbing. I have been experimenting with my self-taught dry-brush inking techniques that apply to different material including different types of raw rice paper and fabric to produce the visual effect that mimics the archaic and austere style of calligraphy engraved on ancient stones and steles (cat. no. 132). I endeavour to relive and capture the so-called *jinshi qi* (金石氣), or "metal and stone aura", yet at the same time create visually refreshing imageries that express contemporarythoughts and personal aspirations.

My black-tiger calligraphy is characterized by its overall approach to the interplay between black and white on the one hand, and positive and negative spaces on the other, attempting to achieve the age-old notion of "void-solid reciprocity" as evident in my new experimentation in the intriguingly illusionist effect of alternating positive (black) and negative (white) legends (cat. no. 121 and 122). There have been various theories on "void-solid reciprocity" in traditional Chinese aesthetics. Perhaps one of its early origins can be traced back to the concept of "*yin-yang*" in ancient Chinese philosophies. According to the Chinese dictionary *Cihai* (辭海), *yin* and *yang* originally referred to the directions of facing or away from sunshine, of which "facing the sun" is *yang*, and "away from the sun" is *yin*. Later these terms were borrowed by thinkers to explain the prevalence of dualities in the nature and their contradictory-complementary relationship. In *I-Ching* 易經 (The Book of Changes), there is a saying that "one *yin* and one *yang* constitute what is called *Dao* (the way of the universe, or Oneness)"[15]. Branching off from this is a dialectic system of thought about unified dualities like *yin-yang* (negative-positive) and *xu-shi* (void-solid). Under the influence of such traditional philosophies about the union between *yin* and *yang*, the aesthetic theory of "void-solid reciprocity" is developed.

The duality of the void-solid notion has been deeply embedded in a wide spectrum of interconnected forms, ranging from painting, calligraphy, ceramics, sculpture, architecture, gardening and handicraft, in the prolonged visual culture in Chinese history. Moreover, various Chinese artistic treatises repeatedly emphasize that "void" and "solid" are symbiotic and mutually reinforcing. The ultimate goal of the artist is to achieve a spirit of equilibrium as conveyed by the balance among such elements as positive and negative spaces, line, texture, colour, shape and form. This is well exemplified by the courtyard in Hanzhong Municipal Museum (漢中博物館) (Fig. 5). Expressed in a naturally harmonious architectural language, every manmade structure and natural element interacts with each other to form a tranquil and self-sustaining realm, while the spirit of unity is further reinforced by the geometric wooden frame of the entrance. When walking through the wooden frame and entering into the courtyard, one can without doubt experience the omnipresent idea of void-solid reciprocity which is intrinsically conveyed through the balance between symmetrical and asymmetrical, organic and inorganic, circle and square – as symbolic representations of heaven and earth, light and shadow, and most fundamentally *yin* and *yang*.

The relatively abstract relationship within the aforementioned intriguing void-solid inter-complementation can be more easily understood in the openwork of a nineteenth-century wooden window frame from Jiangxi Province (Fig. 6). Formed by different parts of the bodies of two mythological animals, an interweaving net-like imagery vividly emphasizes the contrast between the positive shapes, the negative blank spaces are in fact carefully-designed shapes that accentuate the sense of fluidity circulating throughout the whole panel. This engenders an extraordinary degree of vitality that efficaciously captures a whimsical moment in a work that seemingly intends to express a timeless auspicious omen. Undeniably, the captivatingly subtle imagery together with the extremely high level of craftsmanship of this woodcarving by an anonymous artisan is the main subject of appreciation, yet more importantly, one should also pay attention to the less noticeable "cloaked expression" of the intra-penetration between the positive and negative spaces which is exactly an inadvertent visual effect that lucratively communicates the whole idea of void-solid reciprocity.

Although the Chinese reiteration of the artistic conception of void-solid reciprocity in both the prolonged

15 *Zhouyi benyi* 周易本義 (*The Original Meaning of I-Ching*), *Sikuquanshu*四庫全書, *juan* 3, 5a.

multi-faceted visual culture and the rich corpus of literature has not been matched by a similar degree of echo in the Western world, the obvious idea of unity of balance between void and solid can be frequently observed in works of art and historical or religious relics. For instance, the rubbing from a brass engraving housed in All Hallows-by-the-Tower (an ancient Anglican church previously dedicated to St. Mary the Virgin, and located in present day Byward Street in the City of London, overlooking the Tower of London) also perspicaciously transmits a sense of balance between positive and negative lines and spaces that is comparable to the Chinese ideal of void-solid reciprocity (Fig. 7). At first glance, the enchanting expression of the graceful cascade of drapery is brought out by the subtly rich variations in intaglio lines. However, when taking a closer look, one would be amazed at the wonderful sense of design, designating the positive spaces among the intaglio (i.e. negative) lines. In a sense, the universal artistic conception of void-solid reciprocity is ubiquitously embodied in this Western religious work.

In the domain of Chinese calligraphy, the concept of "*xu-shi*" can be understood on three dimensions. The first one refers to the mechanical relationship between the fingers and the palm and that between the arm and the wrist. Once the early Qing calligrapher Song Cao宋曹 (1620-1701) wrote, "there are voidness and solidity in the movement of the brush."[16] What it means is the varied methods of grasping and moving the brush. The second dimension refers to the execution of the strokes. The late Qing calligrapher Zhu Hegeng 朱和羹 (1795-1850) has a detailed explicction on this:

> It is a treasure to see both voidness and solidity in semi-cursive and cursive scripts. If the brushstroke is not void, it would lack fluidity. If it is not solid, it would not be steady enough. Merely using void strokes would lead to floppiness, while applying only solid strokes would result in dull appearance. Seeing both void and solid in play means letting both void and solid reciprocate. Some calligrapher has a secret tip: one's calligraphy is wonderful for it can combine various masters' styles, inspired for it can distinguish itself from the masters. Between combination and separation is where the work becomes both wonderful and inspired. This is when the arrangement of the void and the solidis just right.[17]

The third meaning is to take brush strokes as *shi* (solid) and blank space as *xu* (void) on the dimension of character structure and compositional strategy. Bao Shichen 包世臣 (1775-1855) states that "in the centre of a character there can be solid strokes or empty space"[18]. He assumes each character to be a square, divides the square into nine smaller squares, and takes the central square as the focus of the character's essence. He argues that both the brushstrokes and the blank space can be the essence of a character. In this sense the meaning of *xu-shi* (void-solid) is interrelated with the idea of "*jibai danghei*" (計白當黑), or designating the white space when applying the black ink.

The theory of "*jibai danghei*" originated from the calligraphy master Deng Shiru 鄧石如 (1743-1805): "The sparse areas between the strokes can allow a horse to gallop through, and the densely written areas can block the wind. The wonder of the calligraphy manifests as one designates the white space when applying the black ink."[19] Whenever one practises calligraphy or carve seals, one must pay attention to the densely written character and strokes (solid) as well as to the sparse areas (void) between strokes, characters and lines. The relationship between brushstrokes and the composition of the artwork must be well arranged to achieve a harmony that conveys the spirit of "void-solid reciprocity". There is a common notion that Chinese calligraphy and Chinese painting have the same origin. Therefore the discourses on "void-solid reciprocity" in theories of Chinese painting share similarity with those in theories of Chinese calligraphy. Painter Da Chongguang 笪重光 (1623-1692) of Qing Dynasty writes in his painting treatise that, "when the positions of the objects are in conflict, the painted areas are mainly redundancy; when the void and solid elements are in reciprocity, even the non-painted areas become a marvellous realm."[20] Wang Hui 王翬 (1632-1717) and Yun Shouping 惲壽平 (1633-1690) elaborate on Da's comment that, "people know that the painted areas are painting, but they do not know the white space is also painting. The blank space of a painting is the crux of the whole picture. This is the method of 'void-solid reciprocity'. Most people neglect the blank spaces, but it is exactly the voidness in the whole picture that makes it a marvellous realm."[21] Qing painter and calligrapher Jiang He 蔣和 also remarks

16 Song Cao. *Shufa yueyan*書法約言 (*Calligraphy Rules*), in Wang, Ren & Hu (ed.), *Shuxue jicheng: Qing*, Hebei: Hebei meishu chubanshe河北美術出版社, 2002, p. 2.
17 Zhu, Hegeng. *Linchi xinjie* (*The Insight in Calligraphic Practice*), in Wang, Ren & Hu (ed.), *Shuxue jicheng: Qing*, Hebei: Hebei meishu chubanshe, 2002, p.499.
18 Bao, Shichen. Yizhou shuangji 藝舟雙揖 (*The Two Oars for the Boat of Art*), in Wang, Ren & Hu (ed.), *Shuxue jicheng: Qing*, Hebei: Hebei meishu chubanshe, 2002, p.412.
19 ibid, p.406.
20 Da, Chongguang. *Huaquan*畫筌 (*Interpretation of Paintings*), in Lu (ed.) *Zhongguo shufa quanshu*, vol.8, Shanghai: Shanghai shuhua chubanshe上海書畫出版社, 1993-, p.694.
21 ibid, p. 694.

in his *Miscellaneous Essays on Learning to Paint* that, "space should alternate with density in the arrangement of trees and rocks (objects). In this way the void and the solid are in reciprocity, and this is the wisdom of painting."[22] From these, we can see that *xu* (void) and *shi* (solid) are equally important in the composition of Chinese calligraphy and painting. The elements must be appropriately distributed, so that *yin* and *yang* blend with each other, for the artworks to attain the *Dao* of the aesthetics of "void-solid reciprocity".

Going beyond the domain of traditional calligraphy, I extend my repertoire of the obvious contrast between the clear white brushstroke and the black background, and boldly wander into a new horizon where more spontaneous brush-and-ink relationship and effect are explored in such speedy and relatively more fluid brushwork in such works as *Emptiness*, *Void* and *One Who Has Experienced the Ocean Thinks Nothing of Mere Rivers* (cat. no. 128, 127 and 129). However, I do not draw a clear line between the relatively more abstract expression of "splash-ink" brushwork and the artistic conception of the ancients. This is especially evident in *Emptiness* where the round and forceful brushstrokes of the Chinese character *kong* (空), or "emptiness", which is vaguely suggested bu the rough blank (white) spaces, are inspired by the exact same character *kong* in the stone inscription of the Tomb of the Han General Huo Qubing (霍去病墓) in Xi'an, Shaanxi Province (Fig. 8 & 9).

Last but not least, my experimental calligraphy newly encompasses three-dimensional objects (cat. no. 4 and 5) through which I explore the spatial relationship between the void and the solid. Appearing in the form of a wooden sculpture, the theme of *An Endless Stream* is reinforced by not only the gracefully curvilinear lines and the glossy and intertwining architectonic forms but also the cascading and even free-flowing linesoriginally and naturally appearing on the precious and enchanting *huanghuali* (黃花梨), or yellow rose wood. Taking a closer look, one can easily discover that the three diagonal protuberances are actually intended to mimic the three downward strokes of the simple Chinese character chuan (川), or "stream", rendering this piece a truly experimental calligraphy without using brush and ink. I believe that calligraphy is not restricted to the brush and ink effects on a two-dimensional plane. This is exactly why I introduce my unique approach to a new hybrid artistic mode of calligraphic installation (cat. no. 140 and 22), which is highly effective in expressing multiple concepts and ideas prevalent in contemporary situations and occurrences.

22 Jiang, He. *Xuehua zalun*學畫雜論 (*Miscellaneous Essays on Painting*), in Lu (ed.) *Zhongguo shufa quanshu*, vol.8, Shanghai: Shanghai shuhua chubanshe, 1993-, p. 960.

From Black Tigers to Black-Tiger Calligraphy (Fig.1-9)

Fig. 1 An artisan making an ink rubbing at the Beilin (Forest of Steles) Museum, Xi'an, Shaanxi province. Photography by Daniel C. K. Lau

Fig. 2 The display of the original stone carving of the two Chinese characters *shi men* 石門 ("Stone Gate") and the ink rubbing from it in Hanzhong Municipal Museum (漢中博物館). Photography by Daniel C. K. Lau

Fig. 3 *Slabs Canon of Filial Piety*(石台孝經). Beilin (Forest of Steles) Museum, Xi'an, Shaanxi province. Photography by Daniel C. K. Lau

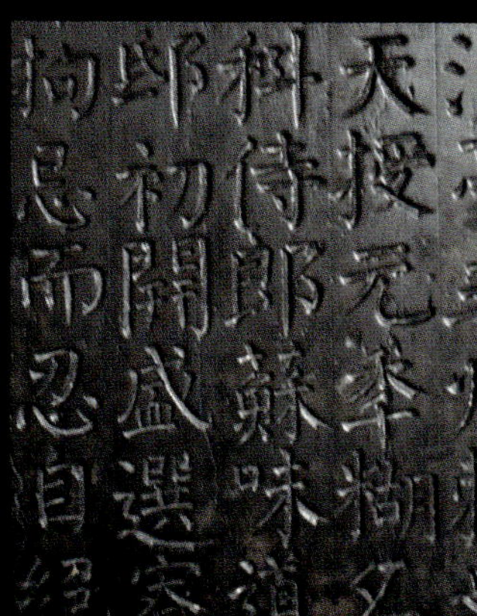

Fig. 4 Detail of Stone Tablet of Yan Family Shrine (顔氏家廟碑), Beili, 780 C.E.), Beilin (Forest of Steles) Museum, Xi'an, Shaanxi province. Photography by Daniel C. K. Lau

Fig. 5 The courtyard in Hanzhong Municipal Museum. Photography by Daniel C. K. Lau

Fig. 6 Detail of the openwork of nineteenth-century wooden window frame from Jiangxi Province. (Collection of Daniel C. K. Lau)¬

Fig. 7 Rubbing from a brass engraving housed in All Hallows-by-the-Tower, London. Photography by Daniel C. K. Lau

Fig. 8 The three characters *zuo si kong*(左司空)in the stone inscription of the Tomb of the Han General Huo Qubing in Xi'an, Shaanxi Province. Photography by Daniel C. K. Lau

Fig. 9 Detail of the rubbing from the stone inscription of the Tomb of the Han General Huo Qubing in Xi'an, Shaanxi Province. Photography by Daniel C. K. Lau

121 *Void-Solid Reciprocity* I
虛實相生

Alternating positive and negative legends
(虛實文相間)
Ink on paper, hanging scroll
94 x 87 cm
2009

紙本墨書，立軸
94 x 87厘米
2009年

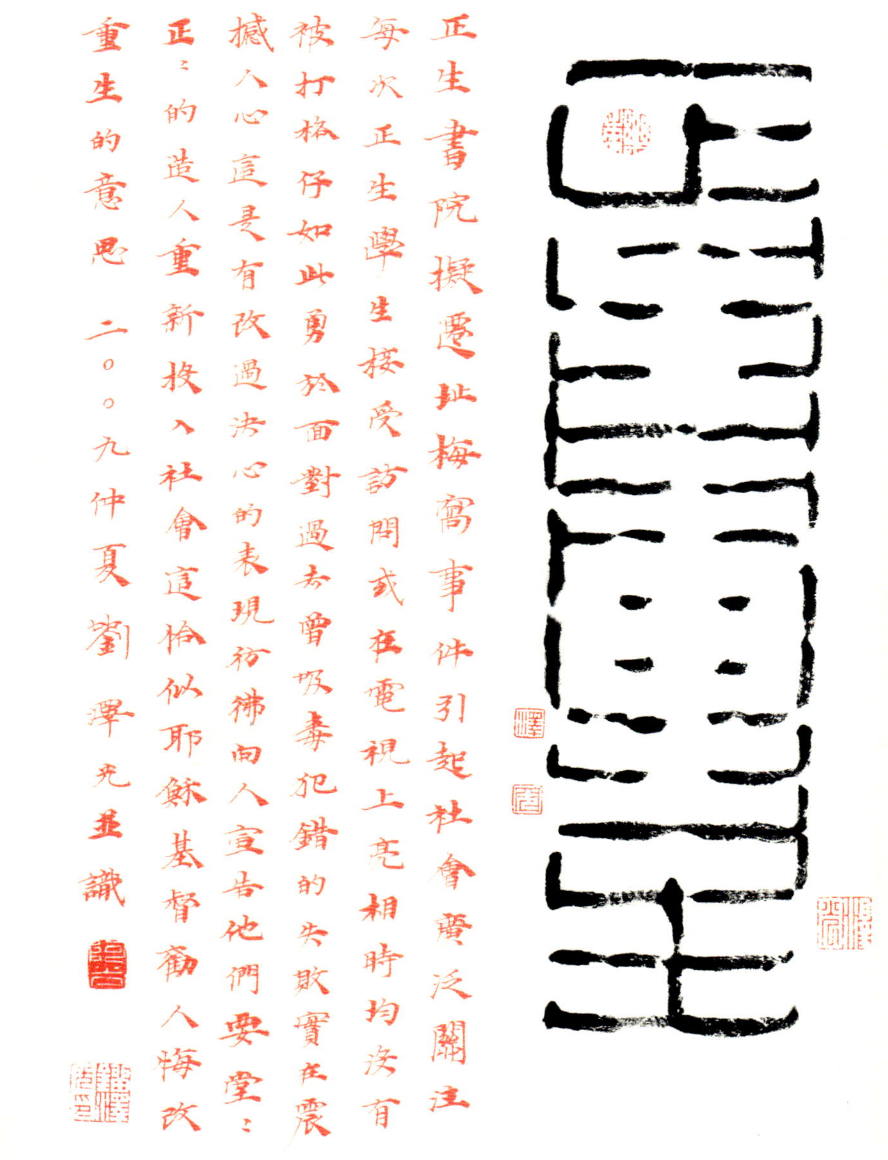

122 *Life Reborn* | 正生重生

Alternating positive and negative legends (虛實文相間)
Ink on paper, mounted and framed
42 x 30 cm
2009

紙本墨書，裱框
42 x 30厘米
2009年

Artist's inscription:
"The relocation of Christian Zheng Sheng College in Mui Wo has been widely concerned in the society. Every time when students of Zheng Sheng are interviewed or appear on television, their faces are never covered with digital mosaic. Their courage to face their drug-taking and wrong-doing past is really striking. This is an indication of their determination to repent and correct, as if they are telling everybody that they are ready to start anew in the society and live with dignity. It is similar to the Christ's encouraging people to repent and be 'reborn'."

題識：
"正生書院擬遷址梅窩事件引起社會廣泛關注。每次正生學生接受訪問或在電視上亮相時，均沒有被「打格仔」。如此勇於面對過去曾吸毒犯錯的失敗，實在震撼人心。這是有改過決心的表現，彷彿向人宣告他們要堂堂正正的做人，重新投入社會。這恰似耶穌基督勸人悔改「重生」的意思。"

123 *Entering the Past, Exiting the Present* I
入古出今

Imitation of rubbing from
stone carving in clerical script
Ink on paper, mounted and framed
33 x 26 cm
2009

墨拓書法・隸書
紙本水墨，裱框
33 x 26厘米
2009年

澤光

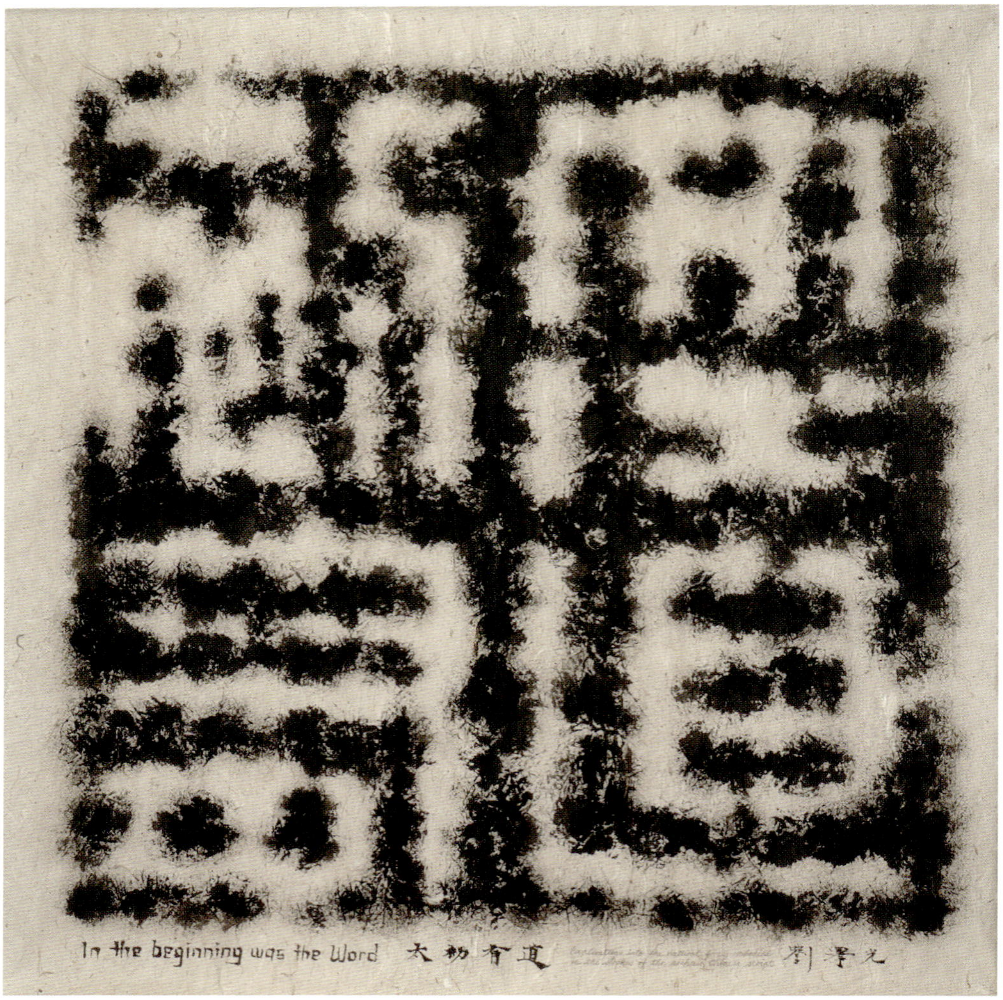
In the beginning was the Word 太初有道

124 *In the Beginning Was the Word* | 太初有道

Imitation of rubbing from
stone carving in clerical script
Ink on paper, mounted on wooden frame
69 x 68 cm
2006

墨拓書法•隸書
紙本水墨，裱框
69 x 68厘米
2006年

力有道
Explorations into the natural forces embodied
in the strokes of the archaic Chinese script
劉澤光

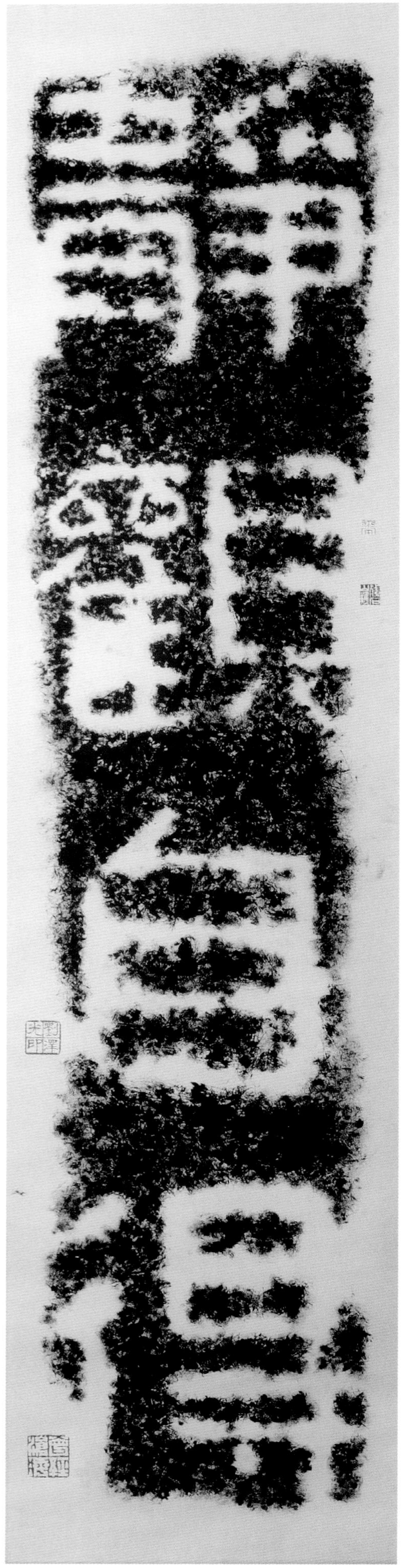

125 *Contentment in Quiet Contemplation* | 靜觀自得

Imitation of rubbing from
stone carving in clerical script
Ink on paper, hanging scroll
225 x 57.5 cm
2007

墨拓書法•隸書
紙本水墨，立軸
225 x 57.5厘米
2007年

126 ***Void and White*** |
虛白

Imitation of rubbing from
stone carving in clerical script
Ink on paper, mounted and framed
43 x 68 cm
2009

墨拓書法・隸書
紙本水墨，裱框
43 x 68厘米
2009年

127 ***Void*** | 虛

Experimental calligraphy with
the character xu (虛), "void"
Ink and water on paper
60 x 38 cm
2009

實驗書法．"虛"
紙本水墨
60 x 38厘米
2009年

128-1 ***Emptiness*** | 空

Experimental calligraphy with the chinese character kong (空), or "emptiness"
Ink and water on chiffon, mounted as a screen
201 x 101 cm
2009

實驗書法・"空"
綢本水墨，裱屏
201 x 101厘米
2009年

128-2 ***Emptiness*** | 空
Daylight | 日光
Koo Ming Kown Exhibition Gallery
Communication and Visual Arts Buliding
Hong Kong Baptist University
香港浸會大學傳理視藝大樓顧明均展覽廳

128-3 ***Emptiness*** | 空
Sunset | 黃昏
Koo Ming Kown Exhibition Gallery
Communication and Visual Arts Buliding
Hong Kong Baptist University
香港浸會大學傳理視藝大樓顧明均展覽廳

129 ***One Who Has Experienced the Ocean Thinks Nothing of Mere Rivers*** |
曾經滄海難為水

Experimental calligraphy with
the character shui (水), or "water"
Ink on paper
119 x 103cm
2009
Collection of University of Hong Kong, 2010.

實驗書法・"水"
紙本水墨
119 x 103厘米
2009年
香港大學藏，2010年

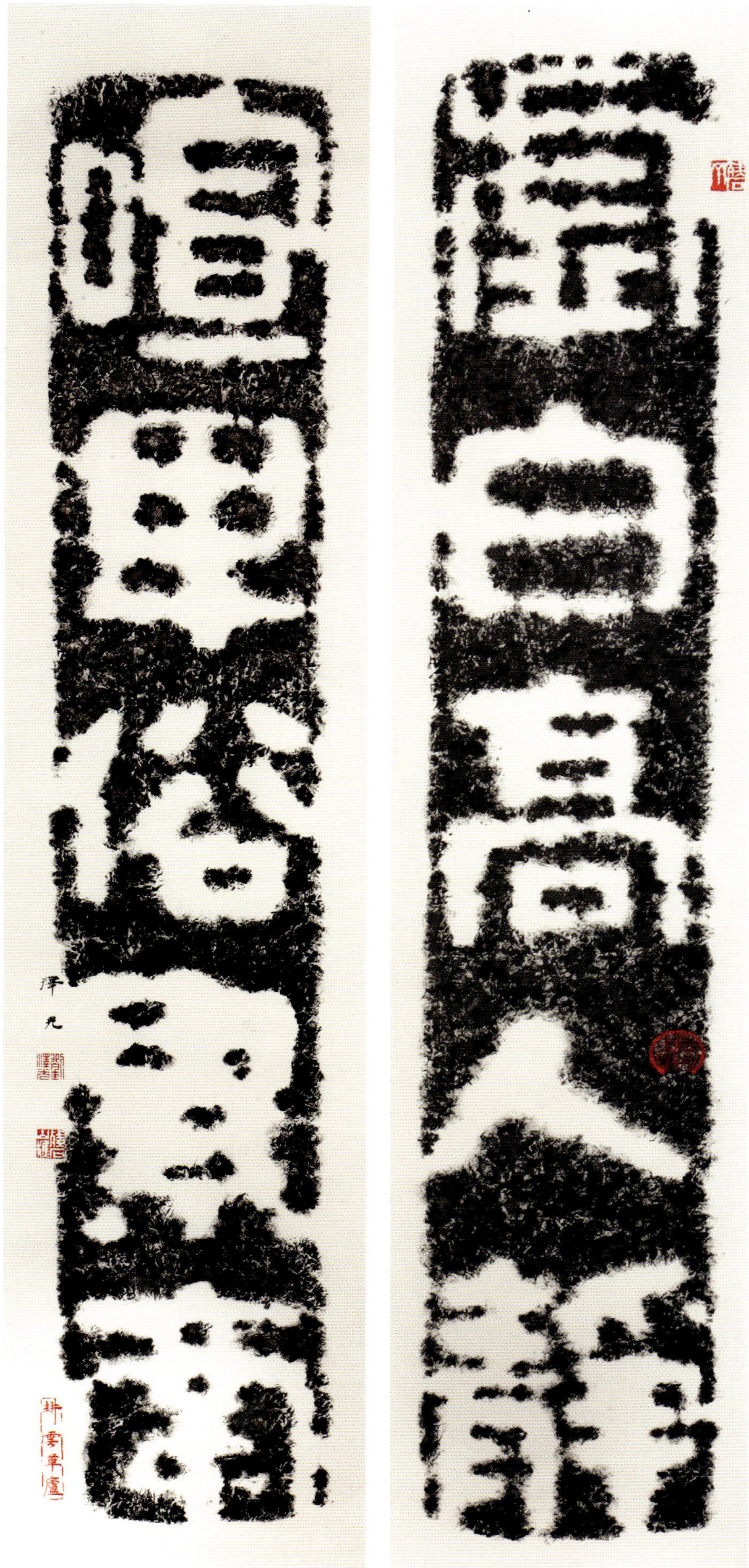

130 *Five-character-line Couplet in the Style of Stele Rubbing Imitation* I
仿石刻體五言聯

Imitation of rubbing from
stone carving in clerical script
Ink on paper, hanging scrolls
2009
135 x 35 cm
2009

墨拓書法・隸書
紙本水墨，立軸
135 x 35 厘米
2009年

Transliteration:
Being free of desire, the lofty hermit remains calm.
In the tumultuous world, one is lingered by secular concerns.
(from Tang poem "Return" of Du Fu (712-770))

釋文：
虛白高人靜
喧卑俗累牽

（唐詩 杜甫《歸》）

131 ***Prologue, Romance of the Three Kingdoms* I**

《三國演義》卷首語

Imitation of rubbing from
stone carving in clerical script
Ink on paper, hanging scrolls
A set of 4 screens, each 264 x 65 cm
1998

墨拓書法・隸書
紙本水墨，立軸四條幅
各264 x 65厘米
1998年

Transliteration:

On and on the Yangzi River rolls, racing east.
Of proud and gallant heroes its white-tops leave no trace,
As right and wrong, pride and fall turn all at once unreal.
Yet ever the green hills stay.
To blaze in the west-waning day.
Fishemans and woodsmen comb the river isles.
White-crowned, they've seen enough of spring and autumn tide
To make good company over the wine jar,
Where many a famed event,
Provides their merriment.

(Translated by Moss Roberts in *Three Kingdoms: A Historical Novel* (Abridged Edition), Berkeley: University of California Press, 1999, p.2)

Artist's inscription:

"Designating the white when applying the black, so that the sparse areas can allow a horse to gallop through, and the densely written areas can block the wind." This is the seal-engraving and calligraphy insight of Deng Shiru (sobriquet: Wanbai Shanren) (1743-1805) of the Qing Dynasty. It means that no matter we carve seals or practise calligraphy, we must pay attention to the treatment of positive and negative spaces. For example, when making white-legend seals, we should consider how we leave the untouched red spaces next to the strokes of the white-legend characters.. This is one of the principles of Chinese painting. As Wang Hui (1632-1717) and Yun Shouping (1633-1690) state in *Commentary Notes for Interpretation of Paintings*, "people know that the painted areas are painting, but they do not know the white space is also painting. The blank space of a painting is the crux of the whole picture. This is the method of 'void-solid reciprocity'. Mostly people neglect the blank spaces, but it is exactly the voidness in the whole picture that makes it a marvelous realm". Therefore Ni Zan's (1301-1374) paintings are fascinating for their likable voidness. The strategies of "blank-leaving" (*liubai*) in Chinese painting and "red-leaving" (*liuhong*) in seal-engraving are common principles of Chinese art. If one grasps this principle, his/her artwork must be of rhythmic vitality. Recent calligraphy and seal-engraving artist Luo Shuzhong (1898-1969) of Guangdong produced "black tigers", which are imitation of stele rubbings, by first outlining the strokes and dots and then filling them with ink. His works are able to achieve the blending of void (*xu*) and solid (*shi*), and his idea is in fact akin to Deng Shiru's idea of "*jibaidanghei*" (designating the white when applying the black).

I started learning calligraphy and seal-engraving at the age of seventeen, which is more than ten years from now. I am particularly fond of the cliff-side and stele inscriptions of Han (206 B.C. – A.D. 220), Wei (220-265) and Six Dynasties (222-589) for the forceful and austere spirit conveyed in the styles of these works of calligraphy. *These works include Erjing Yangliang maishan ji, Lai Zihou keshi, Daji maishandi ji, Yanguang canshi, Hengfang bei bing bei'e, Quxia song, Fuge song, Zhangqian bei, Gaojuli haodawang bei* and *Taishan Jingshiyu jingangjing*. For seal-engraving, I learnt from the seals, sealing clay, brick inscriptions and tile ends of the Warring States Period (ca.470-221 B.C.), Qin (221-206 B.C.) and Han Dynasties (206 B.C. – A.D. 220). I do not have a proper measure of myself, that now I would like to make reference to Mr. Luo Shuzhong's method of creating "black tigers", which bears the styles of the *bafen* script of Han Dynasty (206 B.C. – A.D. 220) and the stele and pottery inscriptions of the Six Dynasties (222-589), mixed together with the white-legend method of seal engraving. But Mr. Shuzhong's works are more like the "polished, black-gold" type of rubbing, whereas mine are akin to the "charcoal" type of rubbing and the "cicada-wing" type of rubbing. Not knowing whether it is good or not, I leave it to the viewers who may have their own understandings.

釋文：
滾滾長江東逝水，浪花淘盡英雄。
是非成敗轉頭空，青山依舊在，幾度夕陽紅。
白髮漁樵江渚上，慣看秋月春風。
一壺濁酒喜相逢，古今多少事，都付笑談中。

題識：
「計白以當黑，疏處可以走馬，密處不使透風」，乃清完白山人鄧石如治印與臨池心得。意謂大凡治印或臨池須注意虛實空間之處理。譬如治白文印時除了注意白文字跡的筆劃之外，還應考慮"留紅法"。中國畫論道理一也。王石谷(1632-1717)與惲正叔(1633-1690)在《畫荃評註》曰：「人但知有畫處是畫，不知無畫處皆畫，畫之空處，全局所關，即虛實相生法；人多不著眼空處，妙在通幅皆靈，故妙境也。」　是故倪高士(1301-1374)畫之引人入勝乃在於其空靈之可愛也。山水畫之"留白"與篆刻之"留紅"乃中國藝術之共通理也。苟能掌握斯理者，其作必氣韻生動。近代廣東書法篆刻家羅叔重(1898-1969)以雙鈎填墨法仿石刻製"黑老虎"[即石刻拓本]。其作能虛實溶和，其意實大類完白山人之計白當黑也。

余十七學書治印，迄今十多年矣。書法尤喜漢魏六朝蒼勁渾穆、鈍拙淳厚一類之摩崖及碑刻，若二京《楊量買山記》、《萊子侯刻石》、《大吉買山地記》、《延光殘石》、《衡方碑并碑額》、《曲狹頌》、《郙閣頌》、《張遷碑》、《晉高句麗好太王碑》及《北齊泰山經石峪金剛經等》。篆刻則學戰國秦漢璽印、封泥、磚文、瓦當。吾不自量，今欲參叔重先生製黑老虎之法，孕漢八分，鎔六朝碑銘、陶、篆刻白文法，一爐共冶。然叔重先生之作近"烏金"拓，吾作則類"煤煙"拓、"蟬翼"拓。工拙不知，惟觀者或各有會心處也。

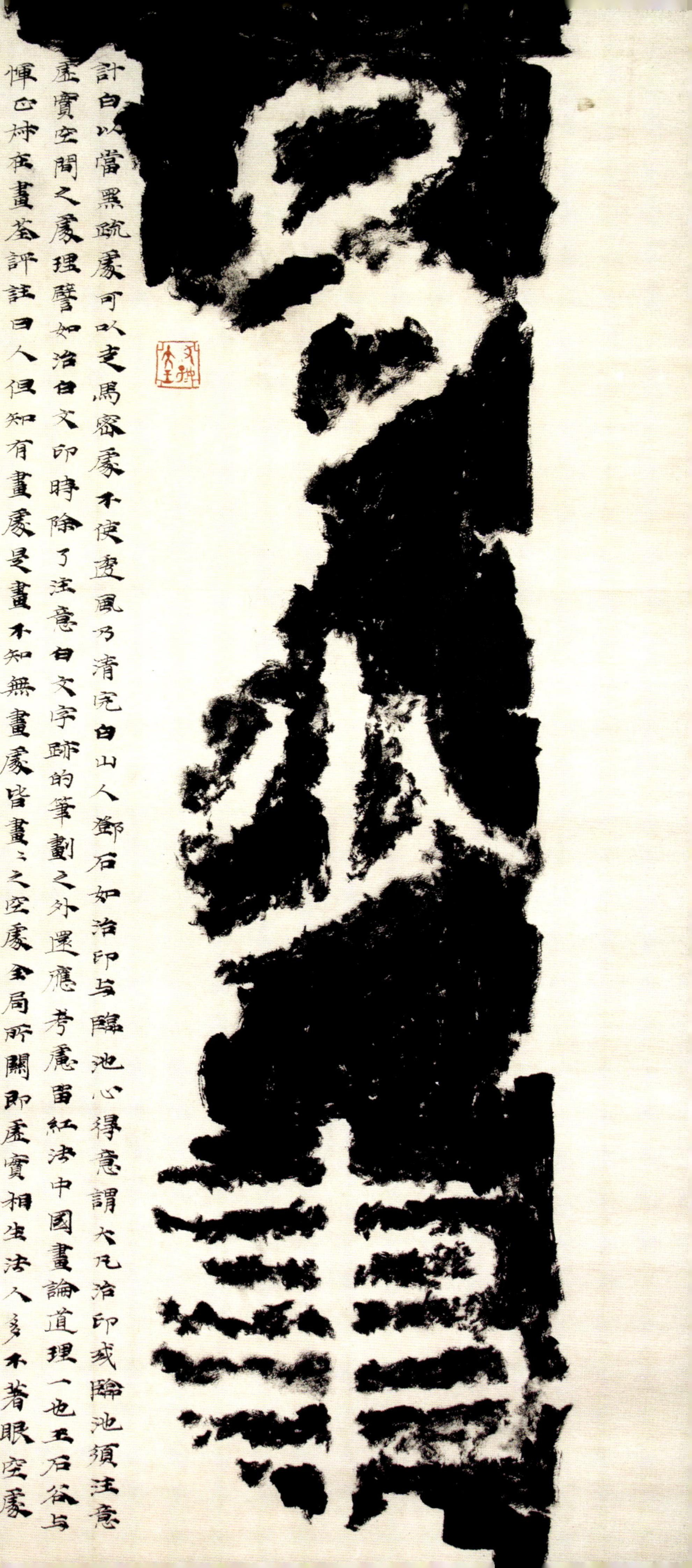

計白以當黑疏處可以走馬密處不使透風乃清完白山人鄧石如治印與臨池心得意謂大凡治印或臨池須注意虛實空間之處理譬如治白文印時除了注意白文字跡的筆劃之外還應考慮留紅法中國畫論道理一也丑石谷與惲正叔在畫荃評註曰人但知有畫處是畫不知無畫處皆畫，畫之空處全局所關即虛實相生法人多不著眼空處妙在通幅皆靈故妙境也是故倪高士畫之引人入勝乃在於其空靈之可愛也山水畫之留白與篆刻之留紅乃中國藝術之共通理也苟能掌握斯理者其作必氣韻生動近代廣東書法篆刻家羅叔重以雙鈎填墨法仿石刻製黑老虎其作能虛實溶和其意實大類完白山人之計白當黑也余十七學書治印迄今十多年矣書法尤喜漢魏六朝蒼勁渾穆鈍拙渾厚一類之摩崖及碑刻若二京楊量買山記萊子侯刻石大吉買山地記延光殘石衡方碑并碑額西狹頌鄐閣頌張遷碑晉高句麗好大王碑及北齊泰山經石峪金剛經等篆刻則學戰國秦漢鉨印封泥磚文瓦當吾不自量今欲叅叔重先生製黑老虎之法爭瀟八分鎔六朝碑銘陶篆刻白文法一爐共冶然叔重先生之作近烏金拓吾作則類煤煙拓蟬翼拓工拙不知惟觀者或各有會心處也

戊寅小寒劉澤光並識於殘石草堂

132 *The Destined Tie to Brush and Ink* | 翰墨緣

Imitation of rubbing from
stone carving in clerical script
Ink on paper, hanging scroll
96 x 43 cm
2009

墨拓書法・隸書
紙本水墨，立軸
96 x 43厘米
2009年

133 *The One and Only Way* | 不二法門

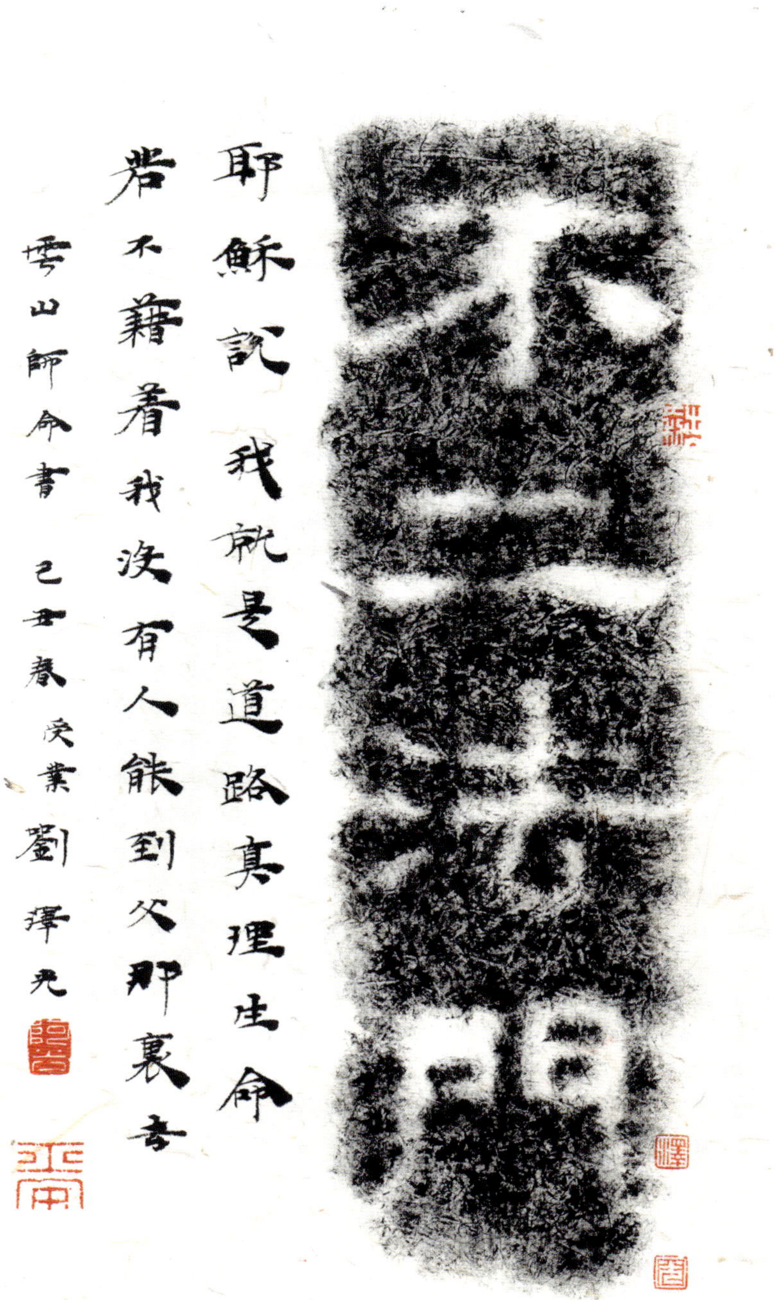

Imitation of rubbing from stone carving in clerical script
Ink on paper
mounted on wood block
48.5 x 30 cm
2009

墨拓書法・隸書
紙本水墨，立軸
48.5 x 30 厘米
2009年

Collection of Mr. Han Yunshan

Transliteration:
Jesus answered, " I am the way and the truth and the life. No one comes to the Father except through me."
(John 14:6)

釋文：
耶穌說："我就是道路真理生命。若不藉著我，沒有人能到父那裡去。"
(約翰福音 14:6)

134 *Extraordinary* | 不常

Imitation of rubbing from stone carving in clerical script
Ink on paper, mounted and framed, 21 x 14.8 cm
2009

墨拓書法・隸書
紙本水墨，裱框，21 x 14.8厘米
2009年

135 *Spiritually Attached to "Private Secretariat" Scholars* | 神交幕客

Imitation of rubbing from
stone carving in clerical script
Ink on paper, mounted on wood block
66 x 56 cm, 2008

Collection of Professor Harold Mok

墨拓書法・隸書
紙本水墨，裱於木板
66 x 56厘米，2008年
莫家良教授藏

Artist's inscription:
"Elder brother Jialiang [Harold] is conducting a research on the calligraphy of the private secretariat (*mufu*, 幕府) scholars. I casually completed this four-character work of calligraphy in the style of imitation of rubbing from stone carving [in clerical script], just want to win a knowing smile from him."

題識：
家良兄近來致力於乾嘉學人書法研究。余偶仿石刻書四字貽之，聊博一粲耳。

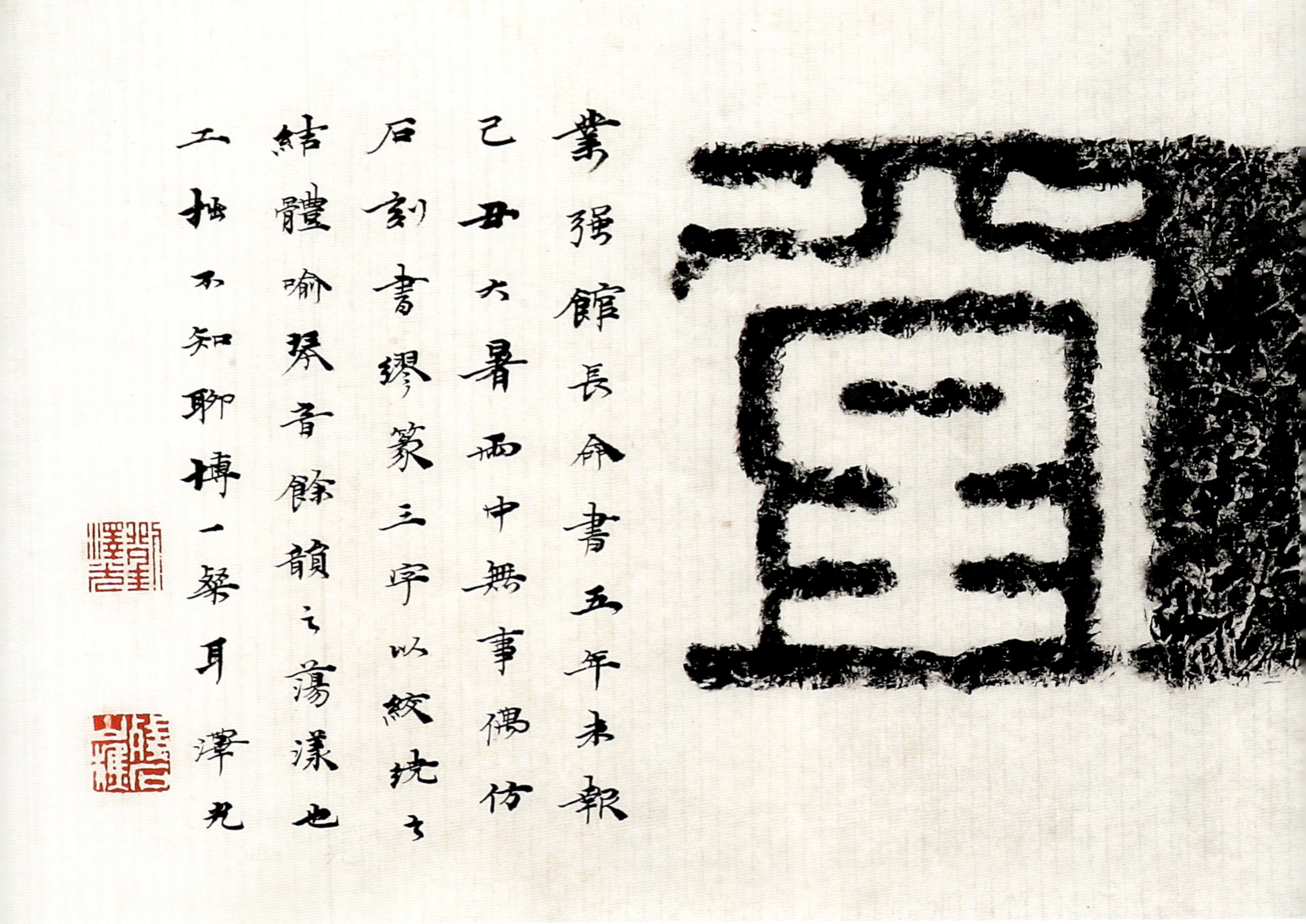

136 ***Studio of Thoughts in Zither-Playing*** |

琴思堂

Imitation of rubbing from
stone carving in clerical script
Ink on paper, mounted and framed
45 x 120 cm
2009

Collection of Mr. Peter Yip-keung Lam

墨拓書法・隸書
紙本水墨，裱框
45 x 120 厘米
2009年

林業強教授藏

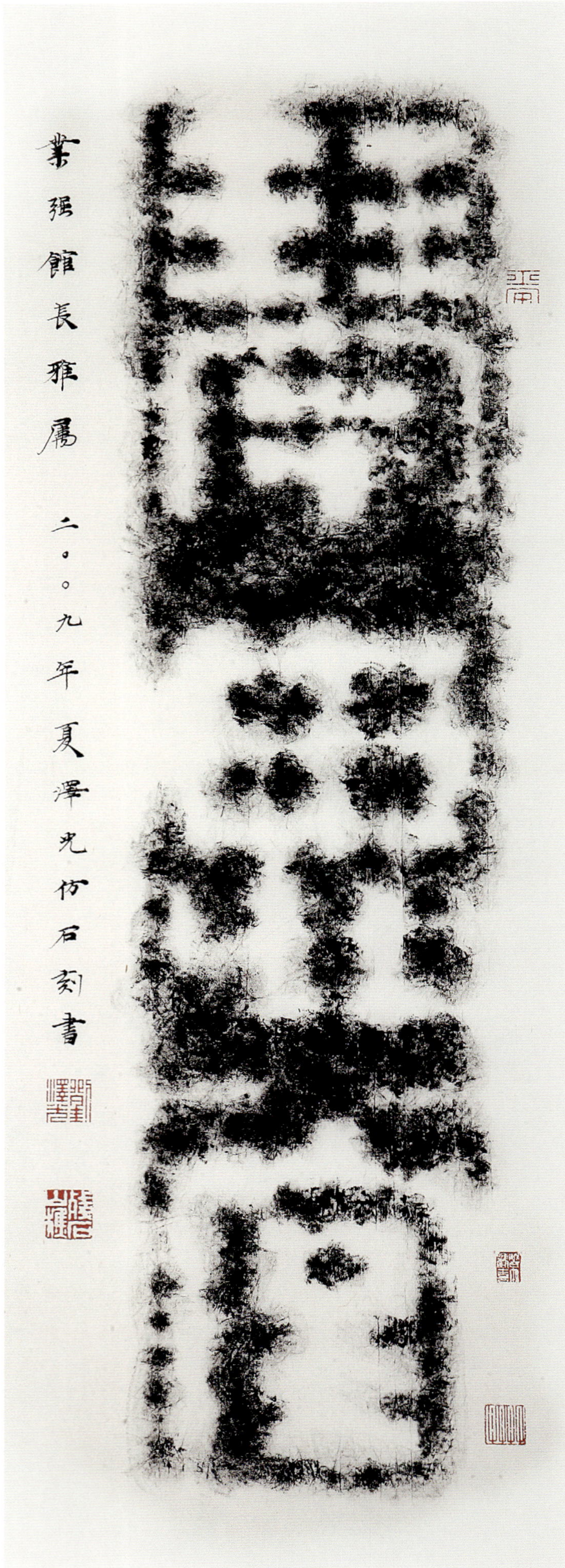

137 *The Studio of Thoughts in Zither-Playing* | 琴思堂

Imitation of rubbing from stone carving in clerical script
Ink on paper, hanging scroll
96 x 44 cm
2009

Collection of Professor Peter Yip-keung Lam

墨拓書法•隸書
紙本水墨，立軸
96 x 44厘米
2009年

林業強教授藏

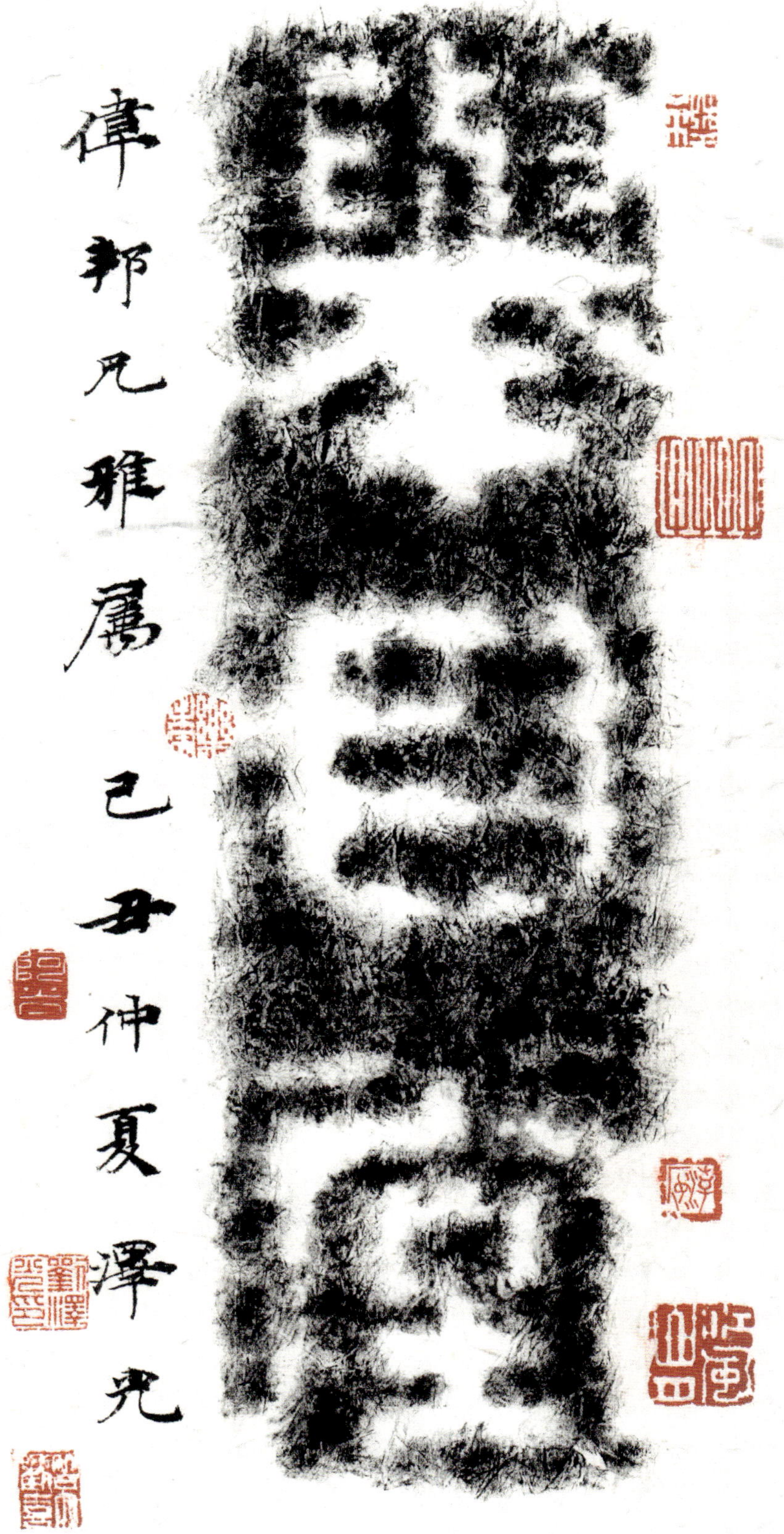

138 ***Studio of Lifting Mine Eyes*** |
舉目堂

Imitation of rubbing from
stone carving in clerical script
Ink on paper,
mounted and framed
42 x 24.9 cm
2009

Collection of
Mr. Koon Wai Bong

墨拓書法・隸書
紙本水墨，裱框
42 x 24.9厘米
2009年

管偉邦先生藏

139 *The Thatched Hut (Studio) Called Broken Stone* | 殘石草廬

Imitation of rubbing from
stone carving in clerical script
Ink on paper, mounted and framed
32.5 x 12.5 cm
1999

墨拓書法・隸書
紙本水墨，裱框
32.5 x 12.5厘米
1999年

Mr. Han Yunshan's inscription:
"The Style of imitation of rubbing from stone carving in clerical script originates from Mr. Luo Shuzhong. Now, my student Chak Kwong also adopts this method to imitate the "coal-smoke" method of making rubbing from the Stele called Hao Dawang bei. The style is completely different from Mr. Luo's, and this can be perceived by the audience."

韓雲山先生題識：
"仿石刻隸書拓本始自叔重羅瑛。今澤光仁弟亦用此法仿好大王碑煤煙拓法，別有面目。觀者當各有會心處也。"

雅与俗

CHAPTER 4/第四章

Elegance & Vulgarity

The Inter-Referencing of Elegance and Vulgarity From Elitism to Contemporary Popular Culture: Daniel Chak-kwong Lau's New Exploration into Calligraphy and Seal Engraving[1]

Prof. WAN Qingli
Director & Chair Professor
Academy of Visual Arts
Hong Kong Baptist University

Calligraphy and seal engraving are the essence of Chinese culture. These art forms appear as repeated pinnacles in history, arising when talented artists excelled in yielding outstanding achievements. The prosperity of calligraphy and seal engraving studies after mid-Qing has once again proved the vitality of the two art forms. In fact, the profound achievements of art in history are not without reason but the result of a fertile accumulation of culture.

Upon the foundation of the great popularity of brush handwriting, a change in literary content, forms and materials inevitably accompanies the emergence of cutting-edge calligraphers with the change in contemporary aesthetics. Before Yuan Dynasty, the major material for seals was bronze. Seals were rarely carved but were made by casting. Materials like jade and gold were used only occasionally for noblemen. After Yuan Dynasty, the use of materials and production method changed with the increasing demands for both official and ordinary seals. Since late Yuan when the literati used huaru stone (a kind of soapstone) for seal engraving, and through the exploration by seal engravers over hundreds of years in Ming and Qing, stone seals have gradually become mainstream, and eventually they came into its golden era in Qing Dynasty, when the study of seal engraving prospered and different schools came into being.

As China enters into modernity after the Republican period (1912-1949), the use of writing brushes is much reduced, and the brush is no longer the most popular writing tool. This is an inevitable challenge to the development of calligraphic art. Nonetheless, the abandonment of the brush as a writing tool does not imply that the rich and profound achievements in the art of calligraphy are meaningless nowadays. Calligraphy can be a fulfilling and compelling artistic activity. Also, it is still and continues to be the source of inspiration and creativity for the artists and art patrons.

Many artists are trying to explore the way to enliven the arts of calligraphy and seal engraving and are experimenting with incorporating the elements of the two into contemporary forms of visual arts. However, without historical knowledge and practical experience in calligraphy, any so-called "modern experiments" in the name of calligraphy are reducible to the surface of forms, and cannot stand the test of time for their shallowness.

By combining the unique visual language of calligraphy and seal engraving with Chinese literary content, artists today can still express their emotions and deliver their ideas. By reworking traditional concepts, calligraphers can present their inner expressions in a fresh new light.

Picking up on this new and intriguing method of creating modern calligraphic works is Dr. Daniel Chak-kwong Lau. His works are infused with the life and thought of modern people, naturally unfolding his taste and inner pursuit on the foundation of traditional calligraphy and seal engraving. Daniel is an artist as well as an art-history scholar. He insists on a balance between artistic creation and theoretical research, and is well-trained by formal institutions and rigorous academic and artistic mentorship in both areas. He was once a research student under my supervision at the University of Hong Kong. Under my supervision, he completed his MPhil thesis on the history of calligraphy and the calligraphic theories of Kang Youwei. After that, he studied abroad at the University of California,

1 A version of this essay was published in: Daniel C.K. Lau ed. *The Inter-Referencing of Elegance and Vulgarity- Daniel Chak-kwong Lau's New Exploration into Calligraphy and Seal Engraving* . Hong Kong: Academy of Visual Arts, Hong Kong Baptist University, 2009, pp. 7-16.

and was awarded his PhD in Art History. During his stay in the United States, Daniel devoted his effort mainly to the studies of Chinese painting, calligraphy and seal engraving of the Qing Dynasty and to research on the interrelated issue of "identity" in selected artistic and cultural circles. Meanwhile, he had also worked as a teaching staff at the University of California at Santa Barbara and the California Polytechnic State University at San Luis Obispo. In 2006, through fair competition and an array of transparent institutional assessments, he was appointed Assistant Professor by Hong Kong Baptist University in its international recruitment of faculty position in Art History and Chinese Calligraphy.

As for his practice of calligraphy and the acquisition of skills involved, Daniel has put in rigorous work. Under the concentrated effort andguidance of the well-known scholar-artist Han Yunshan, Daniel earnestly learnt from tradition and this has laid a solid foundation for his calligraphic pursuit. Meanwhile, he had the exceptional opportunity to access the original works of seal engraving collected by Master Han (which includes the outstanding works by Lu Dinggong (1903-1979), Qiu Siming (1925-1992), Feng Kanghou (1901-1983), Zhang Xiangning (1911-1958), Shang Changzuo (1902-1991) and Lin Qianshi (1918-1990)). These original seals have naturally become the models for Daniel in his study, albeit he has never studied seal engraving under any masters. Through his personal intuition and in-depth study into the styles and techniques of seal engraving, he has developed his own philosophy and style concerning this art form. Moreover, Daniel has studied traditional Chinese painting for many years under Long Ziduo (1917-2008), the painter who retreated in Castle Peak (Tsing Shan) in Tuen Mun. Diligently and perseveringly pursuing the interconnected principles of the so-called "three perfections", namely painting, calligraphy and seal engraving, he eventually gained success thorough an understanding of the inter-relationship between these three forms of art.

Characterized by the pluralistic nature of his artistic pursuit, Daniel never exclusively adheres to any single style or school. His pluralistic style is established on the foundation of his practice of studying a wide spectrum of quality works from past and present and absorbing the essence from various sources in an eclectic manner. Due to the prosperity of "evidential studies" ("textual studies"), the "Stele School" developed rapidly by Qing Dynasty. Since then calligraphers have been categorized into two main camps, belonging to either the Model-book School or Stele School. While the artists in the former school learn from "model writings" reproduced from famous calligraphers' hand-written calligraphic works, those in the latter learn from the rubbings from ancient stele and cliff-carvings. Starting from the Tang and Song Dynasties, the popularity of large projects of productions of big compilations of model writings, as funded by imperial patronages and private sponsorships, greatly facilitated the circulation of calligraphic works as well as the recognition of the works by such famous calligraphers as Zhong You (151-230), Wang Xizhi (303-361), Wang Xianzhi (344-386) and Yan Zhenqing (709-875) as "orthodox". Moreover, the works collected in various model writings were finished by literati, scholar-officials, emperors, high-ranking officials or famous people of the society. Hence these works belong to the category of elite art. By contrast, a large number of calligraphic works from stele was transcribed by anonymous individuals, albeit some were completed by known calligraphers. These works were considered "unorthodox" in the eyes of scholar-officials of the Tang through Ming Dynasties. Daniel, on the one hand, thoroughly studies the "orthodox" Model-book School and the "unorthodox" Stele School; on the other hand, he carefully examines the twentieth-century newly-excavated archaeological artefacts related to ancient writings, such as the writings that appear on the bamboo slips excavated in the deserts and ancient sites of beacon towers in Gansu, Inner Mongolia and Xinjiang Provinces. This category belongs to the writings of the populace in which the literary content is largely related to the real life and episodes of the common people such as the military state of affairs on the frontier, military resources, various types of productions, and medical prescriptions. Moreover, these writings were transcribed by: officials and soldiers on the frontier, accountants, and people with low social status in order to fulfil the requirements of particular jobs. Hence, the writings are unadorned and even rough. Although these writings are commonly considered artistically inferior, Daniel recognizes their aesthetic value. When he sees the images of writings on ancient bamboo slips in any new publications, he will act as if he has discovered treasures. He particularly appreciates the disorderly brushstrokes produced in improvisational circumstances, considering them the embodiment of a special sense of "tasteful crudity" and naivete. In Daniel's eyes, the colloquial calligraphy of the common people and the refined calligraphy of the elite both have their strengths. He believes that in terms of aesthetic value, the differentiation between them does not exist, and that it is inappropriate to exclusively categorize calligraphic works as "orthodox" and "unorthodox". Therefore, regardless of the calligraphic works' elegant and vulgar connotations or the transcribers' identities of elite or nonentity, Daniel endeavours to learn from all of them as long as they are superb works. Hence, his artistic philosophy and practice are contemporary and innovative.

Upon a thorough examination of Daniel's recent works, traces of evidence testify to his earnest study and practice of the seal, clerical, standard, semi-cursive and cursive scripts. He is particularly fond of creating his works in clerical script and the mode of large characters and exceedingly long text composed of small characters in standard script. To decipher his works, one needs to start with tracing the wide spectrum of styles he develops for the writings in different script types. Daniel first started his calligraphic pursuit by learning the standard-script writings of Liu Gongquan (778-865) and Yan Zhenqing. While exploring the brush techniques known as Yan's "tendon" and Liu's "bone", he practices standard script in small characters. His gigantic pieces of standard-script writing in small characters reveal his indebtedness to Ni Zan's (1301-1374) pure yet energetic style, and Zong You's idea of preservation of the structure and brush method of the clerical script. Moreover, Daniel has developed a more flexible brush method, emphasizing the rhythm of the "lifting" and "pressing" of the brush tip, and the variations of visual effect of "heavy" and "light". The resulting style is archaic, elegant and spirited. Additionally, Daniel's other style for his standard-script writing in small characters is modelled after the sutras of the Southern and Northern Dynasties period. Characterized by the speedy execution of one exceptionally long horizontal stroke with a pointed beginning and the exaggeratedly heavy finishing, the square and squat characters show the mixing of clerical and standard scripts.

In his practice of clerical-script writing, Daniel got started with the writings engraved on Han Dynasty (206 BC-AD 220) stele and cliffs, and learned from a wide array of styles ranging from *Zhang Qian bei* 's squareness, *Liqi bei* 's slenderness yet forcefulness, *Xixia song's* honesty, *Shimen song's* recklessness to *Xiyue Huashan miao bei* 's resplendence. He then studied the relatively more flexible and spontaneous brush methods and the naive flavour of the twentieth-century newly-excavated bamboo slips from Northwest China. His large-character writings are austere, natural and fluidly powerful, which largely reflect his indebtedness to his profoundly solid foundation of the Han clerical script as well as his earnest study of the *Diamond Sutra of Mount Tai* of the Northern Qi period and the *Stele of Hao Dawang* of the Jin period. In a sense, Daniel's works bespeak his personal disposition and embody the strength found in him as a person. Moreover, Daniel transforms his forceful style in large-character writings into the style imitating the rubbing from stele or cliff carvings.

Characterized by the application of dry brushstrokes to the negative spaces of the characters and careful predetermination of the distribution of negative and positive spaces, the resulting visual effect of white strokes against a black background is archaic, honest and completely powerful, thus entirely different from the so-called "black-tiger" style (i.e. imitation of rubbings from stele) of his predecessor Mr. Luo Shuzong (1898-1969), and inducing an innovative visual impact on the audience.

As for Daniel's semi-cursive-script writing, the style is reminiscent of Wang Xizhi's and Zhao Mengfu's (1254-1322) approach of combining square and round brushstrokes in a manner that is strong and robust, yet conveying a fluid brush spirit. Daniel's cursive-script writing is developed on the basis of Sun Guoting's (648-730) solid yet variable cursive-script methods. Daniel's brushwork is tinged with Huai Su's (725-785) wild-cursive brush manner and Zhu Yunming's (1460-1526) unusual aura of recklessness. Daniel's draft-cursive-script writings are imbued with the improvisational and candid touches of the Han Dynasty bamboo slips from Northwest China. Emphasizing the unrestrained brush manner, the resulting brushwork is continuously moving and overwhelming, without any disruption.

In addition to his calligraphic pursuit, Daniel excels in seal engraving. Within a square-shape small space, he rigorously examines the negative and positive spaces and the strategy of making spatial arrangement for dots and lines in intriguingly sinuous manner. Upon the foundation of his study of the Qin and Han seals, he has conducted an all-embracing and in-depth study into the styles and blade methods of the Zhe School headed by Ding Jing (1695-1765) and Huang Yi (1744-1802). Daniel employs a technique known as "the blade method of short cutting" that emphasizes sustained delays in the overall rhythm in wielding the carving knife. As a result, the carved lines are solid, refined and forceful. In addition, his works contain many innovative ideas, without being restricted by any masters or schools. For instance, the adoption of the sutra-transcribing style of the Jin Dynasty and the clerical and draft cursive scripts in his seal is unparalleled among the past and present seals. Moreover, he uses English words in his seals, yet the rugged and jerky lines that form the letters are tinged with a strong "metal-andstone" aura. Hence, his seals not only project the breath of the times but also retain the honestly archaic air reminiscent of the past.

With words as their content, works of calligraphy and seal engraving bear literariness and readability. They are more than pure visual arts because they are art objects created from integrated media. Therefore any discussion about calligraphy and seal engraving should not be confined to the styles and the visual effects of strokes and ink, but should also address the literary content of the work. The expression"*Dao revealed through brush and ink*"("筆墨載道", cat. no. 145) has enhanced *dao* ("道") from its original meaning. "*Brush*" and "*ink*" ("筆墨") are the vehicles; dao is the content being carried that transcends its surface meaning. The content of Daniel's artworks is mostly portrayals of little bits of the multiple facets of his life. His works embody thoughts and ideas that vary from projections of his self-image, to significations of friendship and mentorship, and to the life experience of his Christian faith. Expressed through either elegant language or colloquial doggerels and local Hong Kong slang, his works are full of his sincere thoughts and sentiments. For instance, he once encouraged and challenged the intellectual curiosity of his seal-engraving students with a piece of calligraphic work entitled "*Seal-engraving Proverb*". The eight largecharacters reading "*Safety comes first, art comes second*" (安全第一，藝術第二, cat. no. 141), written in clerical script and in the style of Han Dynasty "bamboo-slips" (漢簡) are bordered with calligraphic lines. The resulting visual effect bears a resemblance to a magnified seal. To its left, a long vertical line of small characters of semi-cursive script conveys a doggerel that reads: "Carving a seal needs the synchronization of the hands and the heart [i.e. brain]; the "thrusting" and "cutting" blade methods are both dangerous; boldly wielding the seal-carving knife with careful thoughts; the echo between the mind and the hand [thus] engenderssuperb art." The term "smoke of the teeth" (*yayan* 「牙煙」) adopted in the Chinese text in the verse is a common slang term widely used in Hong Kong that means "dangerous". The slang is vivid and humorous, inducing a knowing smile from the audience.

Daniel is a friendly person, and this is evident in the interaction between him and his students. When teaching the courses of calligraphy and seal engraving, he starts with the rigorous art-historical and the relevant academic topics; however, his students are able to follow his words due to his kind manner and humorous presentation. He treats his students like his friends, respects their personality, interests and individual aspirations, and designs for them flexible course content and a warm mode of teaching. In addition to practical demonstration, he teaches his students step-by-step with patience and guidance. He pays nuanced attention to the strength of each student in order to provide personalized guidance. No wonder he is much loved by his students. Whether it is for teaching or personal artistic pursuits, Daniel accomplishes his job with his greatest passion. His works of calligraphy and seal engraving are exactly a natural revelation of his temperament, which is gentle and courteous, with an additional connotation of the serious attitude of an intellectual in pursuit of profundity.

Insistent on the acquisition of traditional skills with brush and ink, Daniel continuously learns from a wide variety of masterpieces of different dynasties. His works thus indicate experienced and profound techniques with brush and ink, which indeed is rare among the calligraphers and seal engravers of his generation. Nowadays it is common to see Western contemporary art forms and concepts being applied in the creation of calligraphy and seals. Nonetheless, without a foundation in traditional brush-and-ink techniques and the practice of model imitation, and with reckless exaggeration and distortion of Chinese character structure, such self-acclaimed "innovative" works are no different from confusion and ignorance. Compared to this trend, the genuine and thorough traditional flavour in Daniel's works is especially precious. The value and fascination of calligraphy lies in its timelessness, by which people are unconsciously enchanted and influenced. Daniel's works are precisely the proof, and have infused the contemporary art scene with a fresh new dynamic. His effort and achievements in his artistic pursuit are stunningly remarkable, and have started to receive attention from the international art scene. His determination and perseverance in artistic exploration and his passion for life provide the key to his well-deserved success.

雅俗互參──從精英藝術到當代大眾文化：劉澤光書法篆刻的新探索[1]

萬青屴
香港浸會大學講座教授及
視覺藝術院院長

書法篆刻是中華文化的精粹，歷史上曾經屢現高峰，才人輩出，成就驕人。清代中期以后出現的書學中興、印學繁榮，再次顯示書法、篆刻的生命力。實際上，歷史上的藝術高峰，無非是深厚文化積淀的成果，是水漲船高，不會是無緣無故潮落潮漲。在毛筆書寫高度普及的基礎上，書寫內容，形式，工具材質的改變，隨著當時的審美時尚的變化，自然會出現引導潮流的杰出書法藝術家。元代以前，印章的材料主要是用銅，制作以鑄造為主，鑿印少見，只有少數皇室王權使用玉、金材質。元代以后，無論官用還是民用，印章的社會需求大量增加，材質、制作方法逐漸出現變化。元代晚期出現文人以花乳石（今稱葉臘石）刻印，經過明代，初數百年無數印人的探索，工匠的追隨，石印逐漸成為主流，終于在清代出現印學繁榮，流派紛呈的新高峰。

民國以後，中國開始的進入現代，毛筆使用的范圍越來越小，廣泛使用的書寫工具不再是毛筆，這是書法藝術發展所面臨的無法回避的歷史事實。然而，毛筆書寫逐漸退出歷史舞臺，并不意味著豐富的書法藝術成果在今天變得毫無意義。學習書法不僅可以成為有益身心健康的個人藝術愛好，而且對于有創意的藝術家，書法藝術也仍然是藝術探索的靈感來源。

探索如何賦予書法篆刻藝術新活力，如何把書法篆刻藝術元素融入當代流行的視覺藝術形式，是不少藝術家正在進行的嘗試。不過，如果對于書法藝術沒有歷史認識和用筆實踐兩方面足夠的準備，任何用書法名義的所謂現代實驗，往往是流于形式表面，淺薄浮躁，經不起時間的印證。

以書法篆刻獨特的視覺語言因素和中國文字內容的融合，今天的藝術家仍然可以表達意念，抒發情感，創造新境界。劉澤光博士的作品在傳統書法篆刻的基礎上，注入了當代人的生活和思考，自然流露了他內心的追求和個人品味。澤光是藝術家，也是藝術史學者。他堅持藝術創作與理論研究並重，在兩個不同的領域中都受過正規嚴格的訓練。他曾經是我在香港大學任教時的研究生，在我指導下完成了有關書法史和康有為書學理論的碩史論文。後來他赴美就讀加州大學，獲哲學博士(藝術史)學位。留美期間，主要致力於清代書畫篆刻以及所在的文化藝術圈中的身份認同問題的研究，同時亦相繼任教於加州大學(聖地巴巴拉)和加州理工州立大學。2006年，香港浸會大學向國際公開招聘藝術史及中國書法教職，經過公平競爭和透明機制的考量評議，獲聘為助理教授。

在書法技巧層面上，澤光曾下過必要的苦功，在名宿韓雲山先生悉心指導下，認真地向傳統學習，奠定了穩固紮實的基礎。又因常摩挲韓老先生珍藏篆刻名家原石，而有機會與篆刻藝術結緣。澤光雖未曾正式拜師學習篆刻，但是韓老先生所藏的印章(包括盧鼎公、丘思明、馮康侯、張祥凝、商承祚、容庚和林千石等手刻的近百件精品)，很自然的成為澤光的范本，憑他個人對篆刻風格流派和技法的敏銳感悟和深入探究，他發展出自己個人的篆刻風格和藝術理念。習書法篆刻外，澤光亦隨隱居於屯門青山的龍子鐸先生學國畫多年，為探索“書”、“畫”、“印”「三絕」互通之理，孜孜以求，終于能融會貫通，學而有成。

澤光的藝術創作是多元的，從不囿於某家某派。他多元化的書法風格建基於泛覽古今名跡，博採眾長。清代因考據學和金石學的興盛而帶動了“碑學”書法的發展。自此以後，書法家多被分為“帖學派” 或 “碑學派”。前者學習書法的蹊徑是臨摹“法帖”或“刻帖”（“刻帖”指的是把皇室或士大夫收藏的名家墨.刻在石版或木板後，再施以拓印技術所得的“刻帖拓片”，既可供收藏，亦是臨摹範本）；後者則學習刻在古代石碑上的書法和摩崖石刻之“原.拓本”。唐宋以來，由皇家贊助和民間出資刻帖(較大型的稱為“叢帖”或“匯帖”)的風氣盛行，促進了書法的流播，而且更使鍾繇、王羲之、王獻之和顏真卿等“大家”書法風格多被認定為“正統”。再者，法帖中所收的書法皆出自文人士大夫、帝王將相、或是社會中有功名之仕的手筆，屬于精英藝術。相反，碑刻書法雖也有出自記名書法家手筆，但大量作品是由不知名的人所書寫，早在唐至明代的士大夫的眼中，已經被視為非書法的“正統”。澤光一方面對“正統”的“帖學派”和“非正統”的“碑學派”素有研究， 另一方面更留心探究20世紀初以來新出土的與漢字

1 本文曾發表於劉澤光編，《雅俗互參：劉澤光書法篆刻的新探索》，香港：香港浸會大學視覺藝術院，2009年，頁17-21。

相關的考古文物，例如從甘肅、內蒙古、新疆等地的荒漠和烽燧遺址中出土的漢代簡牘。這類屬於平民百姓的書法，文字內容多與民間各種生活實況有關，例如戍邊軍情、戰備物資、各類生產、醫藥處方等，而且多出於戍邊官兵、賬房庫管等社會地位不高的書寫者手筆。往往因工作需要或即興隨意的書寫過程，書法風格不加修飾，予人一種粗糙和樸實的感覺。澤光對這些一般認為藝術價值不高的民間書法卻獨具慧眼，每遇見新出版的刊有簡牘影象的書刊，即如獲至寶，他尤其欣賞在急就或即興的情況下所產生錯落參差的筆觸，覺得它們蘊含一種民間野趣，稚拙天真。在澤光的眼中，俚俗的民間書法和高雅的精英書法各有所長，它們之間並不存在審美觀念上價值高下之分，亦不能單一地以“正統”和 “非正統”來將書法分類。所以無論是雅是俗，無論是出自社會精英或是無名小吏的手筆，只要是佳作，澤光都兼收並蓄，故此他的藝術理念和創作是當代的，是創新的。

綜觀澤光近期作品，可見他在篆、隸、楷、行、草各種書體上都曾經認真臨摹和研究過。他特別喜愛以隸書、長篇小楷和榜書(大字)的形式創作。要解讀他的作品，必先從追溯他各種書體的風格淵源開始。澤光從 公權和顏真卿的楷書入手，探索“顏筋 骨”之同時亦旁兼小楷，從他現時的長篇小楷看來，他尤其得倪瓚清勁之筆意，同時又深得鍾繇帶有隸意的用筆和結體；再加上他個人發展出的一套獨特的筆法 — 即採取較靈活的“提按” ，運筆節奏，而且強調通篇作品視覺效果的輕重強弱變化，最終產生的小楷風格既古雅又瀟灑。此外，澤光有較另類的小楷風格，取法南北朝時經生抄寫的佛教經卷：風格特徵包括強調字中特長的一橫畫以及因快速書寫而形成的露鋒起筆和誇張地重按的收筆，字形扁方，實屬隸楷的混合體。

澤光的隸書從刻於漢碑和摩崖上的隸書作品入手，汲收了《張遷碑》的方整、《禮器碑》的瘦勁、《西狹頌》的樸拙、《石門頌》的奇縱和《西嶽華山廟碑》的華麗俊美等風格特點，繼而取法二十世紀新出土的西北漢簡，兼得較靈活和隨意的用筆和稚拙的趣味。其榜書作品主要得力於其深厚的漢隸基礎，同時亦取法北齊《泰山經石峪金剛經》和晋《好大王碑》。他的榜書創作，風格質樸自然，氣勢酣暢。作品風格在某程度上反映其性情和志向，體現出其內在的魄力。此外，澤光將其氣勢滂博的榜書發展出 “仿石刻書體” — 特點是以乾筆擦出字形的外側，因他對字中筆畫的虛實空間分布早已了然於胸，所以能留白成字，創造出貌似碑刻拓本的作品，風格古樸渾厚，與前輩羅叔重先生的“黑老虎”截然不同，令觀者視覺一新。

至於澤光的行書則掇取王羲之、趙孟頫雄健而方圓兼備的筆法和飄逸流暢的筆意。草書則在孫過庭穩健而多變的草法基礎上兼有懷素狂草筆意和祝允明的縱恣奇氣。他的章草作品融入了西北漢簡的即興和直率的情韻，筆意跌宕，有一氣呵成和暢快淋漓之勢。

澤光於書法創作外兼善篆刻，方寸之間，虛實揖讓，點線迂回，甚為考究。在秦漢印的基礎上，他尤其對以丁敬、黃易為首的浙派印風和刀法，作出了全面而深入的探究。他以強調頓挫的碎刀短切法，加強了運刀時的起伏節奏，所刻出的線條凝練渾厚。此外，他的作品亦自出機抒，不囿諸家流派，例如以晋人寫經書法風格、隸書和章草等書體入印，在古今篆刻作品中是較罕見的。以英文字入印，卻將字母刻成別有金石氣的線條，則既有時代氣息，又不失古拙之風。

書法篆刻以文字為內容，具有文學性，可讀性，是多媒介綜合的藝術，并不是單純的視覺藝術，因此討論書法和篆刻藝術不能只談風格和筆墨的視覺效果而忽略作品中的文字內容。“筆墨載道”(展品145) 一語，提升了“道”的本來意義。“筆墨”是載體，道是承載的內容，是超出表層的涵義。澤光書法篆刻作品的內容大多是他生活點滴的寫照。作品或是個人自我形象的投射，或是師友之情的標誌，或是其基督教信仰的生活體驗，無論透個典雅的語言或俚俗的打油詩和香港俗語，都充滿.他真摯的思想感情。茲舉一例，他曾以一件題為“篆刻箴言”的書法作品來勉勵收讀篆刻課程的學生。「安全第一藝術第二」(展品141)，八個漢簡風格的隸書大字，畫上了框線之後，恰似一方特大印章。左側以小行楷書有打油詩:「刻印心手要合拍，衝刀切刀好牙煙；大膽奏刀細心想，得心應手印藝高。」詩中「牙煙」一辭是香港人常用俗語，謂”危險”。俚語生動傳神，詼諧幽默，使人會心微笑。

澤光平易近人，他與學生講授書法篆刻時，雖從嚴謹的藝術史和學術課題開始，但他態度和善，談吐風趣幽默，待學生如朋友，尊重他們的個性、興趣及個人的意向，設計靈活的授課內容和模式，不單持筆示範，更循循善誘，細心的發掘每個學生的特長而予以個人化的指導。故他深受學生愛戴。無論教學或個人藝術創作，澤光總以他最大的熱情去完成。他的書法篆刻作品正是他本人性情的自然流露，温文爾雅，又不失讀書人求精深博大的認真態度。

他堅持學習傳統的筆墨技法，長期不斷廣泛學習歷代名跡，故他作品中深厚的筆墨功力，實為其同輩書法篆刻家中少見。目前常見有些藝術家套用西方當代藝術形式和觀念於書法篆刻創作中，沒有傳統筆墨和臨摹基礎，將漢字結構任意誇張扭曲變形，自以為“創新” ，無異盲人瞎馬，無知妄為。對比之下，澤光作品中地道的傳統韻味，無疑顯得份外可貴。 書法之可貴與引人入勝，在于耐看，引人入勝，不知不覺中受到感染。澤光的作品正好見証了這個道理，為當今藝壇注入一般清新的力量。他在藝術創作的努力和成績令人矚目，開始受到國際藝壇關注。對藝術探究鍥而不捨的精神和他熱誠的生活態度，正是他的成功之道。

140 *What?* | 咩話？

Imitation of rubbing from stone carving in clerical script (front) & clerical script (back)
Ink on paper, mounted with canvas and wood as a three-dimensional object resembling a monument
119.5 x 60 x 179.5 cm
2008

墨拓書法•隸書（表），及隸書（裏）
紙本水墨，以帆布及木裱成紀念碑狀立體裝置
119.5 x 60 x 179.5厘米
2008年

Shortlisted entry of the "Invitational Competition for the Hong Kong Arts Centre 30th Anniversary Award," (organised by Hong Kong Arts Centre, May 2008), exhibited at the Hong Kong International Arts and Antiques Fair in October, 2008.

Artist's inscription: "The Cantonese expression "咩話" has a twofold meaning: an exclamation of surprise or a question asking literally "what dialect?" Cantonese is a dialect that has "surprisingly" defied the fate of extinction of most minority languages and continues to remain in dominant use in Hong Kong even after the 1997 handover; it helps foster a strong sense of local identity and pride.

To celebrate Cantonese as a distinctive social and cultural phenomenon, I transform the two Chinese characters "咩話" into a visual effect resembling a stone monument rubbing, and evoke an additional sense of historic association through a forcefully archaic and austere calligraphic style, thus taking the age-old and richly vernacular Cantonese dialect through the caverns of time into the dramatic present."

題識： "香港粵語中「咩話」一辭，既表達「驚訝」，亦可指「甚麼方言？」令人驚訝的是：粵方言破解了少數民族語言漸被淘汰的宿命，甚至97回歸後，仍在香港流通使用。這體現出強烈的本土認同和自豪感。為歌頌香港粵語作為獨特的社會和文化現象，我將「咩話」二字轉化為石碑拓本的視覺效果，並藉沉雄古樸的書法風格拱托出一種格外的歷史聯想，將歷史猶久而富濃厚地方色彩的粵方言，帶到戲劇化的現在。"

香港粵語中咩話一辭既表達驚訝亦可指甚麼方言令人驚訝的是粵方言破解了少數民族語言漸被淘汰的宿命甚至九七回歸後仍在香港流通使用這體現出強烈的本土認同和自豪感為歌頌香港粵語作為獨特的社會和文化現象我將咩話二字轉化為石碑拓本的視覺效果並藉沉雄古樸的書法風格烘托出一種格

香港粵語中嘩話一辭既表達驚訝亦可指甚麼方言令人驚訝的是粵方言破
解了少數民族語言漸被淘汰的宿命甚至九七回歸後仍在香港流通使用
這體現出強烈的本土認同和自豪感為歌頌香港粵語作為獨特的社會和文化現象
我將嘩話二字轉化為石碑拓本的視覺效果並藉沉雄古樸的書法風格烘托出一種格
外的歷史聯想將歷史猶久而富濃厚地方色彩的粵方言帶到戲劇化的現在 劉澤光書於香江

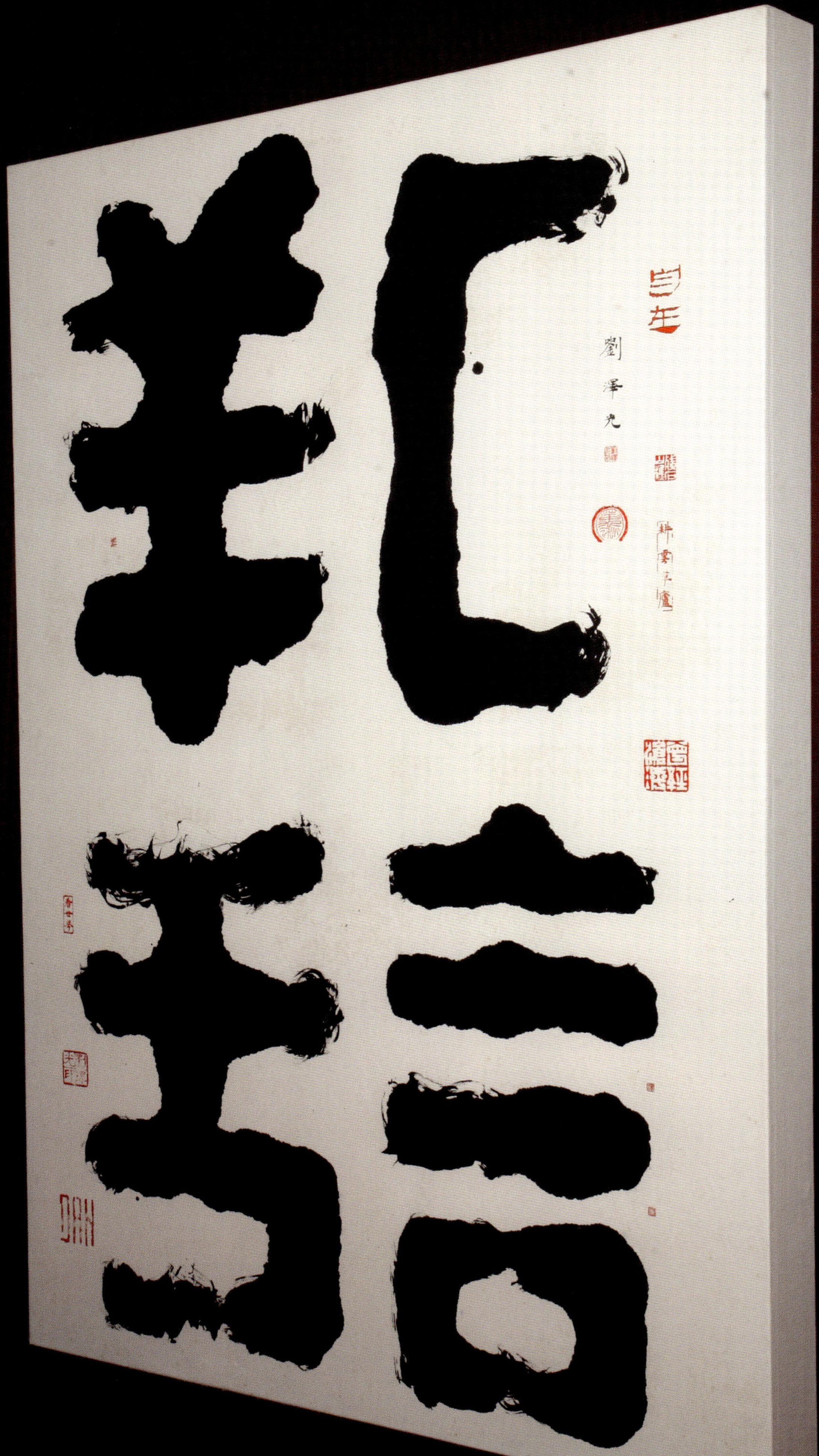
劉澤光

141 *Seal-Engraving Proverb* | 篆刻箴言

Clerical script
Ink on paper, mounted on
wood block
74 x 43 cm
2008

隸書
紙本墨書，裱於木板
74 x 43厘米
2008年

Transliteration: Safety Comes First,
Art Comes Second
釋文：安全第一，藝術第二

Artist's inscription:
"Carving a seal needs the
synchronization
of the hands and the heart [i.e. brain],
The "thrusting" and "cutting"
blade methods are both dangerous;
Boldly wielding the seal-carving knife
with careful thoughts,
The echo between the mind and the
hand [thus] engenders superb art."

題識：
"刻印心手要合拍，衝刀切
刀好牙煙 ；大膽奏刀細心想，得心
應手印藝高。"
按："牙煙"一辭是香港人常用俗
語，意思是"危險"。

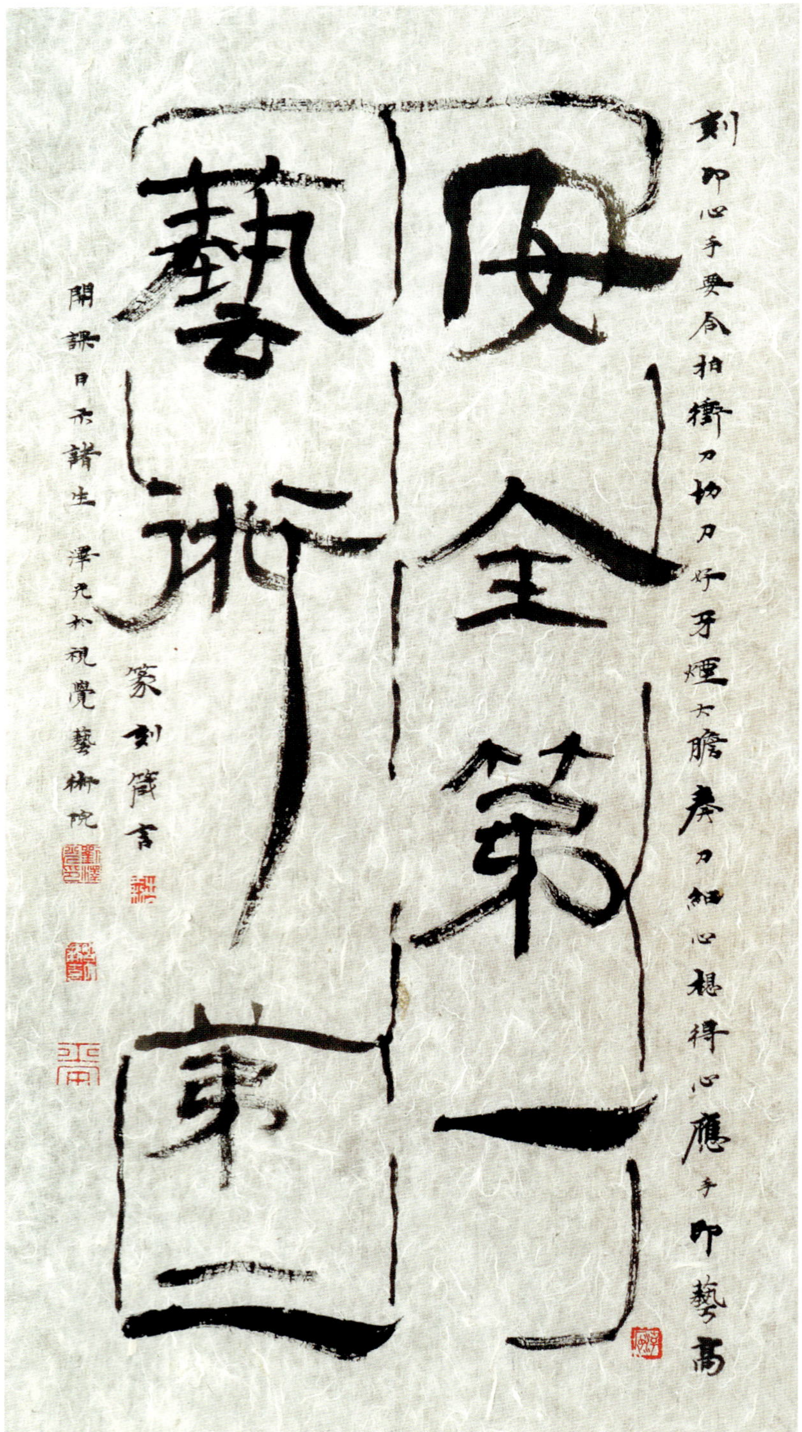

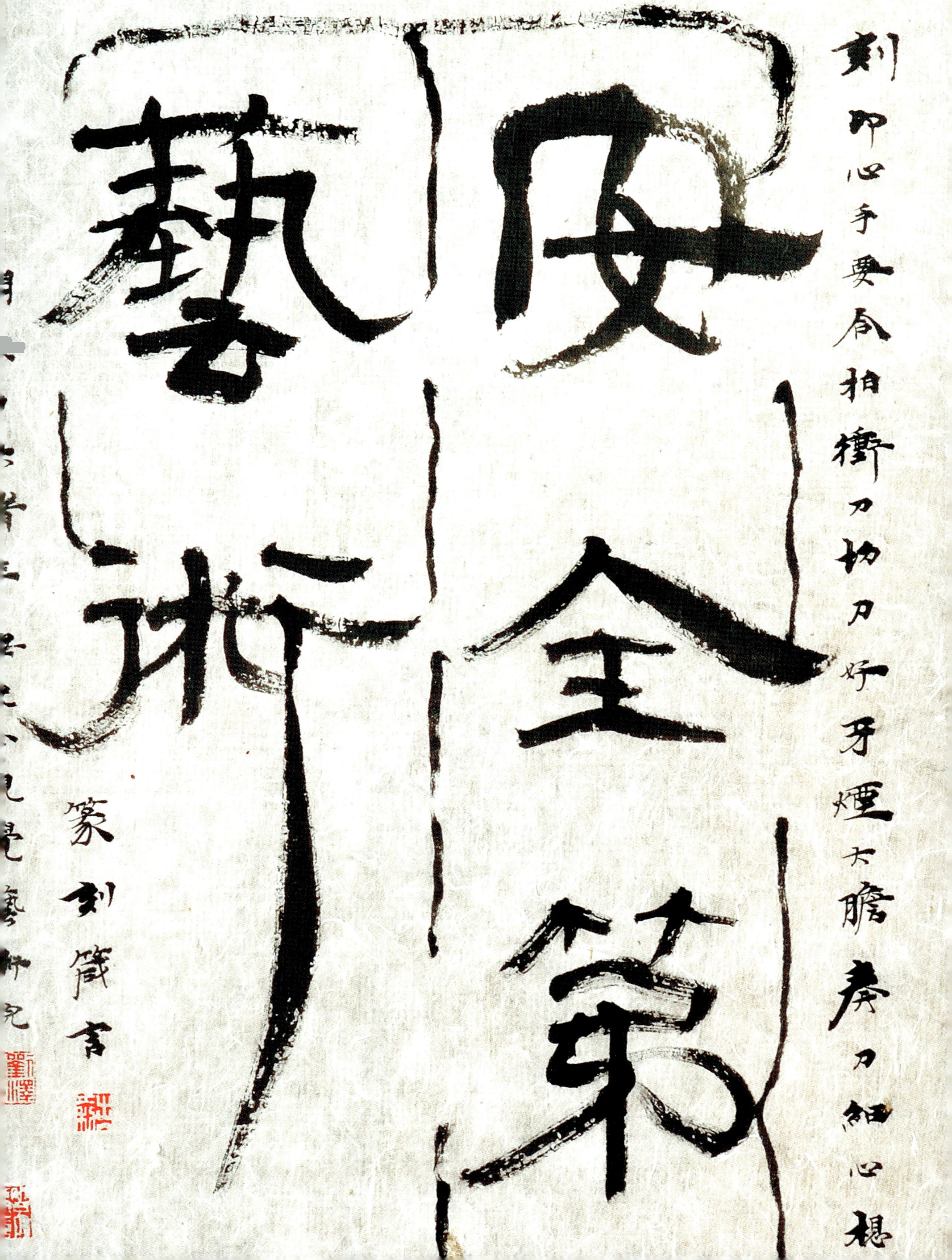

安全篆刻藝術
刻印心手要合拍衝刀切刀好牙煙大膽奏刀細心想
篆刻箴言

142 *To Relax and Enjoy Life*

嘆世界

Clerical script
Ink on paper,
mounted on wood block
91.5 x 37cm
2008

隸書
紙本墨書，裱於木板
91.5 x 37厘米
2008年

嘆

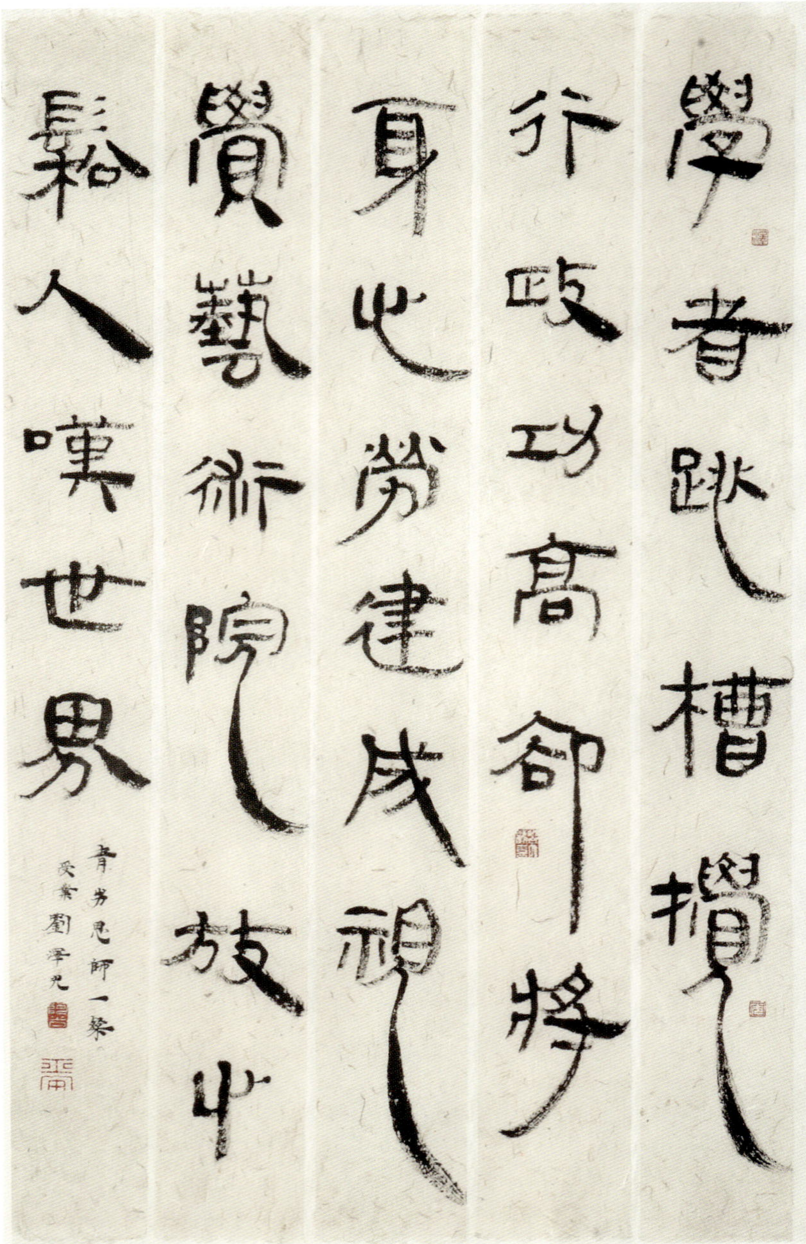

143 *Go Away to Relax and Enjoy Life* I

鬆人嘆世界

Clerical script
Ink on paper,
hanging scroll
a set of five slips,
each 76 x 9 cm
2008

隸書
紙本墨書，立軸五條幅
各76 x 9厘米
2008年

Collection of Professor
Wan Qingli
萬青屴教授收藏

Transliteration:
The Scholar changed his job to engage in administrative work.
Through these tasks thus far, he has attained great achievements, but his body and mind are becoming exhausted;
When the Academy of Visual Arts has become well established,
He will then be at ease, and can relax and enjoy life, knowing that his work is done.

Artist's inscription:
"For the knowing smile of my respected mentor, your student Lau Chak-kwong."

題識："青屴恩師一粲。受業 劉澤光"

釋文：
學者跳槽攬行政，
功高卻將身心勞；
建成視覺藝術院，
放心鬆人嘆世界。

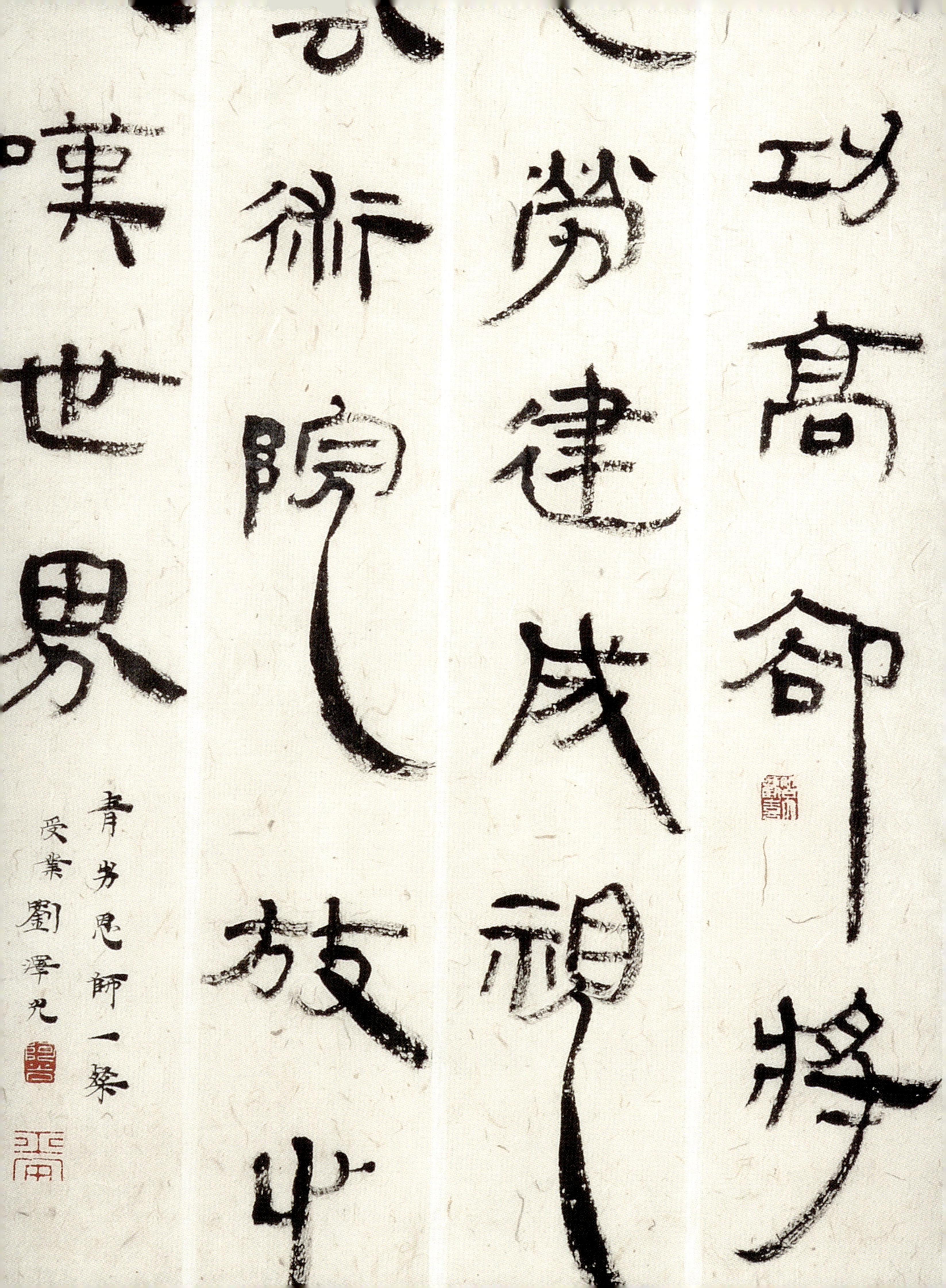
功高卻將
勞建成視
術院技
嘆世界
青芳恩師一粲
受業劉澤光

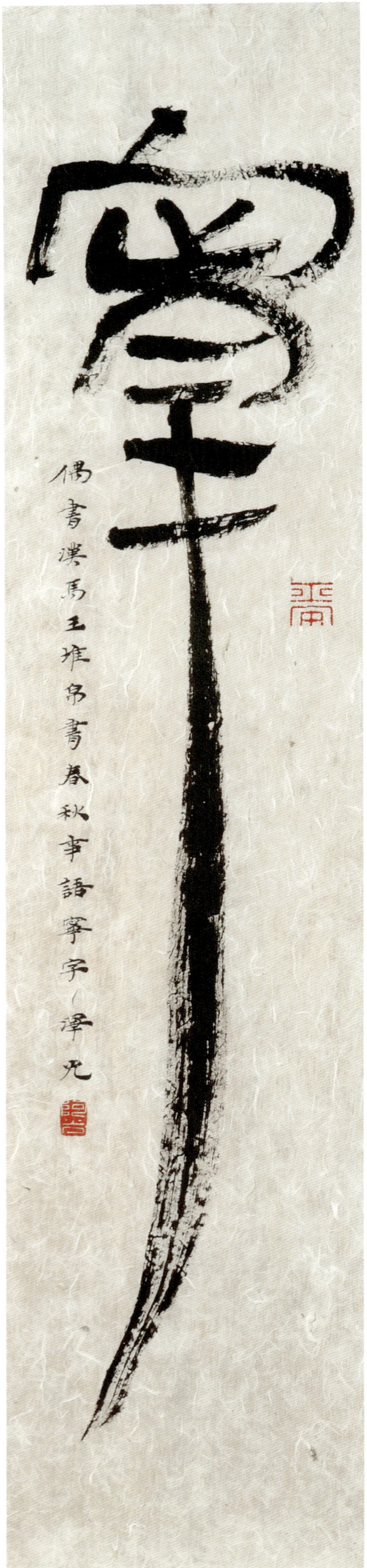

144 ***Tranquility*** | 寧
Clerical script
Ink on paper,
mounted on wood block
73 x 17 cm
2007

隸書
紙本墨書，裱於木板
73 x 17厘米
2007年

145 ***Dao Revealed through Brush and Ink*** I

筆墨載道

Clerical script
Ink on paper, mounted on wood block
78 x 71 cm
2008

隸書
紙本墨書，裱於木板
78 x 71厘米
2008年

146 ***Happy is He who is Content*** |
知足常樂

Clerical script
Ink on paper, hanging scroll
239 x 64 cm
2007

隸書
紙本墨書，立軸
239 x 64厘米
2007年

147 *The Principles of Heaven and Earth Held in Wonderful Hands* I

妙手乾坤

Clerical script
Ink on paper, hanging scroll
180 x 48 cm
2008

隸書
紙本墨書，立軸
180 x 48厘米
2008年

Collection of University Museum and Art Gallery, The University of Hong Kong

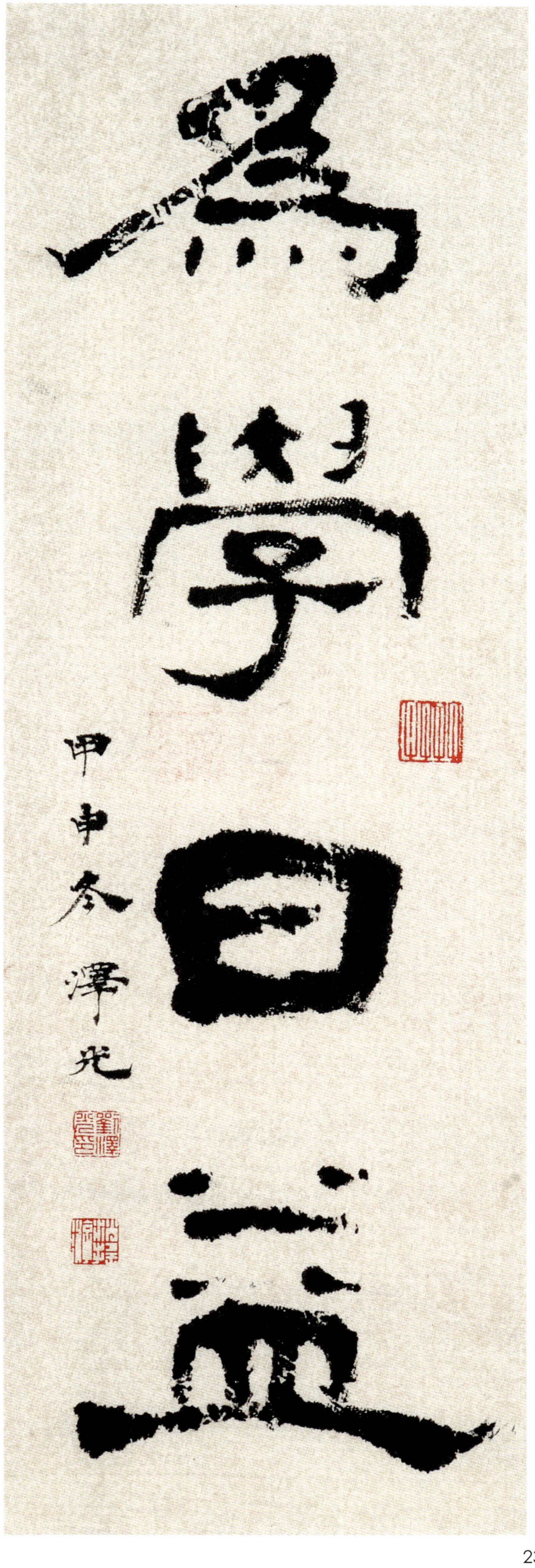

148 *The Pursuit of Learning is to Increase Day after Day*

為學日益

Clerical script
Ink on paper, mounted on wood block
65 x 20.5 cm
2004

隸書
紙本墨書，裱於木板
65 x 20.5厘米
2004年

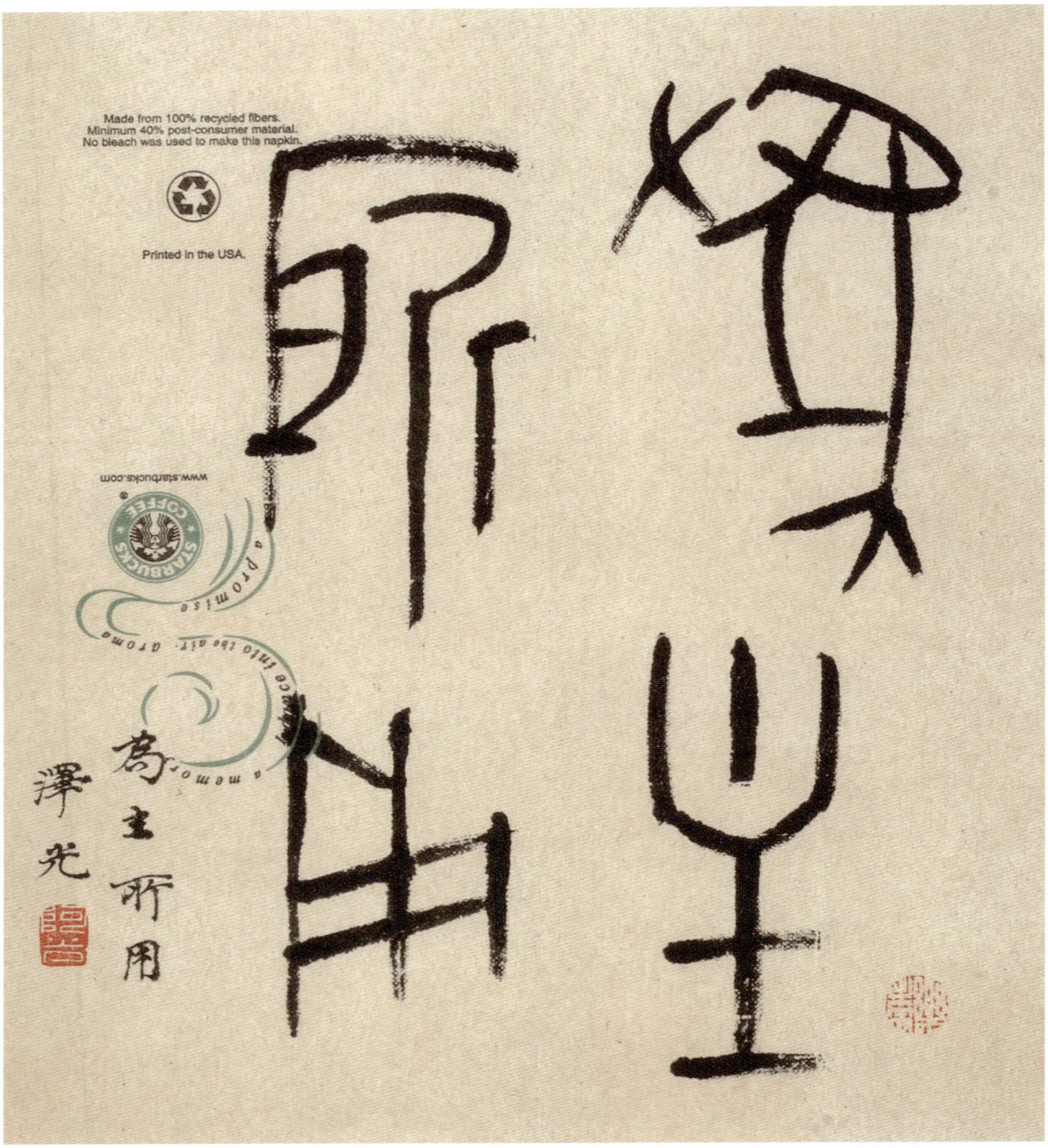

149 ***Service to the Lord*** | 為主所用

Oracle-bone script
Ink on paper, mounted and framed
30 x 30 cm
2006

甲骨文
紙本墨書，裱框
30 x 30厘米
2006年

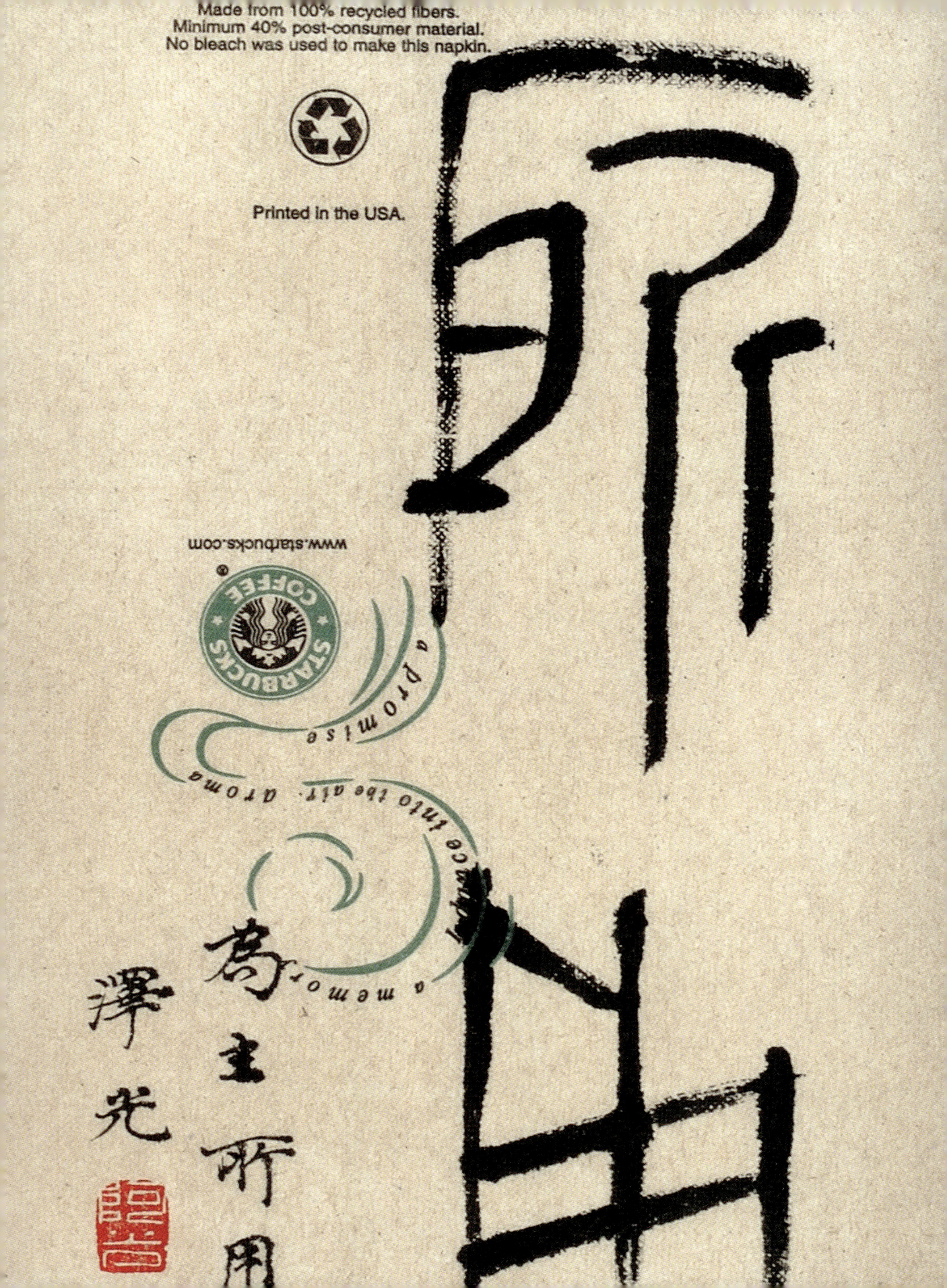
Made from 100% recycled fibers.
Minimum 40% post-consumer material.
No bleach was used to make this napkin.
Printed in the USA.
www.starbucks.com
STARBUCKS COFFEE
a promise
into the air. aroma
a memory
為主所用
澤光

150 ***The Auspicious Image*** |
吉祥之象

Great-seal script
Ink on paper,
mounted on wood block
56 x 9 cm
2007

大篆
紙本墨書，裱於木板
56 x 9厘米
2007年

151 ***The Never-Ending Song*** **|** 未央歌

Seal script
Ink on paper, mounted and framed
50 x 15 cm
2006

篆書
紙本墨書，裱框
50 x 15厘米
2006年

152 *The Method of No-Method* | 無法之法

Seal script
Ink on paper, mounted and framed
22.5 x 52 cm
2006

篆書
紙本墨書，裱框
22.5 x 52厘米
2006年

153 *Ecclesiastes* | 傳道書

Seal script
Ink on paper, mounted and framed
100 x 250 cm
2006

篆書
紙本墨書，裱框
100 x 250厘米
2006年

Artist's inscription:

According to the Dictionary of Bible edited by the Shanghai Christian Literature Society for China (Guangxuehui) in 1916, "Ecclesiastes" originates from a Latin word translated in Septuagint (the ancient Greek translation of the Jewish scriptures), meaning "one who addresses an assembly". This is meant to be included in the bible since 100 B.C. Ecclesiastes documents the lamentation of a wealthy Jewish person who lived around the second centuries B.C. Although wealthy, he had lots of sorrow and disappointment in life. He was already an old man when he wrote the book. Hence, the utterance that the enjoyment of life and wisdom are important aspects of life was his memory. His view on the empty and transitory nature of life is profoundly incisive as he believes that no one can have complete control of life and that one cannot achieve his or her goal with his or her own effort. However, there are opportune moments to turn things around in circumstances of great distress as the author clearly states that through getting to know God and living a devoted life, one can experience the true meanings to life and enjoy the happiness within.

作者題識：

據上海廣學會1916年所編聖經大辭典，傳道書之名，自七十博士所譯之拉丁文而出，即當會眾演說之意也。
為列經之書。是書所記，乃寫一猶太富人之衷曲，則公元前第二世紀也。雖甚豐富，而其愁苦失望之事亦多。考其立言之時，已至垂暮之年，觀言娛樂與智慧二者為性命之源，已成追憶之辭。其言人生之虛空幻變，極為深刻，以為人生無論如何不能引導一己以自達其目的。然而，此憂患之境當有扭轉之契機。作者言明，人可憑認識上帝並虔誠度日，能親歷生命之真義，享受其中歡樂。

傳道書

在耶路撒冷作王大衛的兒子傳道者的言語傳道者說虛空的虛空

益處呢一代過去一代又來地卻永遠長存日頭出來日頭落下急歸所

不滿江河從何處流仍歸還何處萬事令人厭煩人不能說盡眼看〻不

一件事人能指著說這是新的哪知在我們以前的世代早已有了已

色列的王我專心用智慧尋求查究天下所做的一切事乃知上帝叫世

曲的不能變直缺少的不能足數我心裏議論說我得了大智慧勝過我

慧狂妄和愚昧乃知這也是捕風因為多有智慧就多有愁煩加增知識

時都是虛空的你趁着年幼衰敗的日子尚未來到就是你所說我月亮星宿變為黑暗雨後雲彩反回看守房屋的發顫有力的屈身推叫人就起來唱歌的女子也都衰微人怕高處路上有驚慌杏樹開花蚱蜢斷金罐破裂瓶子在泉旁損壞水輪在井口破爛塵土仍歸於地靈仍歸將知識教訓眾人又默想又考查又陳說許多箴言傳道者專心尋求可喜釘穩的釘子都是一個牧者所賜的我兒還有一層你當受勸戒著書他的誡命這是人所當盡的本分因為人所做的事連一切隱藏的事無

演說之意也公元前一百年始認定為列經之書是書所記乃寫一猶太富人之衷曲觀言娛樂與智慧二者為性命之原已成追憶之辭其言人生之虛空幻變極為深言明人可憑認識上帝並虔誠度日能親歷生命之真義享受其中歡樂 劉澤光並識 廣學會

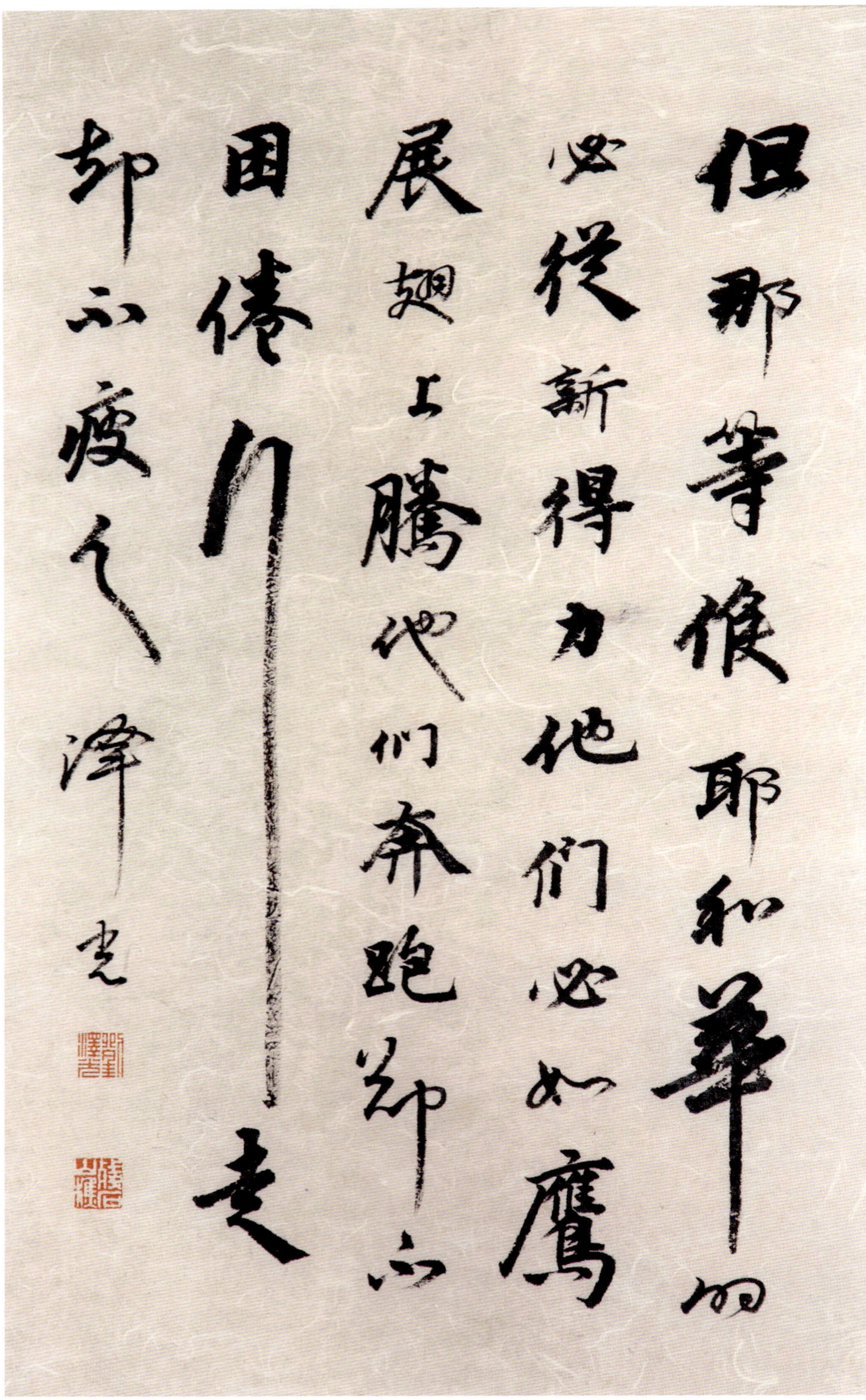

154 ***Isaiah 40:31*** | 以賽亞書 ***40:31***

Semi-cursive script
Ink on paper,
mounted and framed
80 x 45 cm
2009

行書
紙本墨書，裱框
80 x 45 厘米
2009年

Transliteration:
But they that wait upon the Lord shall renew their strength; they shall mount up with wings as eagles; they shall run, and not be weary; and they shall walk, and not faint.

釋文：
但那等候耶和華的，必從新得力；他們必如鷹展翅上騰；他們奔跑卻不困倦，行走卻不疲乏。

耶和華的
他們必如鷹
們奔跑卻不

155 *Lyric by Su Shi* |
蘇軾《水調歌頭・丙辰中秋》

Small standard script
Ink on paper, folded fan
13.5 x 42 cm
2007

蠅頭小楷
紙本墨書，摺扇
13.5 x 42厘米
2007年

Bright moon, when did you appear.
Lifting my wine, I question the dark night sky.
Tonight in the palaces and halls of heaven,
What year is it, I wonder.
Would like to ride the wind, make my home there,
Only I hide i n a jade room of a beautiful mansion,
As I could not bear the cold of high altitudes.
So I rise and dance and play in your pure beams,
This human world — how can it compare with yours?
Circling red chambers,
Low in the curtained door,
You shine on the sleepless.

Surely you bear us no ill will —
Why then must you be so round at times when we humans are parted!
People have their griefs and joys, their togetherness and separation,
The moon has its dark and clear times, its waxings and wanings.
Situations are never ideal since long ago.
I only hope we two may have long long lives,
So that we may share the moon's beauty even though we are a three hundred miles apart.

明月幾時有，把酒問青天。不知天上宮闕，今夕是何年。我欲乘風歸去，又恐瓊樓玉宇。高處不勝寒，起舞弄清影，何似在人間。轉朱閣，低綺戶，照無眠。不應有恨，何事長向別時圓。人有悲歡離合，月有陰晴圓缺。此事古難全，但願人長久，千里共嬋娟。

Translation from:
http://en.wikipedia.org/wiki/Shu%C7%90di%C3%A0o_g%C4%93_t%C3%B3u

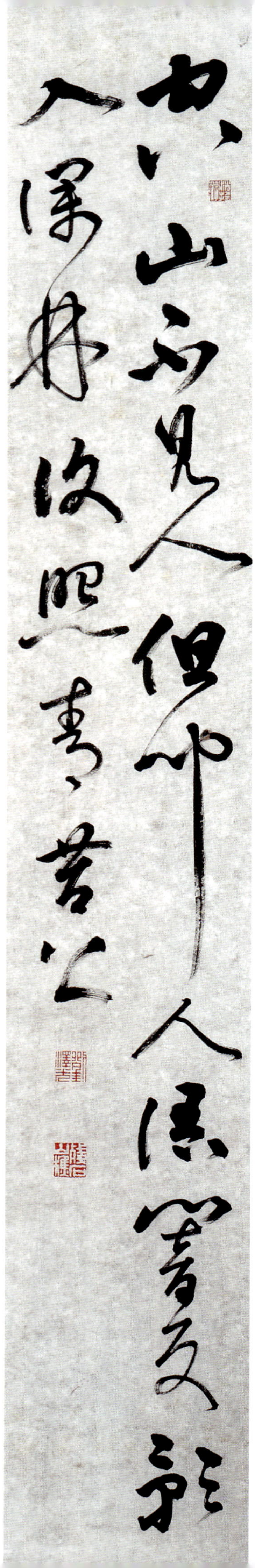

156 *Poem "Deer Enclosure" by Wang Wei* I

王維《鹿柴》

Cursive script
Ink on paper, mounted on wood block
137 x 22 cm
2007

草書
紙本墨書，裱框
137 x 22厘米
2007年

Transliteration:
Hills are empty, no man is seen,
Yet the sound of people's voices is heard.
Light is cast into the deep forest,
And shines again on green moss.

(http://www.chinese-poems.com)

釋文：
空山不見人，但聞人語響。
返景入深林，復照青苔上。

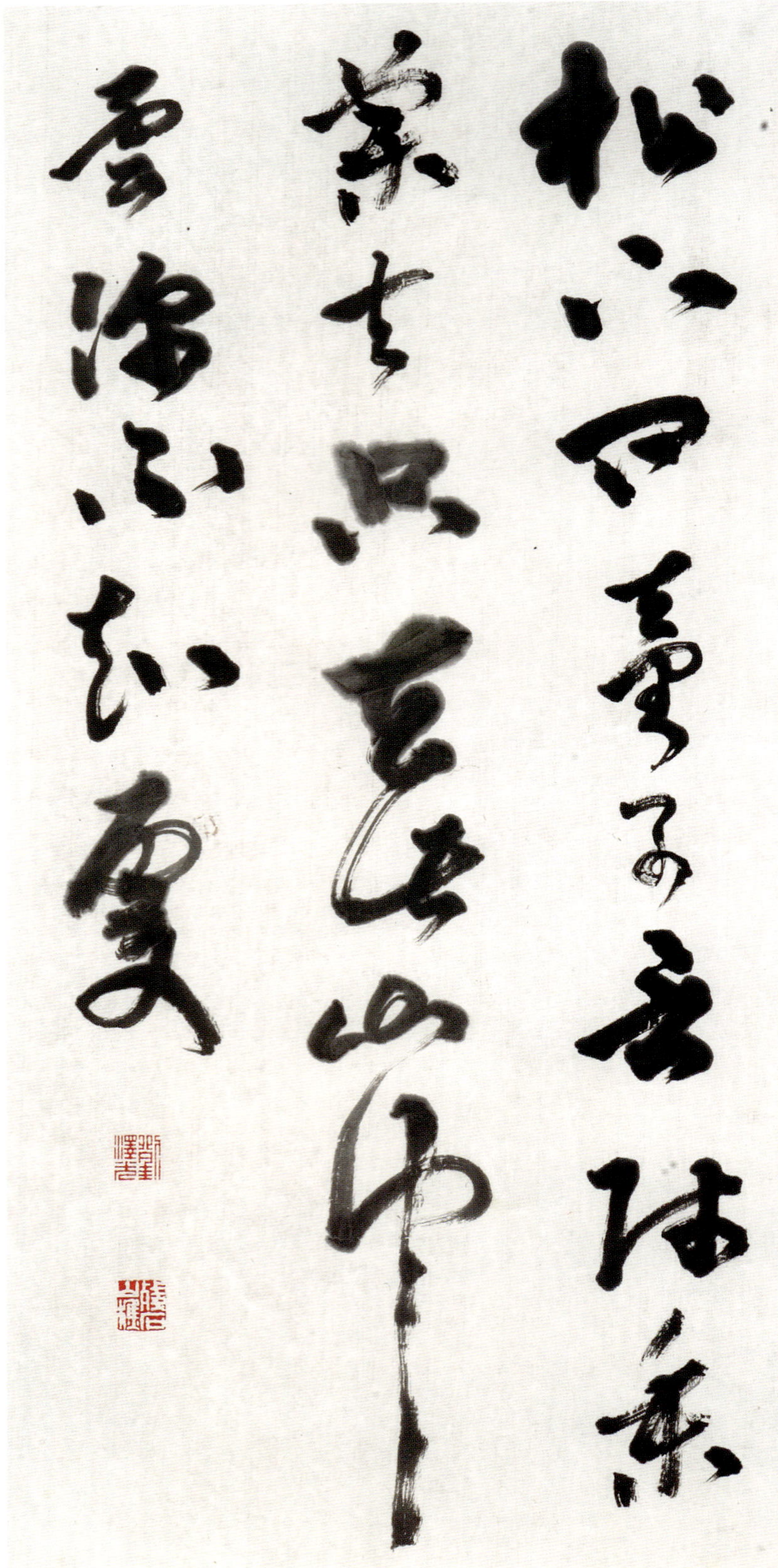

157 *Poem "Looking for the Hermit and Not Finding Him" by Jia Dao* |

賈島《尋隱者不遇》

Cursive script
Ink on paper,
mounted on wood block
95 x 52 cm
2007

草書
紙本墨書，裱於木板
95 x 52厘米
2007年

Transliteration:
Beneath a pine I question a boy.
He says "Master has gone to
gather herbs.
somewhere on the mountain
but who knows where.
The clouds are deep."

(http://www.thedrunkenboat.com/jiadao.html)

釋文：
松下問童子，言師採藥去。
祗在此山中，雲深不知處。

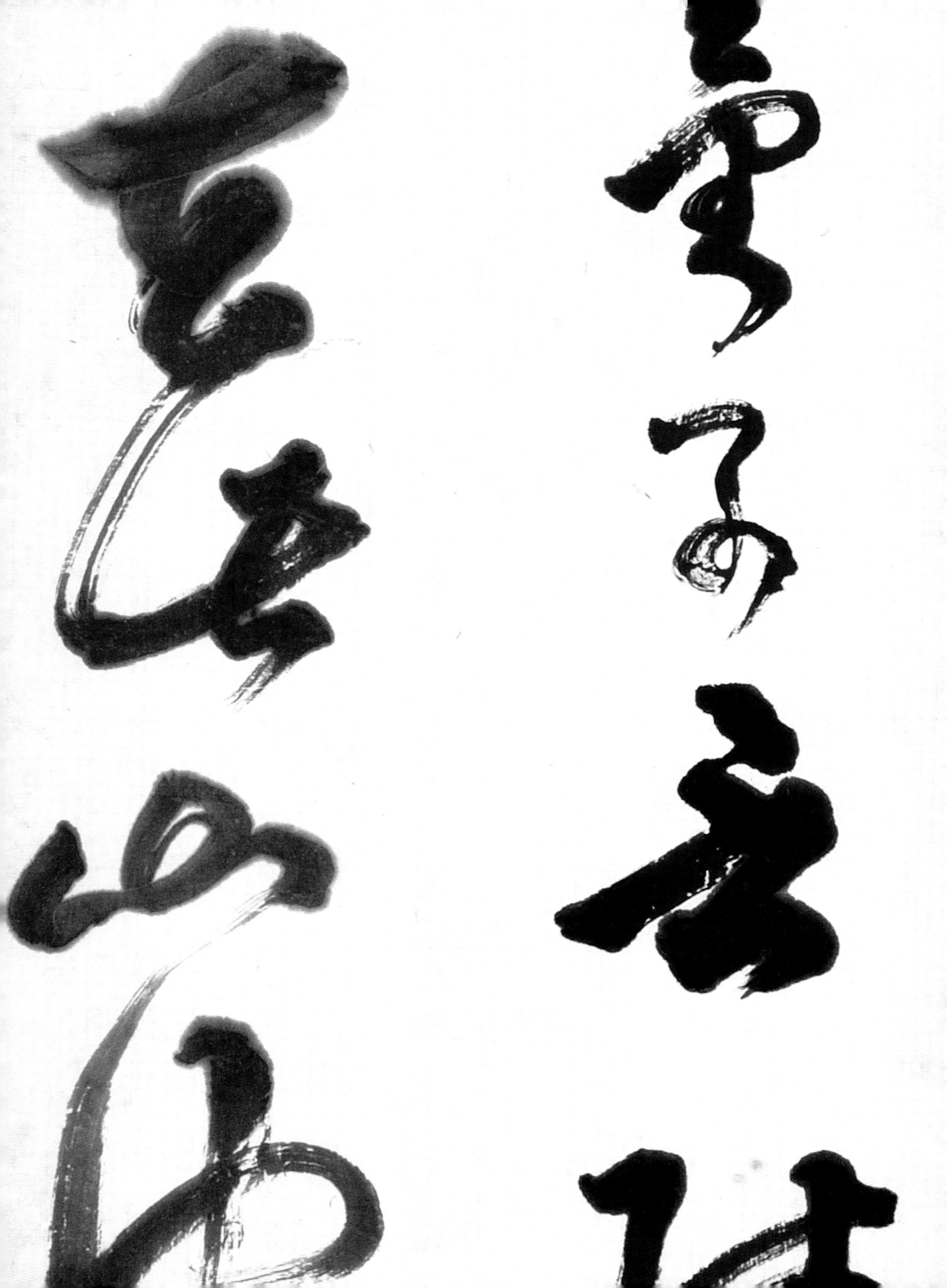

158 *Poem "Through the Yangzi Gorges" by Li Bai* |
李白《下江陵》

Draft cursive script
Ink on paper,
mounted on wood block
73 x 46 cm
2008

草書稿
紙本墨書，裱於木板
73 x 46厘米
2008年

Transliteration/ 釋文:
From the walls of Baidi high in the coloured dawn.
To Jiangling by night-fall is three hundred miles.
Yet monkeys are still calling on both banks behind me.
To my boat these ten thousand mountains away.

(http://etext.lib.virginia.edu/chinese/)

朝辭白帝彩雲間，千里江陵一日還。
兩岸猿聲啼不住，輕舟已過萬重山。

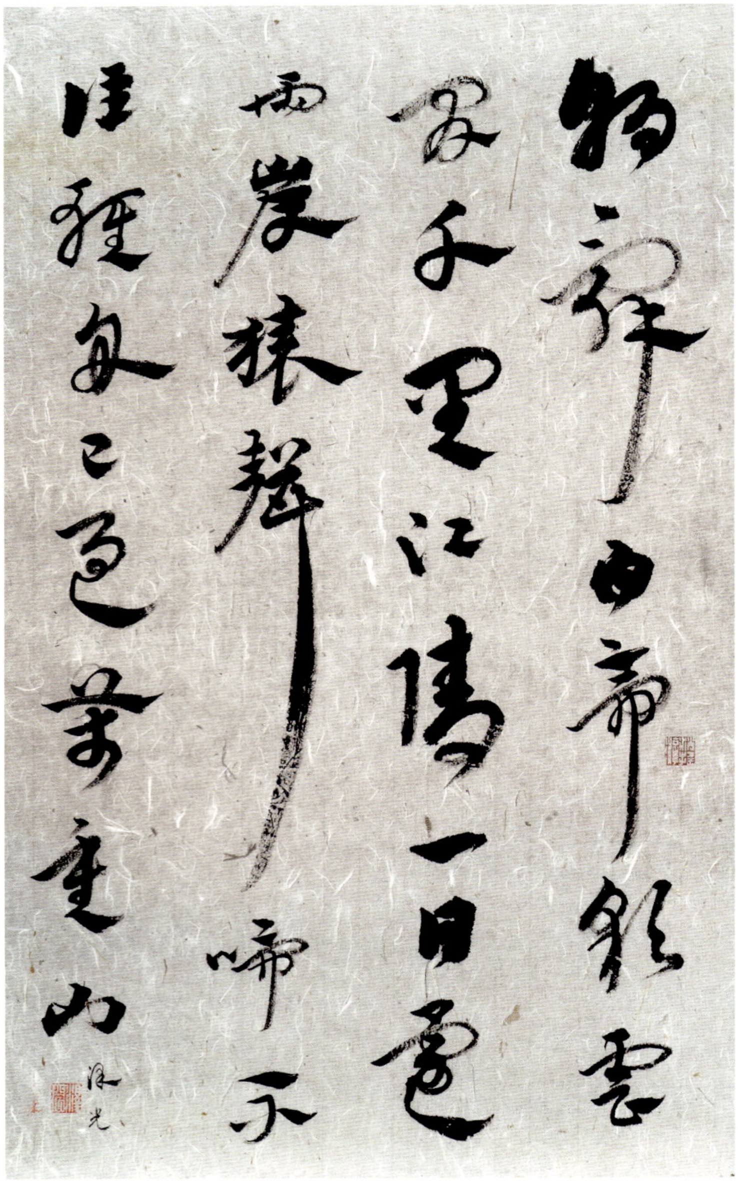

物之拜
要子里

159 ***Lyric by Yan Shu*** |
晏殊《浣溪沙》

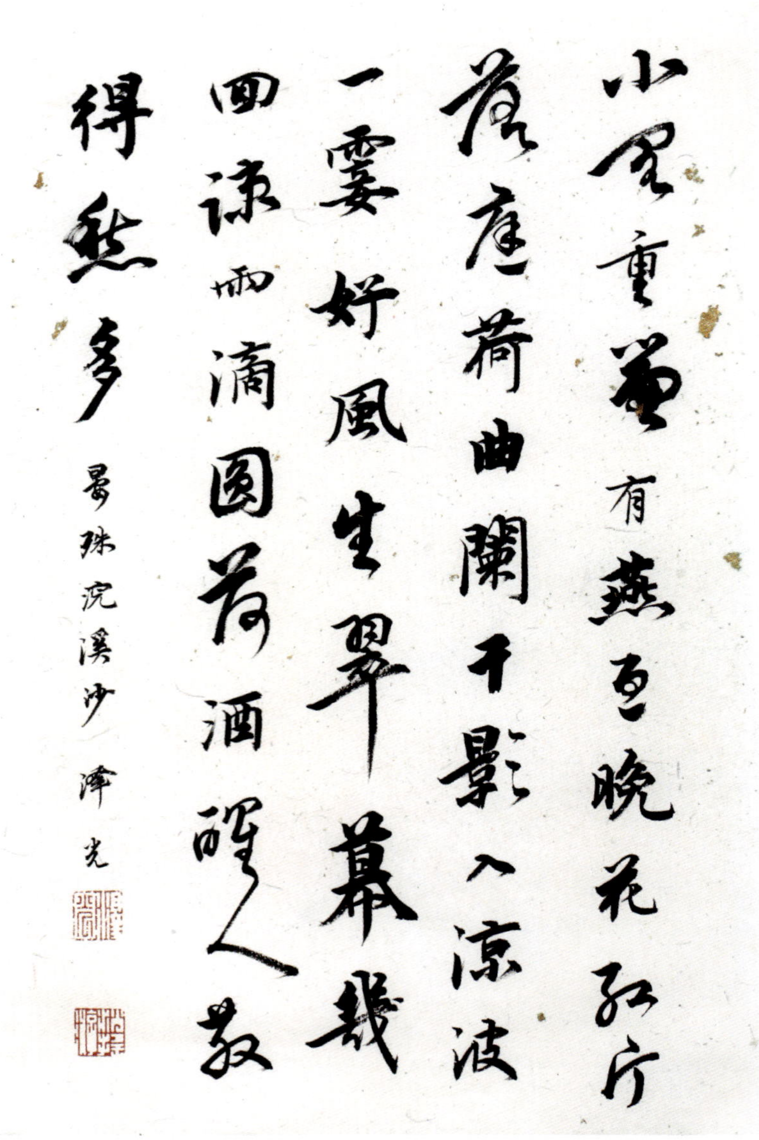

Semi-cursive script
Ink on paper, mounted and framed
42 x 27.4 cm
2009

行書
紙本墨書，裱框
42 x 27.4厘米
2009年

Transliteration:
Lyric "To the Tune of Huanxisha"
by Yan Shu
A swallow flies past the pavilion with layer upon layer of screens.
The red petals of autumn flowers fall down, and make the entire courtyard scarlet.
The wooden railing curves, reflecting on the chill ripples.
Suddenly there blows a strong wind, and all the greens flutter with it.
Some light drizzles drip on the round leaves of lotus.
The guests have sobered up and gone away, leaving more skeins of sorrow behind.

釋文：
小閣重簾有燕過，晚花紅片落庭荷，
曲闌干影入涼波。一霎好風生翠幕，
幾回疏雨滴圓荷，酒醒人散得愁多。

千影入涼波
翠幕幾
何酒醒之數

160 *Lyric "Pounding Clothes by Night" by He Zhu* I
賀鑄《夜搗衣》

Semi-cursive script
Ink on paper,
mounted and framed
42 x 27.4 cm
2009

行書
紙本墨書，裱框
42 x 27.4厘米
2009年

Transliteration:
Folding up the letters and leaving the sewing machine,
The woman brushes off the dust on the fulling block, and starts cloth-pounding in the evening.
The young man riding on horseback, are you still living and well?
When you pass by Guazhou (瓜州), may you see the wild geese flying back towards the south.

釋文：
收錦字，下鴛機，淨拂床砧夜搗衣。
馬上少年今健否？過瓜時見雁南歸。

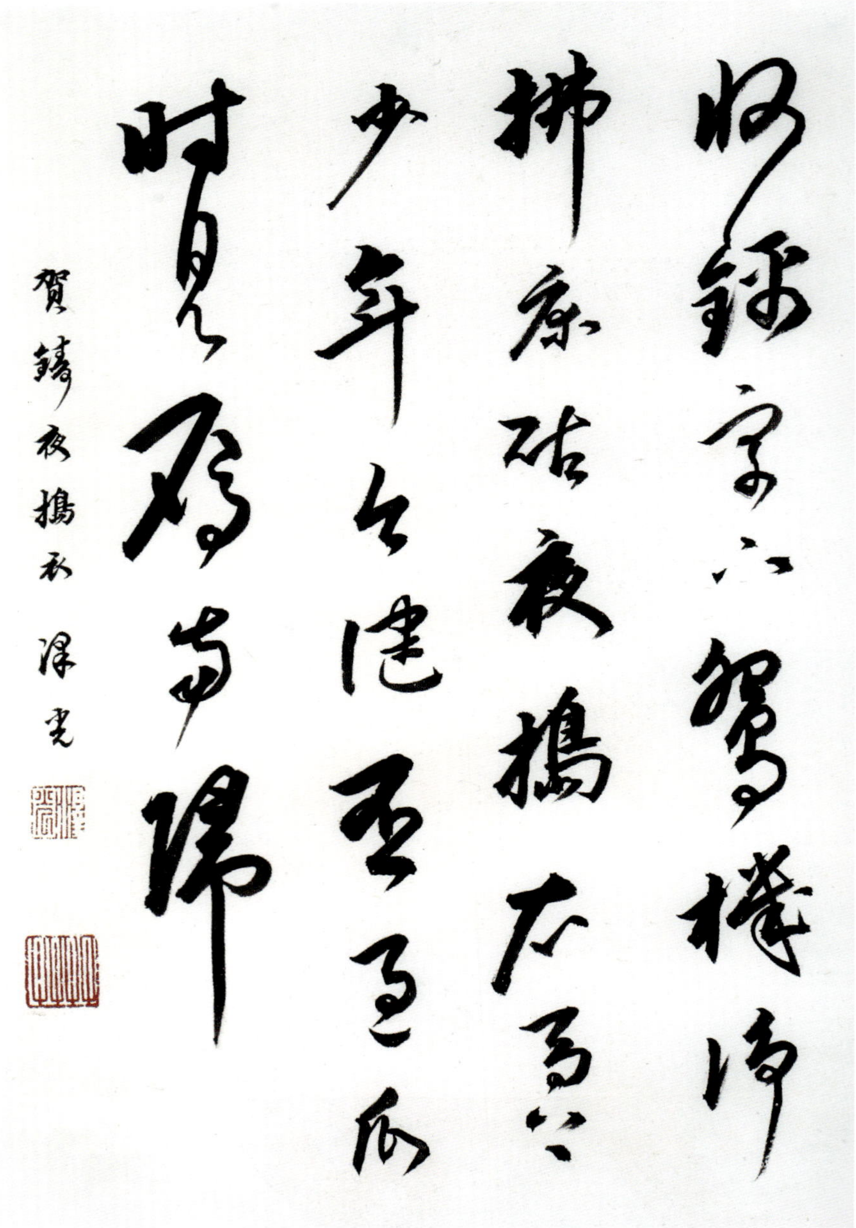

少年亦
时见好

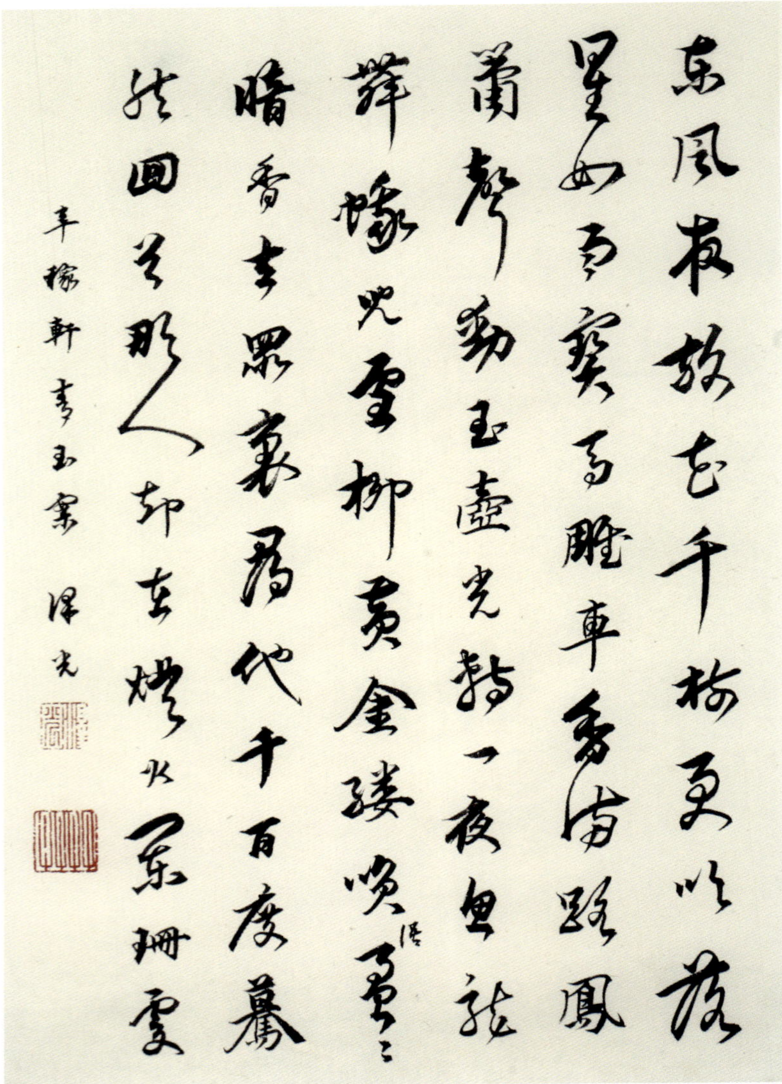

161 *Lyric "Lantern Festival (in the tune of Green Jade Wine Jar)" by Xin Qiji* | 辛棄疾《青玉案——元宵》

Semi-cursive script
Ink on paper, mounted and framed
42 x 27.4 cm
2009

行書
紙本墨書，裱框
42 x 27.4厘米
2009年

Transliteration:
Lanterns look like thousands of flowers aglow;
Later like stars, from the skies, fallen below.
On main streets, horses and carriages ply.
There, ladies shed perfume, as they pass by.
Orchestral music and song greet our ears,
As the moon, slow and steady, eastward veers.
Of the Spring Festival, this night marks the end.
The whole night, capering, carps and dragons spend.
Adorned with ribbons or paper flowers on their head,
Clad in their best raiment, something bright or red,
Women squeeze their way among the festive crowd,
As they talk and laugh; even giggle aloud.
Rouged and powdered;
perfumed to their heart's content,
They cannot but leave behind a subtle scent.
Up and down the main streets, I must have run—
A thousand times or more in quest of one,
Who I have concluded, cannot be found;
For, everywhere, no trace of her can be seen,
When, all of a sudden, I turned about,
That's her, where lanterns are few and far between.

Translation from
www.shigeku.com/shiku/ws/sy/xinqiji.htm

釋文：
東風夜放花千樹，更吹落、星如雨。
寶馬雕車香滿路。
鳳簫聲動，玉壺光轉，一夜魚龍舞。
蛾兒雪柳黃金縷，笑語盈盈暗香去。
眾裡尋他千百度；
驀然迴首，那人卻在，燈火闌珊處。

隊哭雲柳
看書罷歌君
圓去那
却

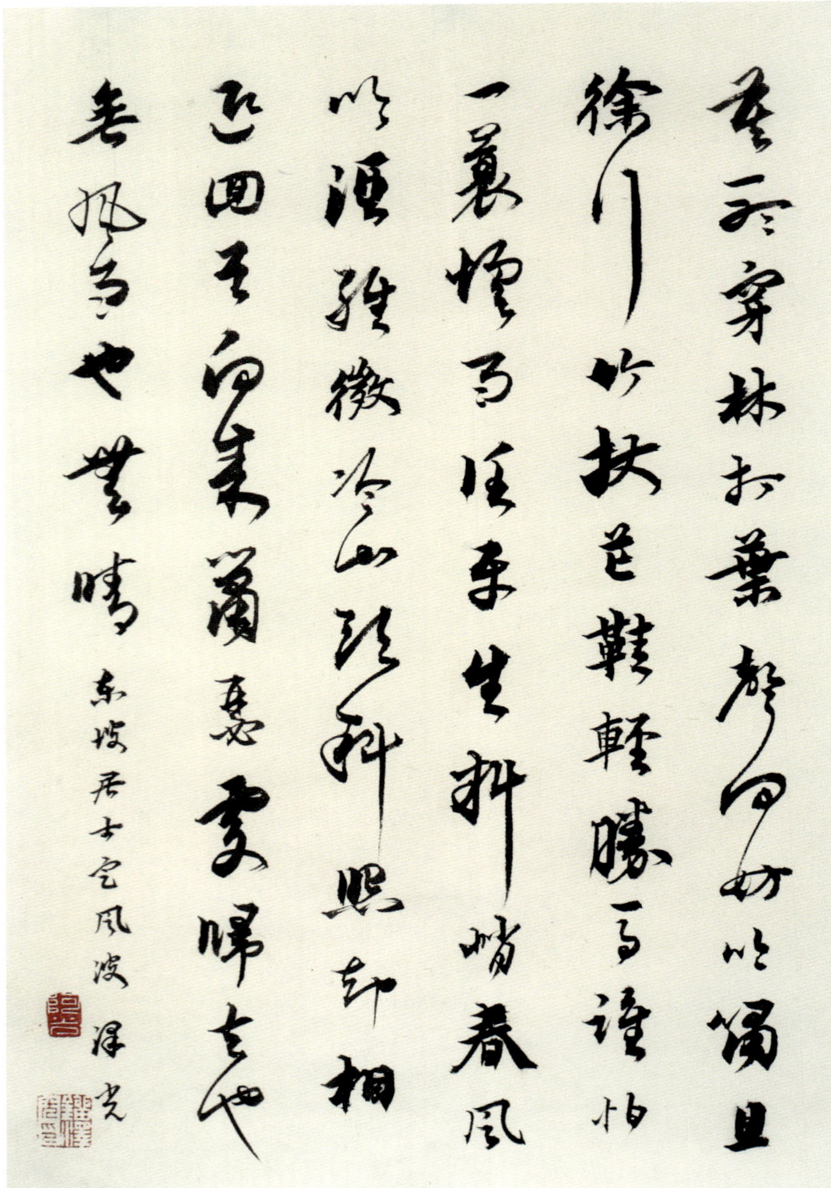

162 *Lyric by Su Shi* | 蘇軾《定風波》

Semi-cursive script
Ink on paper, mounted and framed
42 x 29.7 cm
2009

行書
紙本墨書，裱框
42x 29.7厘米
2009年

Transliteration:
Stop listening to the rain hitting on leaves,
Why not take a leisure stroll, and sing your heart out.
Giving up the horse for lighter gear like sandals and a cane – who cares.
A straw raincoat may just be all I need in misty rain.
The spring breeze wakes me up from drunkenness – a bit chilly.
Luckily the sun setting behind the hill sends me warm welcoming rays.
Turning back, I can still see that windy and rainy place. in.
Now that I have arrived – home at last,
There's no sunshine, no wind and no rain.

Translation from www.asiasentinel.com

釋文：
莫聽穿林打葉聲，何妨吟嘯且徐行。
竹杖芒鞋輕勝馬，誰怕？一蓑煙雨任平生。
料峭春風吹酒醒，微冷，山頭斜照卻相迎。
迴首向來蕭瑟處，歸去，也無風雨也無晴。

任平生料峭
微冷山头斜照
向来萧瑟处归
也无晴
东坡居士定风

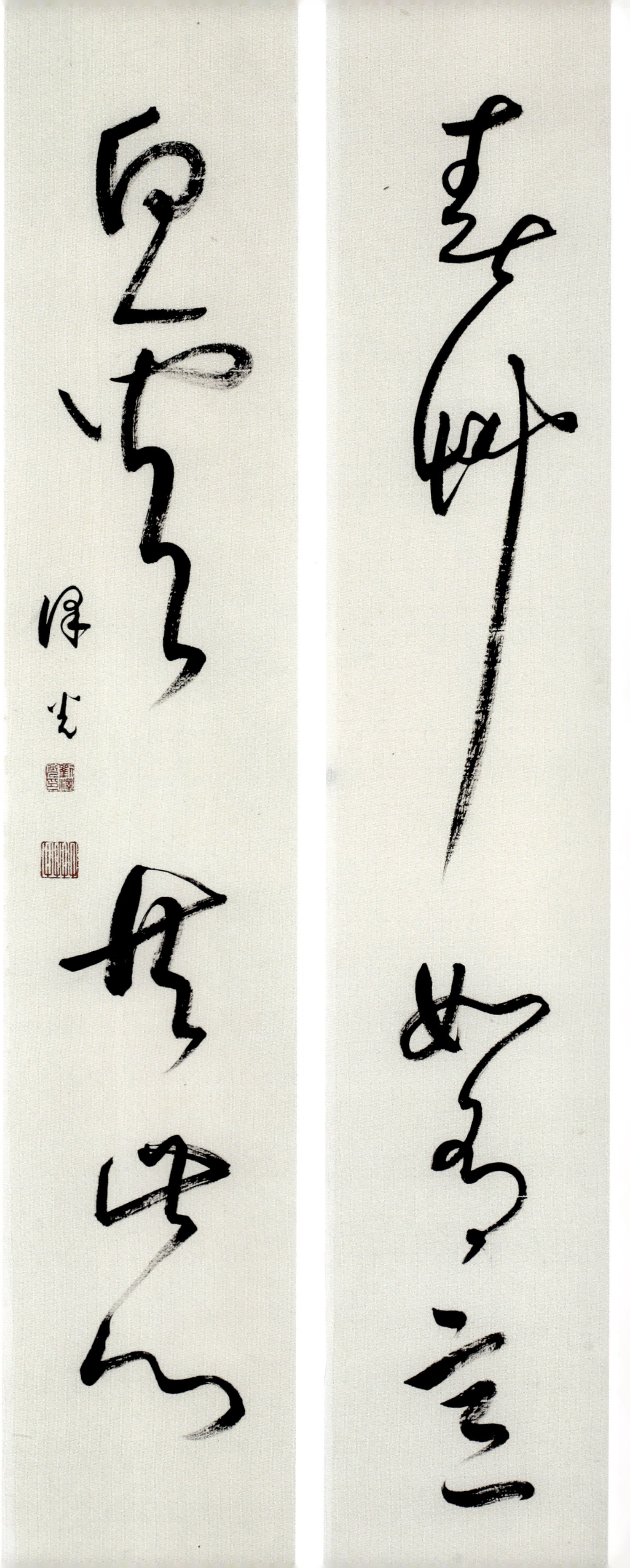

163 *Five-character-line Couplet in Cursive Script* | 草書五言聯

Cursive script
Ink on paper, hanging scrolls
100 x 23cm (each)
2009

草書
紙本墨書，立軸
各100 x 23 厘米
2009年

Transliteration:
Spring grass appears wistful.
White clouds share the same feelings.

(Translation from Jason C. Kuo & Peter C. Sturman (ed.), Double Beauty: Qing Dynasty Couplets from the Lechangzai Xuan Collection, Hong Kong: Art Museum, The Chinese University of Hong Kong, 2003)

釋文：
春草如有意
白雲共此心

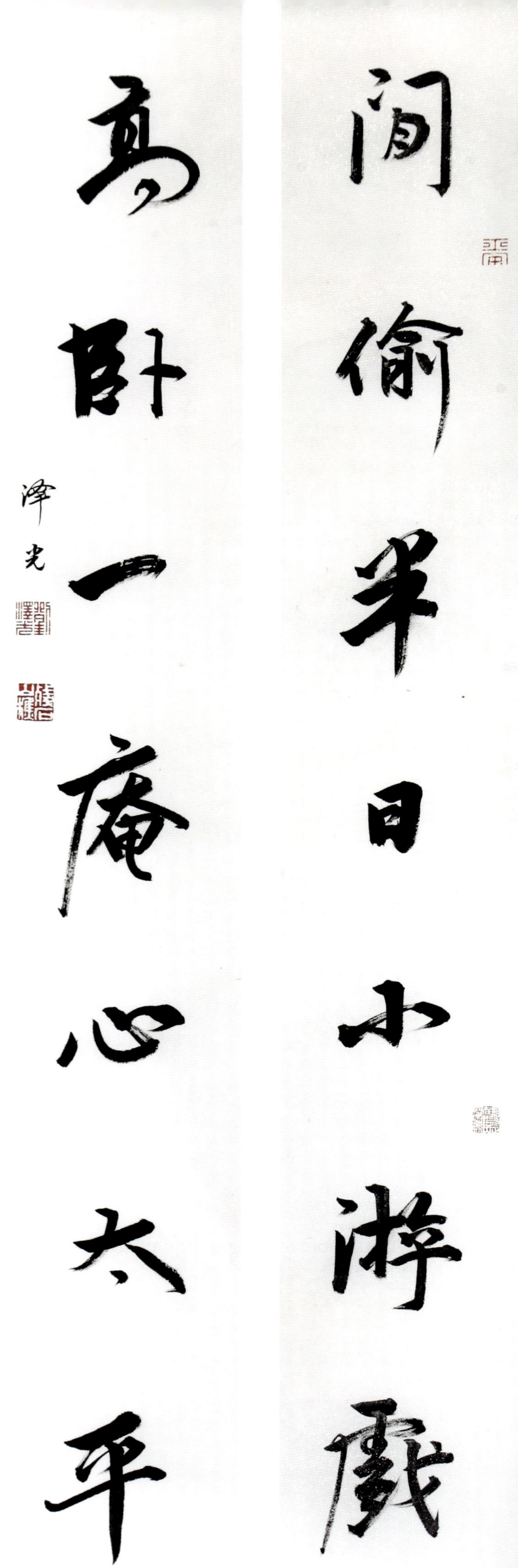

164 *Seven-character-line Couplet in Semi-cursive Script* | 行書七言聯

Semi-cursive script
Ink on paper, hanging scrolls
135 x 25 cm (each)
2009

行書
紙本墨書，立軸
各135 x 25厘米
2009年

Transliteration:
Stealing the leisure of half a day
for a little pay.
Napping away in a lodge and fret
is at bay.

(Translated by Tina Liem in Harold Mok(ed.), Double Beauty II: Qing Dynasty Couplets from the Lechangzai Xuan Collection, Hong Kong: Art Museum, The Chinese University of Hong Kong,2007)

釋文：
閒偷半日小游戲
高臥一庵心太平

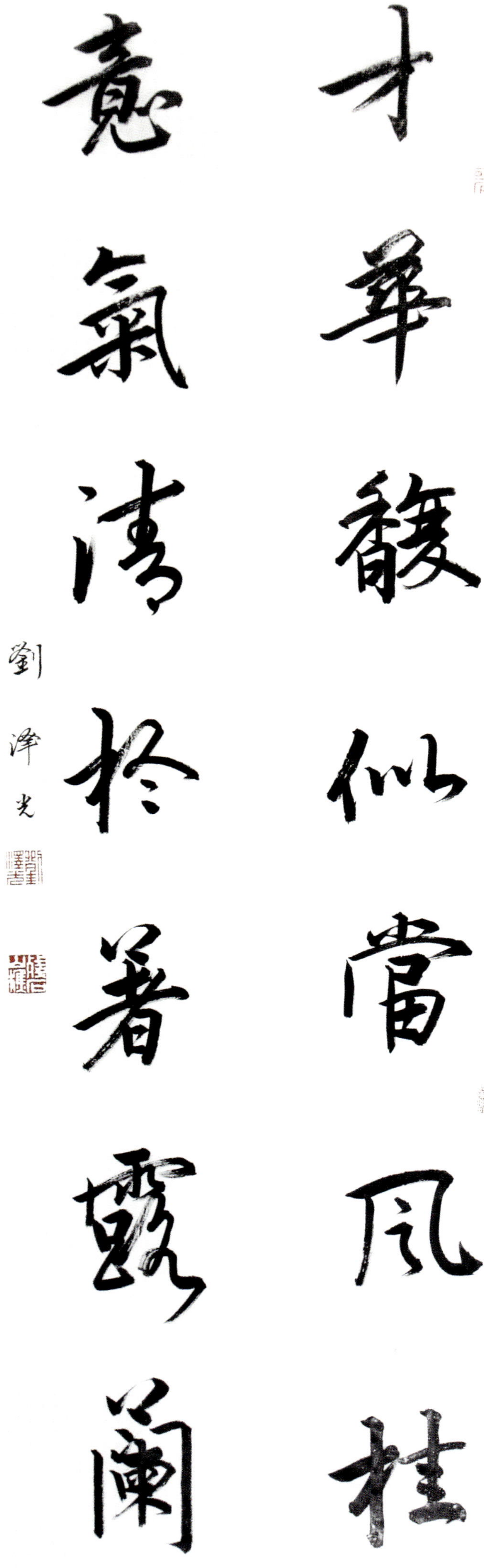

165 *Seven-character-line Couplet in Semi-cursive Script* | 行書七言聯

Semi-cursive script
Ink on paper, hanging scrolls
135 x 25 cm (each)
2009

行書
紙本墨書，立軸
各135 x 25厘米
2009年

Transliteration:
Talents permeating like osmanthus inwind.
Aspirations refreshing like orchid with dew.

(Translated by Tina Liem in Harold Mok (ed.), Double Beauty II: Qing Dynasty Couplets from the Lechangzai Xuan Collection, Hong Kong: Art Museum, The Chinese University of Hong Kong, 2007)

釋文：
才華馥似當風桂
意氣清於著露蘭

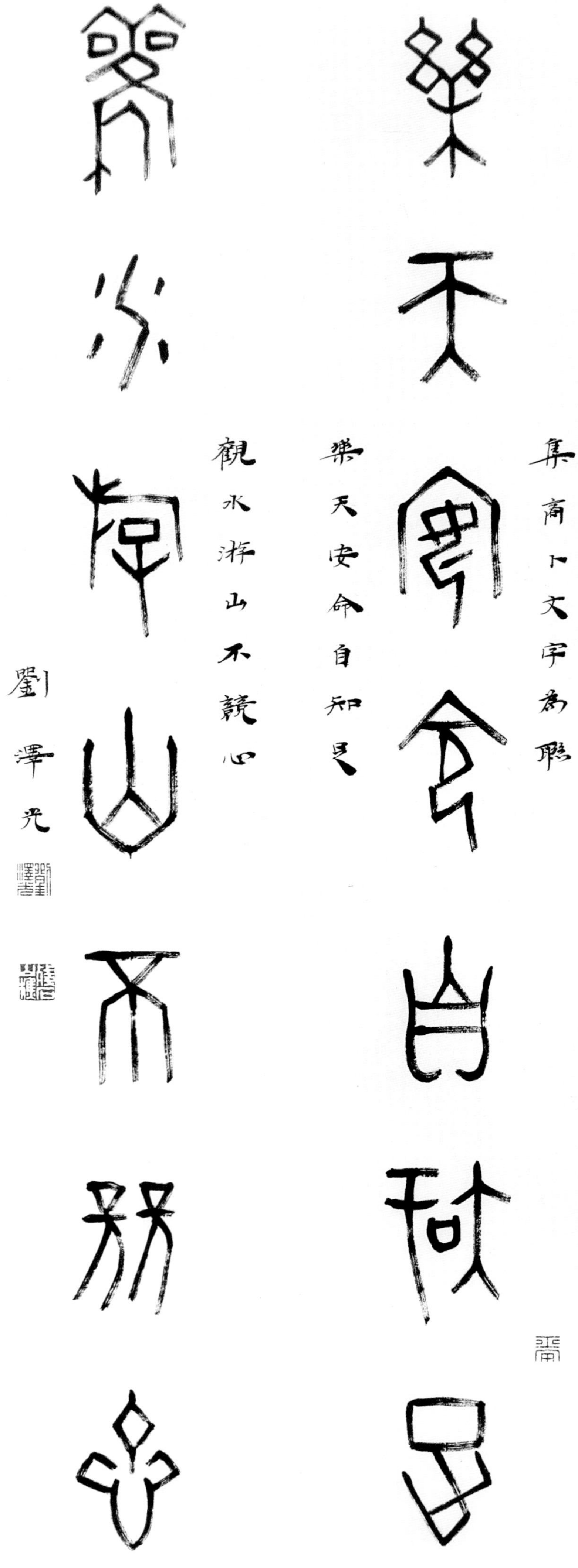

166 ***Seven-character-line Couplet in Oracle-bone Script*** | 甲骨文七言聯

Oracle-bone script
Ink on paper, hanging scrolls
135 x 25cm (each)
2009

甲骨文
紙本墨書，立軸
各135 x 25厘米
2009年

Transliteration:
Enjoy one's life and be contented with one's own lot;
Appreciate the sights of mountains and rivers without intriguing with others.

釋文：
樂天安命自知足
觀水游山不競心

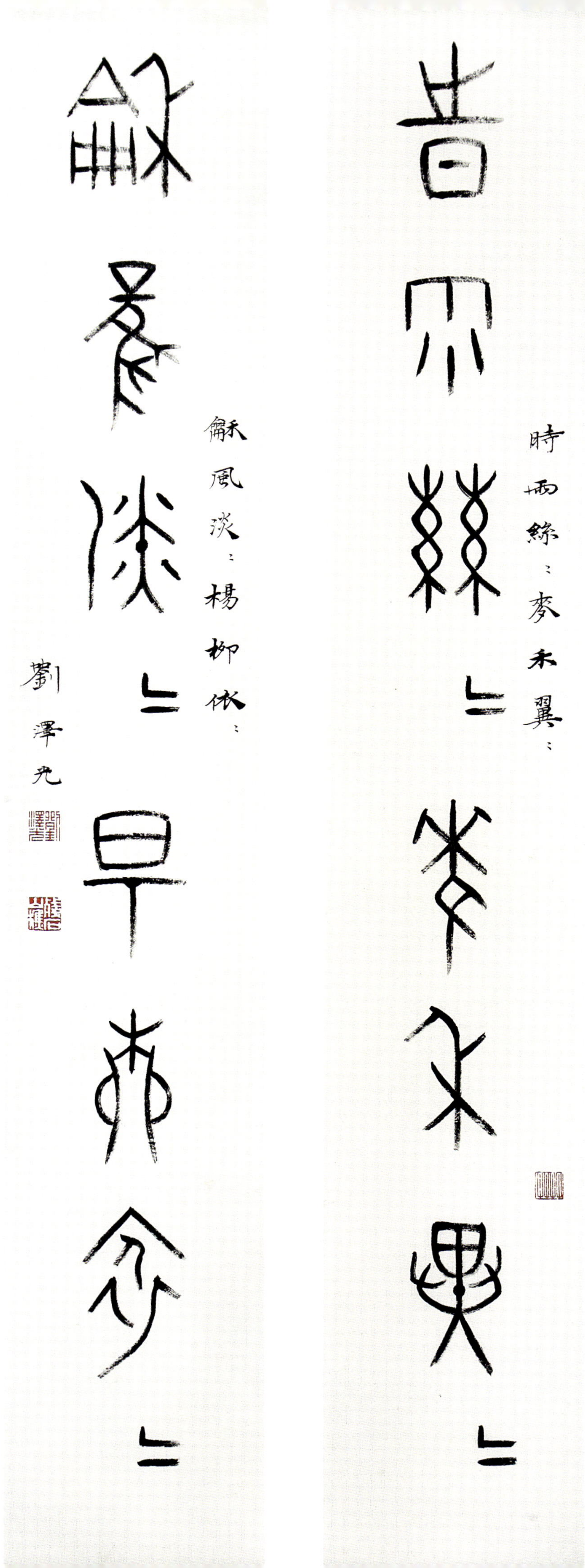

167 ***Eight-character-line Couplet in Oracle-bone Script*** | 甲骨文八言聯

Oracle-bone script
Ink on paper, hanging scrolls
135 x 25cm (each)
2009

甲骨文
紙本墨書，立軸
各135 x 25厘米
2009年

Transliteration:
Timely rain drizzles and wheat seedlings prosper.
Gentle wind breezes and willow branches flicker.

釋文：
時雨絲絲 麥禾翼翼
龢風淡淡 楊柳依依

168 *Five-character-line Couplet in Oracle-bone Script*

甲骨文五言聯

Oracle-bone script
Ink on paper, hanging scrolls
80 x 25 cm (each)
2009

甲骨文
紙本墨書，立軸
各80 x 25厘米
2009年

Transliteration:
Beautiful flowers blossom under the crescent moon.
Homeward birds pass by the declining sun.

釋文：
好花放初月
歸鳥帶斜陽

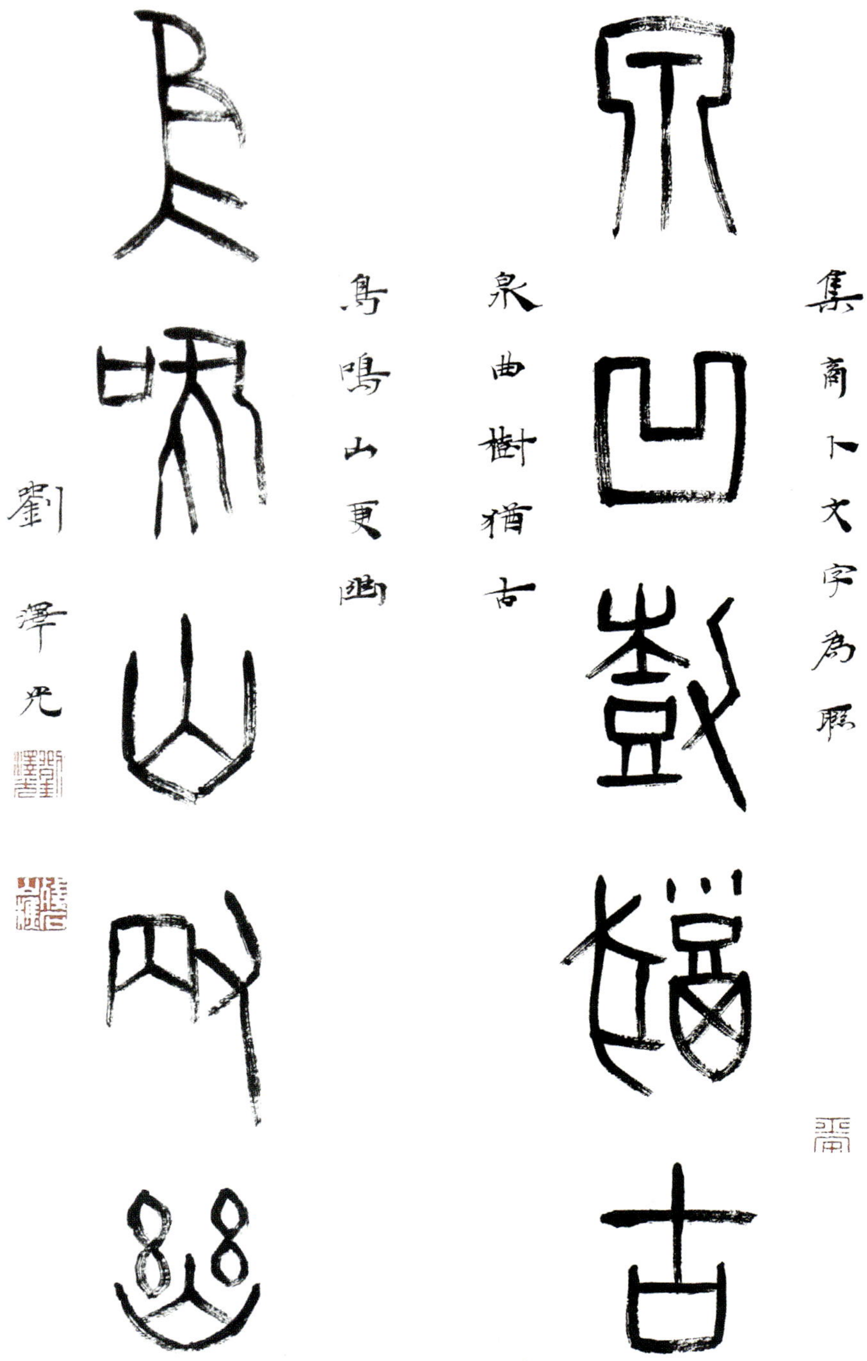

169 *Five-character-line Couplet in Oracle-bone Script* | 甲骨文五言聯

Oracle-bone script
Ink on paper, hanging scrolls
80 x 25 cm (each)
2009

甲骨文
紙本墨書，立軸
各80 x 25厘米
2009年

Transliteration:
Trees look older with the curving streams.
Mountains sound quieter with the twitters of birds.

釋文：
泉曲樹猶古
鳥鳴山更幽

170 *Four-character-line Couplet in Oracle-bone Script* | 甲骨文四言聯

Oracle-bone script
Ink on paper, hanging scrolls
70 x 25 cm (each)
2009

甲骨文
紙本墨書，立軸
各70 x 25厘米
2009年

Transliteration:
It is the refine of substances, the treasure of God.
There are people enjoying longevity, since the times are blessed.

Translation from:
http://en.wikisource.org/wiki/Teng_Wang_Ge_Xu

釋文：
物華天寶
人壽年豐

171 *Four-character-line Couplet in Oracle-bone Script* | 甲骨文四言聯

Oracle-bone script
Ink on paper, hanging scrolls
70 x 25 cm (each)
2009

甲骨文
紙本墨書，立軸
各70 x 25厘米
2009年

Transliteration:
Mentors visit the Tiger Port.
Elites gather at the Dragon Gate.

釋文：
朋游虎皋
人集龍門

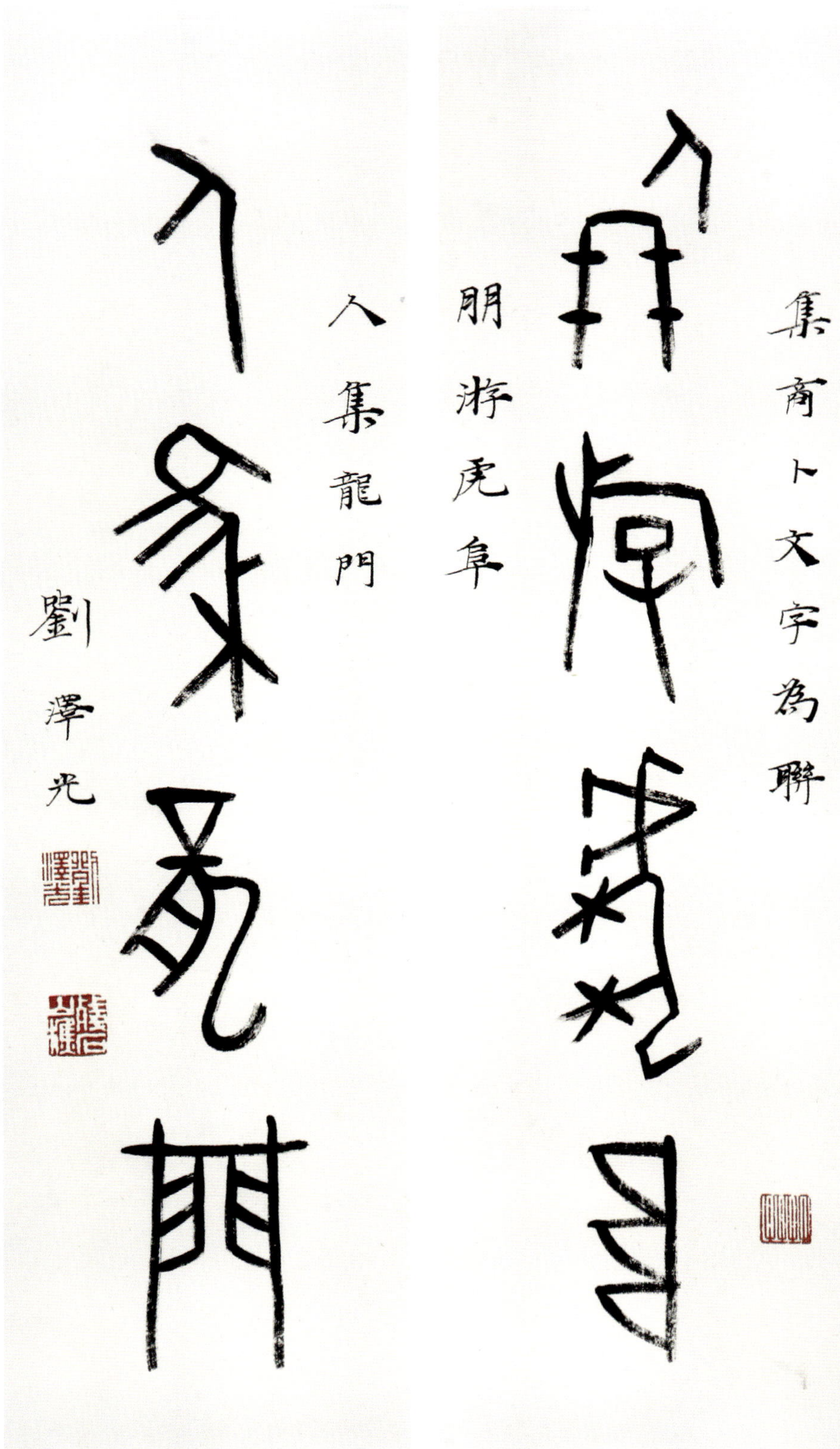

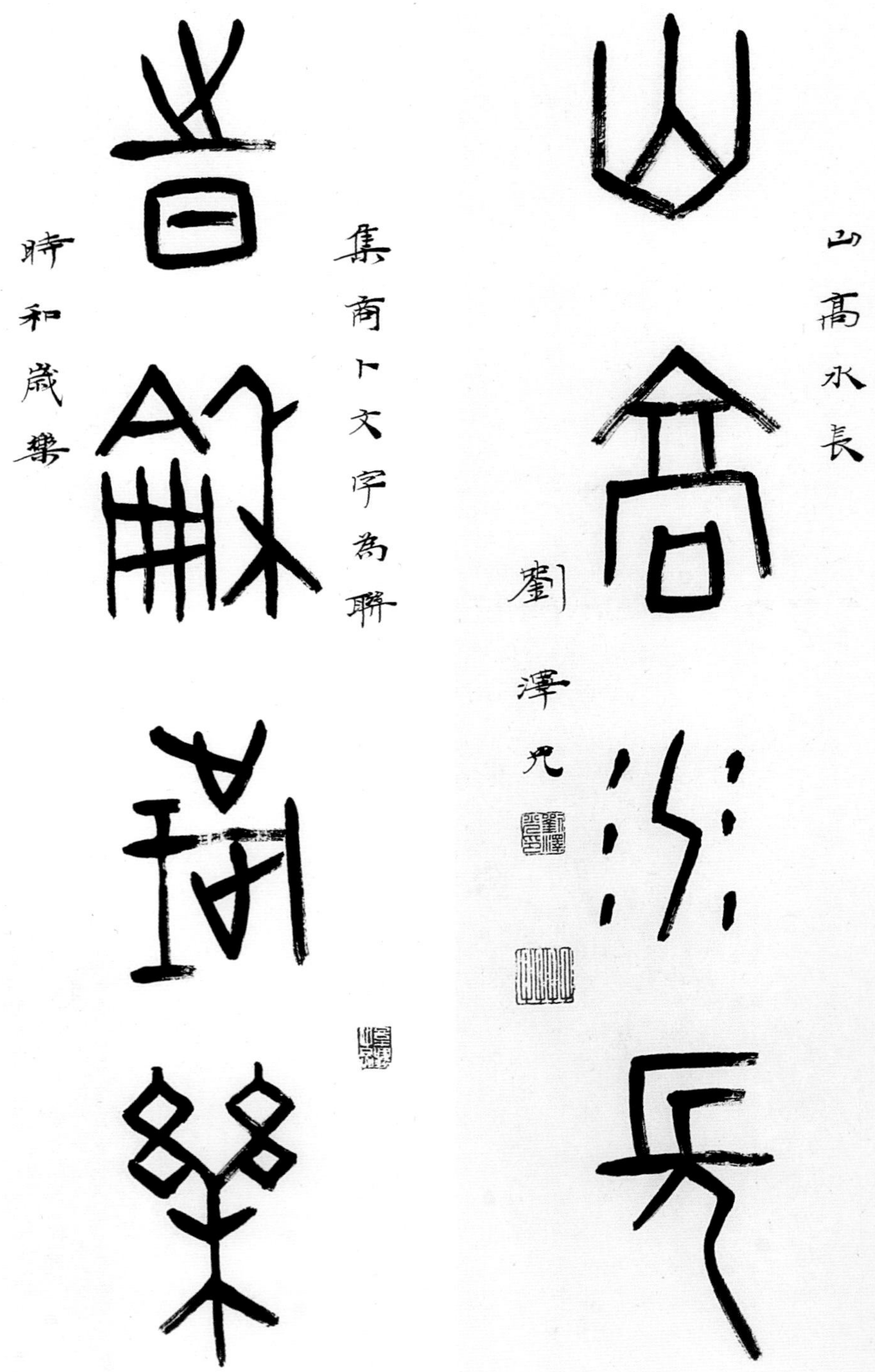

172 *Four-character-line Couplet in Oracle-bone Script* | 甲骨文四言聯

Oracle-bone script
Ink on paper, hanging scrolls
70 x 25 cm (each)
2009

甲骨文
紙本墨書，立軸
各70 x 25厘米
2009年

Transliteration:
The time is peaceful and the year is full of joys
The virtues of a great man are like lofty mountains and mighty streams.

Translation from
http://www.mandarinbook.net/

釋文：
時和歲樂
山高水長

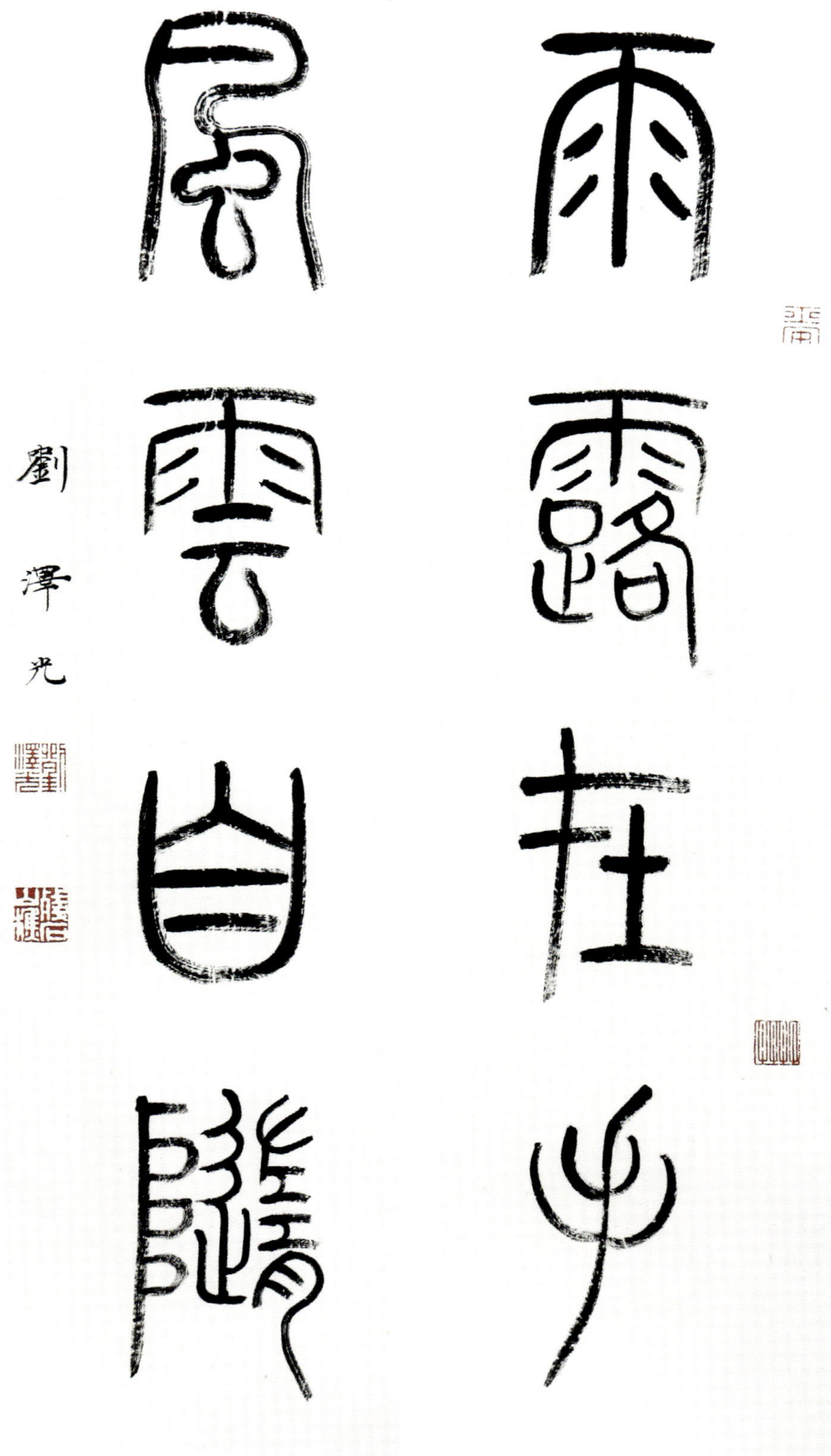

173 ***Four-character-line Couplet in Seal Script*** | 篆書四言聯

Seal script
Ink on paper, hanging scrolls
70 x 25 cm (each)
2009

篆書
紙本墨書，立軸
各70 x 25厘米
2009年

Transliteration:
Rains and dews on hand.
Wind and clouds at ease.

釋文：
雨露在手
風雲自隨

174 ***Ease and Comfort*** | 安樂

Seal script
Ink on paper,
mounted and framed
30 x 12 cm
2007

篆書
紙本墨書，裱框
30x 12厘米
2007年

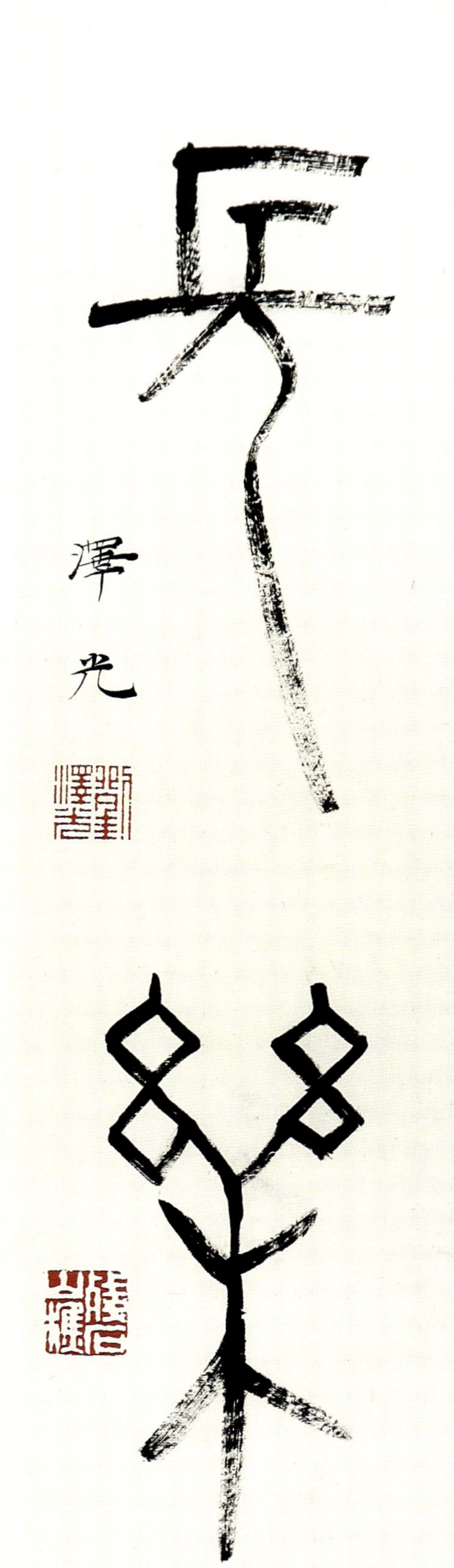

175 ***Stay Joyful*** | 長樂

Oracle-bone script
Ink on paper, mounted and framed
50 x 17 cm
2009

甲骨文
紙本墨書，裱框
50 x 17厘米
2009年

176 *Five-character-line Couplet in Clerical Script* | 隸書五言聯

Clerical script
Ink on paper, hanging scrolls
135 x 33 cm (each)
2009

隸書
紙本墨書，裱框
各135 x 33 厘米
2009年

Transliteration:
Scattered on the sky are thousands of jackdaws.
Surrounding the lonesome village is a flowing stream.

(From *Song* lyric - Qin Guan's "Fragrance filled the Hall")

釋文：
寒鴉千萬點
流水繞孤村

（宋詞 秦觀《滿庭芳》）

177 *Qingli's Memories* | 青岃存念

Draft-cursive script
(Seal-engraving draft)
Ink on paper,
mounted on wood block
59 x 17.5 cm
2008

草書
紙本墨書，裱於木板
59 x 17.5厘米
2008年

Artist's inscription:
In the autumn of 2008, my mentor Professor Wan Qingli instructed (i.e. requested) me to engrave a seal that reads "Qingli's memory". This seal is intended to serve as his "collector's seal". I attempted to use the draft-cursive script in the brush manner of the "Han Dynasty bamboo slips" to make a draft for the seal. I am pleased with this draft because it has a spirit that communicates with the ancients.

題識 ：
戊子秋，青岃師命余刻「青岃存念」印，以作其收藏章之用。遂以章草漢簡筆意試書印稿, 自覺神與古會，頗慊我心也。 澤光補識。

178 ***Investigation of Things*** | 博物

Clerical script
Ink on paper, mounted and framed
30 cm diameter
2009

Collection of Dr. Vivian Ting

隸書
紙本墨書，裱框
直徑30厘米
2009年

丁穎茵博士藏

Artist's inscription:
Indulging in material things ruins one's will.
Investigating things nurtures the aspiration.
This work is dedicated to my good friend Vivian.

題識：
玩物喪志，博物養志。
穎茵好友一粲。

博
看世

179 *How Much is Art? The Price List of Daniel Lau's Works of Caligraphy & Seal Engraving* |

藝術何價
劉澤光書畫篆刻潤例

Semi-cursive script
Ink on paper, mounted and framed
103cm x 26cm
2010

行書
水墨紙本，裱框
103cm x 26厘米
2010年

Transliteration:
The price list of Daniel Lau's works of calligraphy and seal engraving ——

> A flash of the blooming epiphyllum*;
> Acceptance of cheque on the spot upon payment.

Artist's inscription: Those who are aware of real estate advertisings profoundly understand the crux of seizing opportunities to buy and sell valuable commodities.

* Artist's note: Epiphyllum oxypetalum is a special species of flower (cactus) that blooms at night and then withers within a few hours before dawn. Hence, this well-known Chinese idiom uses this flower as a metaphor of impressive yet ephemeral beauty. The artist consciously transformed the negative tone of this Chinese idiom to intriguingly suggest that his artworks will only stay in the market in a short period of time because of the great demand.

釋文：
劉澤光書畫篆刻潤例（價目表）—

曇花一現；
見票即收。

款識：留意香港房地產廣告者，當深明把握機會搶購及割愛心頭好之關鍵。

按：作者以此八字 "曇花一現；見票即收" 作書畫篆刻潤例，以諷刺香港97年前樓價瘋狂的程度，當時房地產代理常以此八字吸引買家，而當時的賣家又真能做到見票即收，樓盤又真的如曇花一現，一瞬即逝（指在持續熾熱的樓市中迅速消失），港式俗語所謂"搶手貨"者也。假若藝術品也能如此"搶手"，這將會是怎樣的世界？

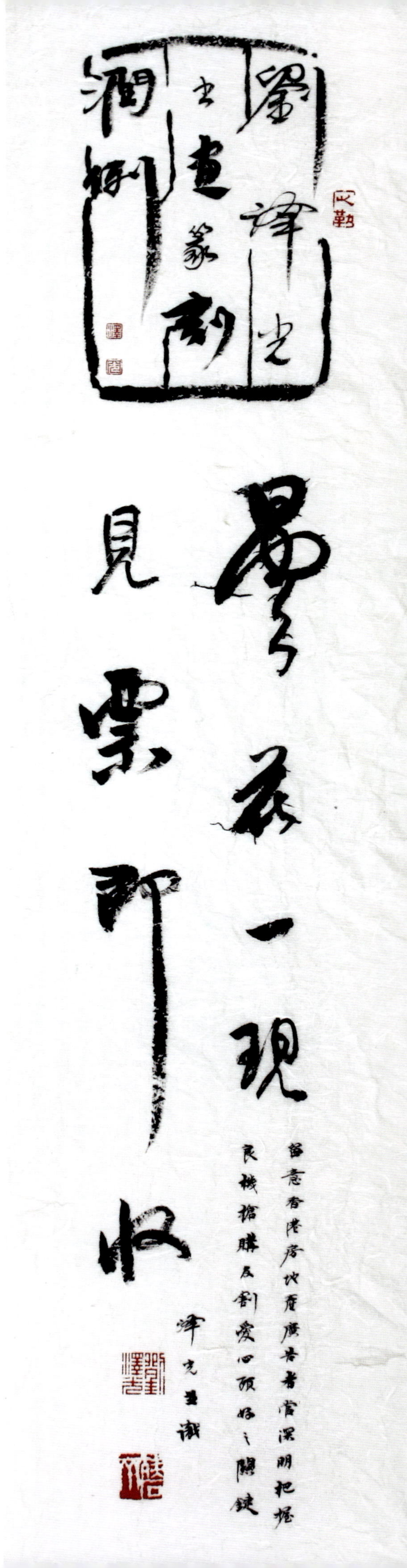

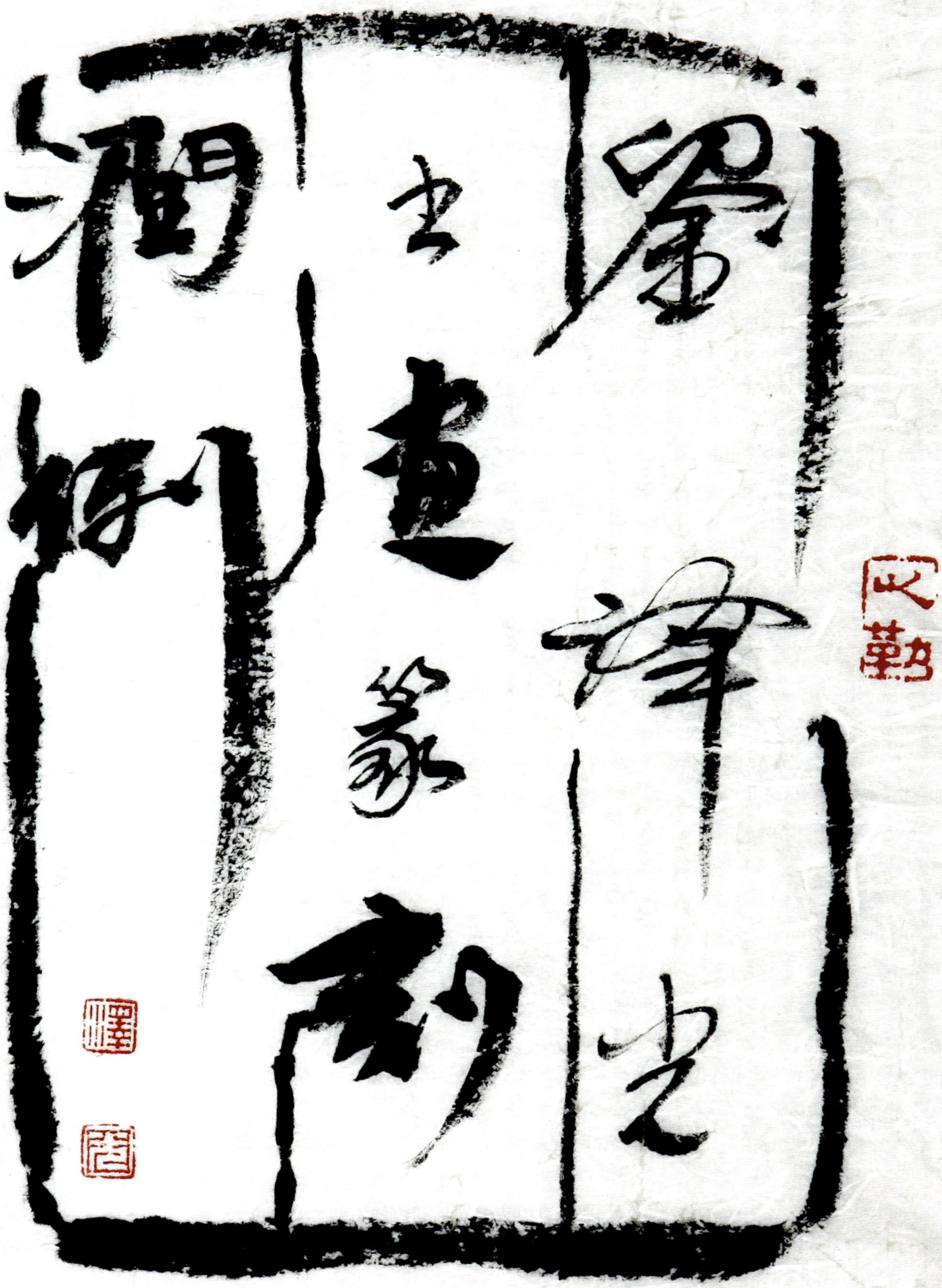

劉燁光
書畫篆刻
潤例

教与學

EPILOGUE/後語

Teach

& Learn

Inheritance and Succession

Lolita Cheung
Curator of "Harmony: Synergy between Tradition and the Contemporary — Chinese Calligraphy and Seal Engraving by Daniel C.K. Lau" Exhibition

Inheritance and succession, is without doubt an important topic in contemporary Chinese art.

I am one of the first graduates from the Master of Visual Arts in Art Administration program offered by the Hong Kong Baptist University. With little experience, I am most grateful to be entrusted by Dr. Daniel Chak-kwong Lau to be the curator for his solo exhibition "Harmony: Synergy between Tradition and the Contemporary — Chinese Calligraphy and Seal Engraving by Daniel C.K. Lau". It not only allowed me to practice what I have leant from class, more notably, provided me an opportunity to ponder the inheritance, and contemplate the future development of Chinese art.

As a scholar as well as a calligrapher and seal-engraver, Dr. Lau's knowledge of the traditional literati art and his artistic talents are evident. Hence the "inheritance" part is well taken care of for this exhibition. However, based on the innovation beaming from his works, I know he would not be contented with a traditional presentation for this exhibition. Dr. Lau has been injecting contemporary thoughts and contents that are with the times into his works, and presents his work in a modernized way while preserving the indispensible elements and essence of Chinese art. His creative orientation is fully reflected in the exhibition.

Traditionally, in calligraphy and seal-engraving, the contact point between the author and the audience is almost always two-dimensional. This is true even for three dimensional artifacts such as steles, tripods and seals, where the appreciation is focused on the implied lifting and pressing action on individual surface of the object. Dr. Lau has taken this to the next level by experimenting with multi-media and adding dimensions to his works. He has demonstrated that modern western elements such as interactive, three-dimensional installation, can be integrated into Chinese art to result in an eye-opening experience for the viewers. I believe that his endeavor to broaden the traditional artistic view, and the creative mindset in pursue of more possibilities, is the attitude we should have for "succession".

I still have much to learn to burgeon into a competent curator, and this has certainly been a very precious learning experience. The most difficult part of this curatorial experience is the need to deny some great works from Dr. Lau's past decade of oeuvre, which I am pleased to see in this catalogue. I would like to take this opportunity to thank Dr. Lau again for his guidance and trust, in helping me make my first and important step into my career in art administration. My gratitude also goes to Roger Ng, Graphic Designer for the exhibition as well as this catalogue, for his professionalism and "can-do" attitude. Last but not the least, my appreciation goes to my husband, who has been very supportive and extremely understanding as I attempt to turn a new page in my career.

承・和・傳

張楚筠
「和：劉澤光古今相生書法篆刻展」策展人

承和傳，毫無疑問是當代中國藝術的其中一個重要課題。

我是香港浸會大學視覺藝術碩士（藝術行政管理）課程的第一屆畢業學生，實屬初出茅廬；有幸得到劉博士的莫大信任，能為他的個人展覽「和：劉澤光古今相生書法篆刻」負起策展人的重責，不但讓我有機會將課堂上的所學所得於以實踐，更難得的是給了我一個珍貴的過程去思考如何承傳和發展中國藝術。

劉博士是一位學者，同時也是一位書法篆刻家，對於傳統文人藝術的理解及創作能力毋庸置疑，使得這個展覽在籌劃之始已充分具備了「承」的條件。但觀乎他作品所展現出的鋭意創新的手法，我知道他是不會滿足於一個傳統展覽模式的－劉博士一直都堅持於作品之中注入與時代接軌的思想內容，將傳統裡各種不能替代的珍貴屬性，以具有現代特色的手法展現，而他這種創作取向亦清晰地呈現於是次展覽中。

不論是傳統書法還是篆刻，作者與觀眾的接觸點自古都多為平面的媒介；就算是立體的碑鼎璽印，每每也只聚焦在個別平面上對提按頓挫的意領神會。劉博士則在這個傳統基礎之上，向更多維的媒介及多元的形式探索，甚至融合現代西方講求立體互動的裝置藝術，進行了一次令人耳目一新的示範。我想，像這種力求拓闊傳統藝術觀賞角度、追尋更多可能性的創作思維，就是「傳」該有的態度方向。

回顧這次策展經驗，自知盡多不足之處，但對我來説絕對是難能可貴的學習機會。整個展覽的候選展品涵蓋了劉博士近十年的佳作，最難的就是如何取捨；藉著一眾佳作付梓成冊，特此再次感謝劉博士給與我的指引和信任，助我實踐了投身藝術行政的重要一步。同時要鳴謝為展覽及本書負責平面設計的伍啓豪，為他的專業態度及有求必應鼓掌。最後，亦要謝謝外子對自己的支持及體貼，令我能放膽去展開事業新的一頁。

A Harmonious Heart Brings Success

Jack Luo

First of all, it is my great honor to have this opportunity to write a short essay about Dr. Lau in this book, which has a profound impact on Chinese calligraphic artwork and academic studies. Originally from Beijing, I am currently a student of the Bachelor of Arts in Visual Arts programme at Hong Kong Baptist University. I hope that my writing can offer everybody a chance to know about Dr. Lau's attitude towards life and his art.

The Aesthetics of "Equilibrium and Harmony"

A man in a neatly pressed suit with a noble look came into the class while carrying tons of Chinese calligraphic works and paintings. The first time I met Dr. Lau was in his art theory course on Chinese art history. I was surprised and could not imagine how this strapping man had any relationship with a type of art that requires a quiet and peaceful heart for studying in the entire process of production of works of calligraphy. In fact, Dr. Lau told us that he used to be a boy with bad temper, but after practicing Chinese calligraphies for many years, he is now a real gentle man. There is an old Chinese saying "a harmonious heart brings wealth". I would like to change this clause into "a harmonious heart brings priceless knowledge". I believe that this newly coined expression can best depict the success of Dr. Lau's unique approach of teaching and his academic and artistic endeavors.

A Harmonious Heart Brings Knowledge

It is of great importance for Chinese calligraphy to show its own chi and momentum in each character. Practice can refine the character with magnificent sweep, but it is more difficult for artist to reach a harmonious heart, which is one of the highest levels of spirit, in his or her artworks. Only with this kind of pure mind, one can be inspired by everyday life to create his or her artwork just as what Dr. Lau does.

Dr. Lau's artworks originate from life, thus he keeps on enjoying life just as enjoying the process of making artworks. Take a class before last mid-autumn festival as an example, Dr. Lau spontaneously got into the mood of creating calligraphic works when he was teaching how couplets were composed. Then he wrote a new couplet in an improvisational manner, with totally new feeling by simply combining one sentence from each of the two old couplets. He also wrote every character in the couplet separately, one character on one small piece of paper, as mid-autumn festival and sent them all to each student. This was why and how the Seven-Character-Line Couplet in Seal Script: "Man becomes an experienced traveler for there have been thousands of miles that he goes; Mid-Autumn Festival comes again as one year has passed quickly." (cat. no. 19) was created. As art students, my classmates and I always want our work to become unique by a way of rebellion against and questioning the daily chores. However, I might never reach the point of moving the beholders that much by only adding pure mood into my artwork like how Dr. Lau did.

To appreciate Dr. Lau's artworks, the beholder who does not have much art research experience may just feel like strolling by the bank of a serene river. It is better for us to have a rest to thinking and enjoy his works..

A Harmonious Heart Brings Successful Teaching

I started learning to draw in Beijing when I was six. After years of studying in Mainland China, I found out that practice is the only way for art or non-art students to pass the entrance examination in order to stand head and shoulders above others and to further chase their goals. Fortunately, I have been lucky enough to meet new teachers and to be educated under new teaching methods here in Hong Kong. I am really thankful to Dr. Lau as he is not only a teacher to me, but also being a friend of mine.

To lay a solid foundation is an indispensable part of learning Chinese calligraphy. I could imagine how Chinese calligraphic class will be taught in Beijing: students would bring the copy book, imitating each character again and again all day, while teachers would play a role as supervisor with the responsibility of correcting any mistakes that the students make. And it is very common to hear phrases like "you should not do this..." It was a totally different experience enrolling in Dr. Lau's course. Dr. Lau guides instead of instructs. We were encouraged to speak out in class. It was not surprising to find out that we were fascinated in discussions about artworks since we knew that there were no right or wrong in art explorations. Surely, Dr. Lau was also pleased when we were trying to use more professional words or phrases like "bold and vigorous brush strokes" when depicting some dark and thick brush strokes. This was a professional attitude that we learned with Dr. Lau's guidance.

Dr. Lau is indeed a modest artist without patronizing attitude. It is very common especially for those scholars majored in studies related to Chinese history to use words in classical Chinese. But Dr. Lau was one of the few who try to avoid this way of talking when giving a lecture. Instead, his speeches were more like chatting with students. Students were all happy in the process of listening and gaining knowledge when we could laugh and talk casually.

The freedom to choose one's own topic for final project is maybe one of the reasons why Dr. Lau becomes popular among students. Take my experience as an example. I got a great support when presenting my idea of calligraphic dance. It was helpful to find out that the idea was respected, and for me to be encouraged in the creative process.

I am not a good writer. The passage above may not be a complete description of Dr. Lau. Still, I hope the readers could share a harmonious heart with me when reading and appreciating the articles and the artworks in this book.

和氣生才 ◣

羅屹昀

能夠受到劉老師邀請在這樣一本影響深遠的書法作品及學術研究專集中撰文實在是受寵若驚，深感萬分榮幸。作為一名從首都北京來到香港求學的藝術學生，雖學業不精、文筆不佳，但也希望借寥寥數語，可以讓大家更加瞭解並接近一個生活中的劉澤光老師。

以和為貴

課室之中，一人行來，此人生得一副燕頷虎頸之相，銅筋鐵骨之形，一言一行中，盡顯粗獷豪雄之氣，身著西裝筆挺，腰間萬卷纏身，真可謂一猛壯書生也。初見我的恩師，是在中國藝術史研究課上，見到講臺後這個身材高大，身形偉岸的男人，很難將他與書法這種需要平和心態進行研究和創作的藝術形式聯繫到一起。後來才知道，老師原來也是個脾氣很大，容易發火的"熱血"青年，經過多年修行書法，才慢慢將火氣修成了和氣。中國有句俗語叫和氣生財，我則將它變成了人才的才，覺得更加可以概括澤光老師的為學和為師之道。

和氣生才學

書法，講求氣與勢的修為，勢是基本功，字形以及用筆的長期訓練則可以顯勢，而氣則是意境的培養，而"和氣"則是一種很難以達到的境界。和，在這裏指平和之心，或換言之，就是生活中所謂的平常心。也只有擁有這樣的心態，才能像澤光老師一樣把創作和藝術生活化。

藝術來源於生活，澤光老師的平常心體現在他作品中一個很重要的特點就是源於他對生活的享受。小舉一例，中秋將至，在課上探討對聯的寫作過程中，興致所至，老師從曾經用於創作的兩幅對聯中各取一句變成一幅新對藉以抒發自己當時與學生們歡聚的情感，後又將一副對聯中的每個字拆開，既當作示範、又當作禮物，送給每個人作為中秋小禮，這便是《篆書七言聯》(萬里因循成久客；一年容易又中秋)(展品19)的創作過程。我身邊的很多同學，都常常希望自己的藝術作品，可以通過反叛或是質疑生活的點點滴滴來吸引別人的關注，然而卻很少有人能像澤光老師的作品這樣，通過純真、質樸的情感來感動觀 。

品味老師的作品，對於不做學術研究的觀眾來說，就像漫步在緩緩的溪流間，氣定神閑，平心靜氣去享受就好了。

和氣生才人

我從六歲就在北京開始學習畫畫，期間間斷著學下來多多少少也對大陸的美術教育有個印象，大部分的藝術生走的道路其實和普通高考生一樣，通過不斷地練習以求從百萬大軍中脱穎而出。我很幸運可以來到香港，接觸這裏的老師和教學方法，尤其是澤光老師，可稱的起名副其實的良師益友了。

書法教學，比起其他科目來説，打下堅實的基礎是必不可少的環節。之前我腦海中浮現的書法課，就是學生每個人一本字帖，從上課臨摹到下課，老師扮演的則是巡視和糾錯員的責任。我常在大陸聽到老師的一句話就是："你這麼做是錯的。"然而上澤光老師的堂則有一種全新的體驗，劉老師扮演的角色只是引導大家。老師常常鼓勵我們每個人都在課堂上發言，從剛剛開始對著一幅作品一言不發，到現在我們每個人都樂於發表自己對於作品的看法。澤光老師讓我們看到，在藝術的探索中，沒有對錯，只有功力的深淺。當然，老師也鼓勵我們多用一些專業術語，比如形容一個顏色很濃，筆劃比較粗的字就可以説這個字運筆渾厚。這些對於我們的職業素質培養，亦很有益處。

其實，我最欣賞老師的一點是他雖然有很高的藝術修養和成就，卻從來沒有一點架子。這種平易近人的和氣之心是我認識的學者中少有的。研究書法避免不了文言文的之乎者也，澤光老師的坐而論道卻多使用幽默的口吻有時甚至是潮語。這種充滿內涵卻又不乏樂趣的演説，讓同學們在娛樂中成長。

對於功課，老師不強求我們的主題，甚至並不要求我們一定要在紙上寫字，可以説這是充分到考慮了對我們個性的培養。我的作品在畫布上用身體進行書法舞蹈得到了老師充分的鼓勵和支援，我覺得在自己個性被尊重的同時，也更加用心去進行創作，這種良性迴圈對學生作品的影響是十分重要的。

結語

學生學識淺薄，草草幾行文字，肯定無法真正讓大家瞭解一個完整的劉老師，卻也希望讀者可以跟我一樣，滿懷一顆和氣之心，去欣賞這本書中的文字和作品。

Biography of Dr. Daniel Chak-kwong Lau

Dr. Daniel Chak-kwong Lau received his Ph.D. (art history), M.Phil. (Chinese art history) and B.Ed. (art education) degrees from the University of California at Santa Barbara, the University of Hong Kong and the University of Gloucestershire respectively. He is currently Assistant Professor at Hong Kong Baptist University and Director of the Master of Visual Arts Programme (MVA), teaching Art History, Chinese calligraphy, painting and seal engraving. Prior to joining HKBU, he taught at California Polytechnic State University at San Luis Obispo and the University of California at Santa Barbara, where he won the GSA Outstanding Teaching Award Honorable Mention in Humanities and Fine Arts (2005-06). In 2008, he was invited as Visiting Scholar of Institute of Modern History of Academia Sinica in Taipei. In 2010, he received a substantial grant (General Research Fund [GRF]) from the Research Grant Council, Hong Kong Special Administrative Region, to support his research on twentieth-century Hong Kong calligraphy, and another grant from the Hong Kong Arts Development Council to publish a bilingual catalogue "Harmony: Synergy between Tradition and the Contemporary — Chinese Calligraphy and Seal Engraving by Daniel C.K. Lau". He is now Member of China Calligraphers Association.

Dr. Lau has published Impression: Seals Engraved by Daniel Chak-kwong Lau, The Void-Solid Reciprocity: Black-Tiger Calligraphy by Daniel Chak-kwong Lau, The Inter-Referencing of Elegance and Vulgarity: Daniel Chak-kwong Lau's New Exploration into Calligraphy and Seal Engraving, Literati Arts - Inheritance and Transformation and more than 40 articles and exhibition catalogue entries, including those contributed to Double Beauty: Qing Dynasty Couplets from the Lechangzai Xuan Collection and Encyclopaedia Britannica (revision of entries on Chinese calligraphy in extended edition 2001).

Dr. Lau learnt calligraphy and Chinese painting from Mr. Han Yunshan and Long Ziduo. He has held four solo exhibitions of Chinese painting and seal engraving in Hong Kong and the USA, as well as several other group shows (including "Dao Revealed through Brush and Ink: Chinese Paintings and Works of Calligraphy & Seal Engraving by Wan Qingli, Daniel Lau Chak-kwong and Koon Wai Bong" and "Calligraphic Works by One Hundred Contemporary Hong Kong Calligraphers"). His works have been shortlisted in significant group shows including "The Power of Word" exhibition (a juried theme show presented by Westmont Reynolds Gallery, Santa Barbara, California, USA, 2005), "Shiji Zhijiao Qianren Qianzuo: The Seventh National Calligraphy and Seal Engraving Exhibition" (organized by Chinese Calligraphers Association, China Art Gallery, Beijing, China, 1999-2000), "The First Guangdong Province Small-Character Calligraphy on Fan" (organized by the Association for the Calligraphers of Guangdong Province, Guangzhou Heritage Garden, Guangzhou, China, 2000), "Exhibition Celebrating The Centennial of the Xiling Seal Engraving Society" (Xiling Seal Engraving Society, Hangzhou, China, 2003) and Hong Kong Art Biennial Exhibition/ Hong Kong Contemporary Art Biennial Awards (1994, 1998 and 2009). His works can be found at museums and art galleries in Hong Kong, the Mainland and the United States of America. He has won many calligraphy awards at national and international competitions.

Courses being taught at Hong Kong Baptist University

- Introduction to Art History
- Elements in Visual Arts & Approaches to Art Criticism
- Introduction to Chinese Art
- The Art of Chinese Calligraphy
- Personality in Semi-Cursive Script
- Chinese Seal Engraving: The Expressive Identity
- Contemporary Vision in Chinese Art Practice

Courses taught at the University of California at Santa Barbara and California Polytechnic State University at San Luis Obispo

- Early Chinese Art (A survey of the art and archaeology of ancient China, from Neolithic times through the Tang dynasty (A.D. 618-906).)
- Survey of Asian Art (Art and Architecture of China, India and Japan)

劉澤光博士簡歷

英國格羅斯特郡大學美術教育學士，香港大學哲學碩士（中國藝術史），美國加州大學聖地巴巴拉分校哲學博士（藝術史）。現任香港浸會大學視覺藝術院助理教授及視覺藝術碩士(藝術行政管理)課程總監，教授藝術史、中國書法、篆刻等科目。加入浸大前，曾任教美國加州大學聖地巴巴拉分校及加州理工州立大學聖路斯奧匹斯堡，並獲2005-06年度加州大學聖地巴巴拉分校GSA人文學及藝術傑出教學獎。2008年，獲邀為中央研究院近代史研究所訪問學人。2010年，獲香港政府研究資助局(Research Grant Council, H.K.)資助其關於二十世紀香港書法之研究計劃；又獲香港藝術發展局資助其中英雙語出版：《和 ： 劉澤光古今相生書法篆刻》。現任中國書法家協會會員 。

著作有《印象：劉澤光篆刻》、《虛實相生：劉澤光黑老虎書法》、《雅俗互參：劉澤光書法篆刻的新探索》、《文人藝術之承傳與轉化》及四十多篇論文和展覽圖錄的文字說明(包括《合璧聯珠：樂常在軒藏清代楹聯》的中英雙語展品說明)，並為2001年版的《大英百科》修訂了有關中國書法的條目。

從韓雲山、龍子鐸兩先生習書法、國畫。曾在香港、美國舉辦書畫、篆刻個展4次，及多次聯展(包括“筆墨載道：萬青屴、劉澤光、管偉邦國畫、書法及篆刻展”及“書苑掇英——當代香港百人書法展”)，並多次入選在中國、香港、美國等地舉行的大規模聯展，包括“The Power of Word” Exhibition, Westmount College, Santa Barbara, California. (A Juried Theme Show presented by Westmont Reynolds Gallery, Santa Barbara, California, USA, 2005)；“世紀之交千人千作全國第七屆書法篆刻展”(中國書法家協會主辦，北京中國美術館，1999-2000)；“廣東省首屆扇面書法小字展”(廣東省書法家協會主辦，廣州文化公園，廣州，2000)；“西泠印社百年華誕國際印學社團精品博覽”(西泠印社，杭州，2003)及香港當代藝術雙年展(1994、1998、2009)。作品為中國、香港、美國等地著名藝術博物館所收藏，並曾獲多項全國及國際書法及藝術獎項。

在香港浸會大學任教之科目
- 美術史導論
- 視覺藝術元素及藝術評賞方法
- 中國藝術導論
- 中國書法藝術
- 行書中的個性
- 中國篆刻：具表現力的身份
- 中國藝術實踐中的當代視野

在美國加州大學聖地巴巴拉分校及
加州理工州立大學聖路斯奧匹斯堡任教科目
- Early Chinese Art (A survey of the art and archaeology of ancient China, from Neolithic times through the Tang dynasty (A.D. 618-906).)
- Survey of Asian Art (Art and Architecture of China, India and Japan)

cklau@hkbu.edu.hk
www.net12.hkbu.edu.hk/cklau/index.html

List of Artworks/ 作品目錄

Daniel Chak-kwong Lau, Ph.D.
Assistant Professor &
Programme Director
Master of Visual Arts (MVA)
in Art Administration
Academy of Visual Arts
Hong Kong Baptist University
Member of China Calligraphers Association

劉澤光博士
香港浸會大學
視覺藝術院
助理教授及視覺藝術碩士(藝術行政管理)課程總監
中國書法家協會會員

cklau@hkbu.edu.hk
www.net12.hkbu.edu.hk/cklau/index.htm

Artworks Sale Enquiry
danielcklau@gmail.com

和
劉澤光印